EMBRACING THE NONHUMAN
IN THE GOSPEL OF MARK

SEMEIA STUDIES

Jacqueline M. Hidalgo, General Editor

Editorial Board:
Eric D. Barreto
Jin Young Choi
L. Juliana M. Claassens
Rhiannon Graybill
Emmanuel Nathan
Kenneth Ngwa
Shively T. J. Smith

Number 102

EMBRACING THE NONHUMAN IN THE GOSPEL OF MARK

Dong Hyeon Jeong

Atlanta

Copyright © 2023 by Dong Hyeon Jeong

All rights reserved. No part of this work may be reproduced or transmitted in any form or by any means, electronic or mechanical, including photocopying and recording, or by means of any information storage or retrieval system, except as may be expressly permitted by the 1976 Copyright Act or in writing from the publisher. Requests for permission should be addressed in writing to the Rights and Permissions Office, SBL Press, 825 Houston Mill Road, Atlanta, GA 30329 USA.

Library of Congress Control Number: 2023947569

CONTENTS

Acknowledgments vii
Abbreviations ix

1. Introduction: A Confession within the Four Walls 1

2. Marked by the Beast: The Wild Beasts of Mark 1:13b 33

3. Vegetal Lessons: How Mark's Plants Teach Us about
   God's Empire 53

4. And Say the Sea of Galilee Responded? 81

5. The Animal Masks of the Syrophoenician Woman and the
   Markan Jesus 103

6. Conclusion: (Re)animating the Biblical Epistemic Ground ... 125

Works Cited 135
Ancient Sources Index 163
Modern Authors Index 170
Subject Index 174

ACKNOWLEDGMENTS

This book owes its birth and sustenance from the lessons provided by the nonhumans. They crawl, prowl, bark, and claw the pages of this book. Many tree pulps bestowed their vegetal generosity literally (by becoming paper) and relationally by imparting the wisdom that ideas are seeds who at first seem to be buried in darkness, but with the generous actancy of humans, nonhumans, and even the divine sprout into trees that provide shade and fruit for others.

Speaking of human actants (human linguistic), words cannot express my gratitude to Stephen D. Moore, Laurel Kearns, and Tat-siong Benny Liew for their guidance and support in completing this book. The intensities of their collective wisdom encouraged me to craft a project that tries to break free from the traps of anthropocentrism. They gave me wings to fly and traverse the jungles of biblical scholarship and ecology and religion.

All of the chapters in this book were presented in various conferences, annual meetings, and colloquia. During those events, I thank the invaluable critiques and encouragements provided by Robert Seesengood, Jennifer Koosed, Ken Stone, Timothy Eberhardt, Jared Beverly, George Aichele, Althea Spencer-Miller, Kenneth Ngwa, John W. Herbst, Rodolfo Nolasco, Anne Wonhee Joh, K. K. Yeo, and other colleagues and mentors whom I have not mentioned here. I am very grateful to Jin Young Choi (my manuscript editor) for her invaluable feedback and words of encouragement. Her embodiment of wisdom is truly liberating and empowering. Also, I thank Steed Davidson and Jacqueline Hidalgo (Semeia Studies editors-in-chief) for the opportunity to publish my manuscript in the series that inspired me to think and act in postcolonially critical and liberating ways.

And, of course, Eric Thomas, Brian Tipton, Peter McLellan, Nicholas Johnson, Ashley Bacchi, Phil Erwin, and Beth Anderson, with whom I grew up with intellectually, emotionally, and spiritually. They know the joys and pains of this journey. To them I say, yasas!

My inspiration for this project was the Philippines. The inception of my thoughts began inside your womb. Your nonhumans showed me the way; your humans taught me to care. To my nonhuman companions I left behind in order to write about them, the irony of things. Thank you for the warm welcome whenever I have come back home. To the islands in the Philippines who animated my spirit and imagination, I still remember dreaming about this book on the ford of Underground River, on the valleys of Taal volcano, and under a mango tree.

To my fellow NoDAPL water protectors, I raise my fist in solidarity with you. I still remember the birds and the buffalos.

To my spiritual discipline, Rhian, I owe you my life and my devotion. You tell me the truths in a world that is too polite. My life is interesting because of you. We cowrote this book. Maybe, as you said, there should a "couple/partner hermeneutics." I also thank my in-laws, Candace, Mark, Chelsea, and Kendall, for taking care of Yuri and Jimin when I needed that time to finish things up. You are the best in-laws anyone could ask for.

To my beloved Yuri and Jimin, you changed my life for the better. Watching you smile, eat, play, and sleep washed away all of my worries. You gave me the energy to push on, even with many sleepless nights. I cannot wait until the day we can talk about the horizons, the possibilities, that life brings us.

To my patrons, my parents: Doo-Hai Jeong and Dong Hee Seo-Jeong. I sing your praises every morning! It took too long for me to get this far. I had several difficulties along the way, but your prayers and support kept the fire burning. Maraming Salamat po! Mahal ko po kayo!

ABBREVIATIONS

Ancient Sources

Ab ubre cond.	Livy, *Ab urbe condita*
Agr.	Cato, *De agricultura*; Tacitus, *Agricola*
Alex. fort.	Plutarch, *De Alexandri magni fortuna aut virtute*
An.	Aristotle, *De anima*
Ant.	Josephus, *Antiquitates judaicae*
Apoc. Mos.	Apocalypse of Moses
Astr.	Manilius, *Astronomica*
b.	Babylonian Talmud
Barn.	Epistle of Barnabas
Bell. Jug.	Sallust, *Bellum jugurthinum*
B.J.	Josephus, *Bellum judaicum*
C. Ap.	Josephus, *Contra Apionem*
Cal.	Suetonius, *Gaius Caligula*
Chers.	Demosthenes, *De Chersoneso*
De abst.	Porphyry, *De Abstinentia* (*On Abstinence from Animal Food*)
Dig.	Justinian, *Digesta seu Pandectae*
Eph.	Ignatius, *To the Ephesians*
Eth. Nic.	Aristotle, *Ethica Nicomachea*
Geogr.	Strabo, *Geographica*
Gos. Thom.	Gospel of Thomas
Hist. plant.	Theophrastus, *Historia plantarum*
Hist. rom.	Appian of Alexandria, *Historia romana*; Dio Cassius, *Historia romana*
Il.	Homer, *Ilias*
Jos. Asen.	Joseph and Aseneth
Jub.	Jubilees
Ketub.	Ketubbot

m.	Mishnah
Metaph.	Aristotle, *Metaphysica*
Nat.	Pliny the Elder, *Naturalis historia*
Od.	Homer, *Odyssea*
Phaedr.	Plato, *Phaedrus*
Phil.	Cicero, *Orationes philippicae*
Plant.	(Pseudo-)Aristotle, *De plantis*
Pol.	Aristotle, *Politica*
Rom.	Ignatius, *To the Romans*
Rust.	Varro, *De re rustica*
Shabb.	Shabbat
Sat.	Juvenal, *Satirae*
Smyrn.	Ignatius, *To the Smyrnaeans*
T. Benj.	Testament of Benjamin
T. Iss.	Testament of Issachar
T. Naph.	Testament of Naphtali
Theocr.	Demosthenes, *In Theocrinem*
Tim.	Demosthenes, *Contra Timotheum*
Verr.	Cicero, *In Verrem*
Vit. Apoll.	Philostratus, *Vita Apollonii*

Secondary Sources

AB	Anchor Bible Commentary
ABD	Freedman, David Noel, eds. *Anchor Bible Dictionary*. 6 vols. New York: Doubleday, 1992.
ACME	AMCE: An International E-Journal for Critical Geographies
ATI	*American Theological Inquiry*
BAGD	Bauer, Walter, William F. Arndt, F. Wilbur Gingrich, and Frederick W. Danker. *Greek-English Lexicon of the New Testament and Other Early Christian Literature*. 2nd ed. Chicago: University of Chicago Press, 1979.
BBR	*Bulletin for Biblical Research*
Bib	*Biblica*
BL	Bible and Liberation
BMW	The Bible in the Modern World
BP	The Bible and Postcolonialism

BR	*Biblical Research*
BTB	*Biblical Theology Bulletin*
BZ	*Biblische Zeitschrift*
C21	Center for Twenty-First Century Studies
CBQ	*Catholic Biblical Quarterly*
Colloq	*Colloquium*
CR	*CR: The New Centennial Review*
Crit Inq	*Critical Inquiry*
EcR	*Ecumenical Review*
EDNT	Balz, Horst, and Gerhard Schneider, eds. *Exegetical Dictionary of the New Testament*. 3 vols. Grand Rapids: Eerdmans, 1990–1993.
ExpTim	*The Expository Times*
Fem Form	*Feminist Formations*
Sim.	Shepherd of Hermas, Similitude(s)
HeyM	Heythrop Monographs
Int	*Interpretation*
JAAR	*Journal of the American Academy of Religion*
JBL	*Journal of Biblical Literature*
JFSR	*Journal of Feminist Studies in Religion*
JJS	*Journal of Jewish Studies*
J. Philos. Educ.	*Journal of Philosophy of Education*
JRS	*Journal of Roman Studies*
JSOT	*Journal for the Study of the Old Testament*
JSOTSup	Journal for the Study of the Old Testament Supplement Series
JSNT	*Journal for the Study of the New Testament*
JSNTSup	Journal for the Study of the New Testament Supplement Series
Kunapipi	*Kunapipi: Journal of Postcolonial Writing and Culture*
Language	*Language: Journal of the Linguistic Society of America*
LNTS	The Library of New Testament Studies
MELUS	*Multiethnic Literatures of the United States*
NCBC	New Century Bible Commentary
NIB	Keck, Leander E., ed. *The New Interpreter's Bible*. 12 vols. Nashville: Abingdon, 1994–2004.
New Lit. Hist.	*New Literary History*

NIBCNT	New International Bible Commentary on the New Testament
Phoenix	*Phoenix: Journal of the Classical Association of Canada*
Pelican	The Pelican New Testament Commentaries
PMLA	*Publications of Modern Language Association*
RBS	Resources for Biblical Study
ResQ	*Restoration Quarterly*
RevExp	*Review and Expositor*
SemeiaSt	Semeia Studies
SNTSMS	Society for New Testament Studies Monograph Series
SocAnim	*Society and Animals*
SozW	*Soziale Welt*
SP	Sacra Pagina
Stud. World Christ.	*Studies in World Christianity*
SymS	Symposium Series
TDNT	Kittel, Gerhard, and Gerhard Friedrich, eds. *Theological Dictionary of the New Testament*. Translated by Geoffrey W. Bromiley. 10 vols. Grand Rapids: Eerdmans, 1964–1976.
TLZ	*Theologische Literaturzeitung*
TTC	Transdisciplinary Theological Colloquia
USQR	*Union Seminary Quarterly Review*
WBC	Word Biblical Commentary
WUNT	Wissenschaftliche Untersuchungen zum Neuen Testament

1
INTRODUCTION:
A CONFESSION WITHIN THE FOUR WALLS

Hiss, bark, growl, bellows the Asian body. Blunted skulls, blighted bodies.

On the unforgiving streets smeared with racism and xenophobia, Asian bodies kiss the asphalt with our bloodied carcasses. We gasp for air to breathe. No, the myth of model minority did not spare us. As a matter of fact, we are easy targets because of perceived meekness; we are hunted down because they assume that we do not bite back.

Am I next? The next animalized other?

I hate the animalization of my body. I feel like I am part of a game in the white supremacist's hunting ground, dodging bullets and arrows sanctioned by racism in its vile manifestations during the COVID-19 pandemic.

I am not an animal, far from it.

And yet, my body, my spirit, feels animalized. I want to say and prove that I am not an animal. I am a human being, fully and unequivocally.

So, I cower and hide within the four walls. Far from the Karens/Kens and their sharpened xenophobic rhetoric, I think that I am safe. Alas, far from it, I am wrong. The transcorporeality of racism and hatred pierce through the walls. They devour my sensibilities even through the cyberfold. Watching the daily news of another violated Asian descent invades my body and psyche—the haunting never stops. The affective reach of racism and hatred transgress through borders, cinder blocks, and even internet firewalls. The trauma of animalization is visceral, porous, aggressive, and unrelenting.

I am an animal, I am animalized after all.

The permeability of my body and my being to the animalizing rhetoric of anti-AAPI (Asian Americans and Pacific Islanders) hatred have made me realize that my being as a human—a being of Asian descent—is being deconstructed every moment. What does it mean to be Asian when my emotions are clouded and traumatized by racism? Is there such a thing as autonomous Asian body when my body aches because I saw the news that a grandmother a thousand miles away has been hospitalized from being clobbered on her head?

An instantaneous response against racism is to distance myself from the white supremacist's claim that I am an animal, a lesser human. My gut instinct is to proclaim my full and unequivocal humanity. I am not a dog. I am far superior than the animals. But by doing so, I have fallen into the white supremacist's trap because I have succumbed to their colonial and speciesist technique of animalizing the other. I have also proclaimed, just like how the colonizers have been doing, my so-called greatness by denigrating the animal other.

This defense mechanism, as Ecclesiastes teaches, "is nothing new under the sun" (Eccl 1:9, NRSVue). We had to differentiate ourselves from the animals as a first-response survival technique against racism. However, that legacy of differentiation lingered more than it should have. As someone who cares for the earth and all of the creatures in them, I have caught myself resorting to a first-things-first approach of caring for Asian bodies. Caring for the earth, particularly the nonhumans (animals, plants, and inanimate entities), is given attention when I have the leisure to do so, which barely happens. Every time I have participated in seminars and retreats on ecojustice, I have been the only Asian descent in the space. It has surprised me that I have never found another racially minoritized person(s) in the room with me. The absence does not imply lack of concern. We, racially minoritized persons, do care. It is just that we have to deal with the unending reemergence of oppressive systems that haunt our communities. The absence is a manifestation of our racialized and animalized bodies stretched to their limits. Unfortunately, the stress that comes with fighting the good fight in various fronts has inadvertently resulted in the neglect of the nonhuman others, much to the chagrin of many AAPI persons who care for the earth. Such neglect has also trapped us into the colonial technique of crab mentality in which the racially minoritized have to claim superiority over the nonhumans in order to justify our humanity.

A lesson I have learned throughout the COVID-19 pandemic is that my Asian body and being is never in a silo, never atomized from outside influences. The color of my skin, the shape of my eyes, the figure of my body, the family name I carry, do not solely identify me as Asian. Rather, my identity as Asian is always contested by the affective reach of those that surround me near and far. Most of all, the nonhumans affect me. The nonhumans penetrate my being *not* because the white supremacists said so. Rather, the nonhumans and I have an affective bond because we share the same trauma and pain of being othered. They have survived and lived through anthropocentrism since the beginning of time. Their scars resemble our scars. Their trauma echoes ours. So, instead of shunning the nonhumans as the other, a way to heal the wounds caused by racism through animalization is to embrace the denigrated other/self. To embrace is to acknowledge the reality of colonization/animalization in each other and to subvert the oppressive systems by invoking the life-giving responsivity between humans and nonhumans. In particular, as a biblical scholar, I choose to participate in this embrace by reimagining and reconfiguring our relationality with all of the creation (animals, plants, and inanimate entities) with the Gospel of Mark.

Tracing the Marks of the Nonhumans

So, once again, I contemplate and read the Gospel of Mark. This time, I am reading it with the intent of embracing the nonhumans from my racially minoritized perspective. I seek to read with a new relationality not just with my fellow AAPI communities but also with the nonhumans who frolic around and transgress through my porous abode. And so, I try to see and feel how the nonhumans are hissing at, crawling through, clawing back, and pollinating the pages of the Gospel of Mark. Alongside their paw prints, I have also noticed how the colonized *ethne* (ἐθνῆ), the colonized people of the Roman Empire, intersect or keep on emerging with the nonhumans in Mark.[1] The nonhumans intersect particularly with women, the disabled, the enslaved, the poor (Galilean peasants), and others who are colonized through animalization. Unfortunately, they also intersect as objects of animalization by the colonizers/oppressors. By animalization I follow Neel Ahuja's (2009, 557) definition as a process that "involves contextual comparisons between animals (as laborers, food, 'pests,' or 'wildlife') and the bodies or behaviors of racialized subjects."[2] Tracking

---

1. This book defines *ethne* as (human) people, groups, or community. See chapter two for further elaboration. Interestingly though, Homer in the *Iliad* (1924) used *ethne* as a collective noun for nonhumans such as μελισσάων (tribes of thronging bees, 2.87), ὀρνίθων (tribes of winged foal, 2.459), and μυιάων (tribes of swarming flies, 2.469).
2. Ahuja references in turn Ritvo 1997, 121–27; and Pratt 1992, 208–13.

these intersections throughout Mark, I have found several Markan passages that manifest the complex relationality of the nonhumans and the colonized *ethne* (people or group) in their various colonized assemblages.³ I have noticed that the Markan Jesus and the empire of God are reconfigured as bestial messiah and vegetal empire of God accordingly.⁴ These reconfigurations are not always positive. As colonization through animalization is deeply ingrained in psyches, discourses, and systems, Mark depicts his Jesus on a few occasions as mimicking the colonizers' animalization of the colonized *ethne* and the nonhumans.

I have read Mark in this way because my approach to antiracism is to become antispeciesist. To care for the Asian self is to care for the nonhumans. To care for the Asian self is to embrace and double down on relating oneself with the nonhumans. To care for and read with the nonhumans does not neglect the need to strengthen the citation politics of supporting Asian descent writers (Liew 2008). It also supports the importance of cross-racial biblical interpretation (Smith and Choi 2020; Wongi Park 2021; and Liew and Segovia 2022, just to name a few). To embrace nonhumans through biblical interpretation is not about assuming that one comprehends how nonhumans think or feel in the Bible, let alone how they would read the Bible. Rather, nonhuman biblical interpretation is about valuing the *responsivity* of nonhumans, to use Jacques Derrida's term (2008, 33, 124–25). Nonhumans respond and not just react; they affect and influence other entities, including and especially humans. So, the question then becomes: How are we, particularly those of Asian descent, responding to and recognizing their responsivity as they are found with(in/out) the Bible? Could we read the Bible as those of Asian descent by opening the borders of intersectionality that invites affective relationality with the

---

3. I define assemblage preliminarily with Bennett's (2010, 24) definition: "Assemblages are ad hoc groupings of diverse elements, of vibrant matters of all sorts. Assemblages are emerging confederations that are able to function despite the persistent presence of energies that confound them from within ... Assemblages are not governed by any central head ... An assemblage thus not only has a distinctive history of formation but a finite life span."

4. I am following Moore's preference to use *empire* instead of *kingdom* or *kin-dom*. As Moore argues, himself being influenced by such scholars as Wes Howard-Brook and Anthony Gwyther (1999): "I believe that *basileia* in Mark, as in other early Christian texts, is best rendered in English by the term 'empire' rather than by the more innocuous 'kingdom,' a term whose political edge has been all but rubbed smooth by centuries of theological usage" (Moore 2006, 37 n. 29).

nonhumans? Could we become Asian descent without anthropocentrism and navel-gazing?

Aside from these philosophical reasons, an ecojustice argument is more viscerally immediate in supporting this hermeneutics. Due to climate change, environmental degradation caused by various pollution, factory farming, and increasing unethical profiteering at the expense of the nonhumans, biblical interpretation cannot and should not be limited to anthropocentric readings anymore. As a matter of fact, my nonhuman reading of the Gospel of Mark not only takes ecological and nonhuman readings as valid ways of reading Mark. I also take this reading one step further by intersecting nonhuman reading with the perspectives of colonized *ethne*. To elaborate, my approach is about reading Mark with the relationality between the nonhumans and the colonized *ethne*. This relationality cares for nonhumans even to the point of philosophically blurring ontologies (in order to efface the Cartesian logic of human superiority over nonhumans). This blurring is my way of embracing the other, their whole self, even their "ontolog(y/ies)."

Confessions and Questions

Before the COVID-19 pandemic, I had already experienced animalization in various circumstances.[5] During my early years of graduate studies in the southern United States, I was subjected to racial slurs whereby strangers aimed animal sounds (hisses, dog barks, and monkey screams) against me. But what really opened my (Asian) eyes to the power of animalization was reflecting upon how this bestial logic operated in my childhood in the Philippines. Although a Korean born in South Korea, I grew up around Manila. As fellow colonized *ethne*, one might assume that our solidarity would protect us Koreans and Filipinx[6] from lashing out at each other. Particularly since both of our nations celebrate independence from cruel Japanese occupation and still struggle with the US and Chinese imperialism, I had naively believed that our histories had taught us to avoid such

---

5. My experience echoes Ngũgĩ Wa Thiongo's Nigerian colonial education. Thiongo abhorred the punishment his fellow students received in British schools in Nigeria for speaking Gikuyu. The punishment was wearing a sign that said "I am a Donkey" (1994, 437).

6. I chose *x* over *o/a* in writing/describing Filipinx because *x* is a signifier that includes and recognizes the presence of queer Filipinx persons and communities.

animalizing colonial tactics. Yet, as a matter of confession, my Filipinx brothers and sisters and I used animalization to demean each other. I did not target the powerful oppressor(s) but hurled verbal assaults at my Filipinx friends. I had not taken into account that my East Asianness socially separated me from Southeast Asianness. As a Korean residing in the Philippines before the influx of Korean immigrants, I felt isolated and belittled for my difference. Meanwhile, my Filipinx community read me as a young man of privilege. In the world of colorism, my paler skin complemented, rather than challenged, dominant standards of a valued body. Unaware of these internalized whiteness standards within Asian groups, I participated in perpetuating these hierarchies by animalizing my Asian neighbors. Was this a residue of colonial neurosis (à la Fanon 1967) that desired the oppressors' methods? Was this a colonial mentality in which I chose to mimic the oppressors in order to escape my (former) colonized reality through demeaning others?

Such self-realization helped me recognize other manifestations of racism when I migrated to the West Coast of the United States. A white seminary student commented that she felt as if she needed a passport to travel to California because UC Berkeley felt like Asia. In fact, in 2007, a New York Times writer communicated concerns of over-representation of Asians at prominent institutions of higher education and specifically cited UC Berkeley as an example (Egan 2007). The same writer accused admissions offices of converting top ranked American universities into "Little Asias." When I arrived in California, I continued to hear about Asians as the "model minority," a stereotype meant to subjugate/silence the minoritized with racist and empty flattery (Wu 2014). And, indeed, I partook in fulfilling those expectations of being an "ethnic, but neutral" body: the virtue of "mainstream multiculturalism" (Egan 2007).

Even in academia, scholars feign interest in my perspective, my gaze, my optics—an extension of the obsession with Asian eyes as the corporeal defining imprint of my Asianness. One time when I described myself as Asian American, a white American corrected me saying that I was not a US citizen and therefore could not be American. "You are an Americanized Asian. Perhaps a Westernized Asian if you will." In other words, as I transgressed national borders, I did not enter an empty stage. My body was haunted by the ghosts of orientalism, through and against which I would be viewed. These specters of orientalism manifested themselves often through animalization. Not only are colonized *ethne* understood in animalistic language, we are read in the context of our stage, our environment, that environment in turn being regularly conceived as fit only for animals, a step closer to the natural world than the habitat befitting proper humans.

These stories and questions are the impetus for my desire to intersect nonhuman studies and the experience of animalization by the colonized *ethne* in reading the Gospel of Mark. I find animality, vegetality, and new materialism in the form of animacy theory liberating and invigorating, and yet my other optic *squints* critically in order to always remember the hauntings of bestial logics that linger around the desire of nonhuman studies for ontological fluidity among all actants.

This haunting is nothing new. Rachel C. Lee (2014) in *The Exquisite Corpse of Asian America* discussed the "*zoe*-ification" of Asian Americans. Zoe comes from Giorgio Agamben's concept of *zoe* versus *bios* in which the latter is a label for those who are politically worthy of life while the former reduces entities (mostly humans) to the level of the dispensable like rodents, insects, or microbes (Agamben 1998). Lee traces the bodily *zoe*-ification of Asian Americans in literature. Carlos Bulosan's (1943) *America Is in the Heart* expresses the pain of being labeled as monkeys by racist Americans. The outpouring of lament against the animalization of Asian Americans persists in Maxine Hong Kingston's *Woman Warrior* (1976), Jessica Hagedorn's *Dogeaters* (1990), and R. Zamora Linmark's *Rolling the R's* (2006).

Even before Derrida wrote *The Animal That Therefore I Am*, Aimé Césaire in *Discourse on Colonialism* (2001) had already questioned the ontological essentialism manifested by (western European) humanism. Cary Wolfe (2003b, ix–xxiii) also accuses the liberal philosophical tradition of theorizing and redefining the human too easily, resembling the privileged mobility of "those who are on top" who do not have to deal with oppressive structures. In other words, intersecting animality with race/ethnicity/gender had become an afterthought at best when it should have been a point of departure.

African Americans have struggled side by side with Asian Americans against racialized animalization. What if Agamben, Foucault, and Derrida took the Middle Passage as the starting point for their theories rather than the precincts of Europe? Césaire, Frantz Fanon (1963, 1967), Lewis Gordon (1998), Zakiyyah Iman Jackson (2013, 2020), Sharon Patricia Holland (2012), Hortense J. Spillers (1987, 2003), Alexander G. Weheliye (2014), and Sylvia Wynter (2003) had already been disrupting the concept of enlightenment man before and alongside French theories(/ists). They did not need to be convinced about the blurring of the human-nonhuman divide because the ontologies of their racial/ethnic environments were forcefully blurred by animalization. Their starting point was already posthuman if not unhuman. That is why nonhuman studies have to bring to the forefront the struggles of the colonized and animalized other (Jackson 2013, 674).

Bringing such struggles to the forefront is not about following Marjorie Spiegel's (1996, 30) suggestion in which human suffering is simply equated with animal suffering. Sweeping the history of denigration under the rug by arguing that such comparison is only offensive to speciesists does not resolve the anthropocentric oppressive systems and issues. And yet, the reconfiguration of ontologies by nonhuman studies as fluid or as transgressing the boundaries between humans and nonhumans (i.e., as removing anthropocentric philosophical or essentialist differences between humans and nonhumans) needs more nuanced explanation. To claim this fluidity demands first and foremost acknowledgment of the histories of racism, sexism, colonization, ableism, and other oppressive structures that have used animalization as their tool of choice. Taking the lead from Wolfe's (2010, 99) argument in *What Is Posthumanism?*, a nonhuman reading of Mark should avoid the mistake of applying animality theory (or, by extension, vegetality theory and new materialism) too quickly to marginalized and colonized groups without at least recognizing their unresolved colonial-animalizing issues. In the United States, for example, minorities have been animalized as a form of oppression and segregation. W. E. B. Du Bois (2007, 75–83) fought against the horrible treatment of African Americans in schools (see Boisseron 2018) as they were treated like animals, as creatures in between humans and cattle. Animalization is so prevalent in contexts of oppression that Fanon (2004, 7–8) had to narrate the "discovery of humanity" by the colonized as a way to combat their animalization by the colonizers.

Moreover, this book's intersectional quest does not seek a foolproof way to include all who are oppressed, let alone solve their animalization, in the name of nonhuman studies. Using Judith Butler's concept (1990, 143), I resort to the "embarrassed *et cetera*," the shorthand way of, in this case, expressing my failure to include all who are oppressed and the failure to completely resolve the issue of animalization. This failure is not avoidable, and yet should not be an ongoing reason to continue the exclusion of those who are not mentioned in this book. As a matter of fact, I hope that they will be discussed in other works. Nevertheless, my embarrassed *et cetera* admits the difficulty of finding fully adequate ways to assert ontological fluidity between humans (particularly those who are animalized) and nonhumans. Moreover, my other embarrassed *et cetera* is my conversation partners in regard to the theories I have used in this book. I hope that the next iteration of my work will have more racially minoritized scholars as the primary interlocutors. I also hope that the readers of this book will be encouraged to uplift those that I have missed and upon which I have been unable to fully expound.

Embracing my Ecoinfluencers

The names and publications below do not represent a literature review. Rather, this is my version of land acknowledgment, my way of acknowledging the academic land in which I reside and from which I benefit. I acknowledge them because I am grateful and accountable to the ancestors of this terrain whose liberatory work and presence provided spaces of emergence for persons like me. As an Asian descent, I am grateful for this opportunity to express myself, centering myself as the primary voice of my own writing destiny. At the same time, I am haunted by my Asian (Korean-Filipinx) upbringing that teaches to always remember my ancestors and from where I came. My Korean name is a constant reminder of my family lineage (the "Jeong" clan, "Dong" generation, and my name is "Hyeon"). My Filipinx community taught me the enduring lesson of "utang na loob" or debt of one's inner self (obliging to the people who helped me through positive reciprocity and social responsibility). I am not arguing that Asian writing does not prioritize the self or the liberatory work of writing that represents the voice of the oppressed. Rather, I write as I am: intersectional and ontologically fluid. My writing reflects my constant transgressions of cultural sensitivities and academic borders/walls, negotiating these spaces willingly and unwillingly. I am also inviting the biblical studies field to write literature review neither as stones to step on, nor as relics to profit from, nor as straw figures with which to critique. Rather, what if we could write and read literature review as a celebration of the richness of one's community? Could the politics and art of choosing which literature to mention be based on affective encounters of a particular circumstance(s), of activism that lists and reviews for decolonizing ends? With that in mind, I begin with my nonhuman companions: *ganda* (my canine companion), the Underground River, Taal volcano, and the mango tree of Maranatha seminary.

Second, I acknowledge my advisor and mentor, Stephen D. Moore. Inasmuch as biblical studies (at least in the United States) is anthropocentric and dominated by white(ness), I was able to study (post)posthumanism with the New Testament and write their intersections through this book because Moore gave me wings to fly and express myself. As a matter of fact, Moore (2011, 71–93) had already more than a decade ago begun acknowledging the complexity of the presence of nonhumans in the Gospel of Mark far beyond being labeled as flat or dispensable characters. Moore's (2017a, 1) *Gospel Jesuses and Other Nonhumans* paves the way in defamiliarizing anthropocentrically interpreted "overly familiar texts, excavations of their incessantly erased strangeness." He and many other ecoinfluencers have planted the seeds that allow interpretations to give voice and value to nonhumans, even blurring ontological boundaries between humans and nonhumans. I have jumped onto this bandwagon by rereading select narratives of Mark through animality, vegetality, and animacy theory.

Third, the Roman Catholic institution where I taught while writing this book made me aware of the cornucopia of ecojustice work done by various churches (particularly the Roman Catholic Church). Among the plethora of publications I could quote here, I limit myself with two quotes. First from *Sollicitudo Rei Socialis* (On social concerns) article 34, Pope John Paul II writes that we must participate in

> acquiring a *growing awareness* of the fact that one cannot use with impunity the different categories of beings, whether living or inanimate—animals, plants, the natural elements—simply as one wishes, according to one's own economic needs. On the contrary, one must take into account *the nature as each being* and of its *mutual connection* in an ordered system, which is precisely the "cosmos." (Baum and Ellsberg 1989, 36)

Here, Pope John Paul II echoes the clarion call to reject the commodification of nonhumans. This rejection is an invitation for the church and the society to take into account that the nonhumans are also divinely created entities worthy of life and dignity. Second, Pope Francis's (2015, 57) second encyclical, *Laudato Sí: On Care for Our Common Home*, amplifies the Roman Catholic Church's work on ecojustice by dismantling the human-nonhuman hierarchy: "Yet it would also be mistaken to view other living beings as mere objects subjected to arbitrary human domination." Although these quotations do not fully reflect a philosophical critique of agency, their ecojustice concern for the restoration of familial relationship with the earth resonates with activists and scholars seeking to establish the intrinsic worth of nonhumans.

Fourth, the Earth Bible Team and their various projects (Habel 2000, 2001; Habel and Wurst 2000, 2001; Habel and Balabanski 2002; Habel and Trudinger 2008) have courageously challenged the anthropocentricity of the field of biblical studies through their ecojustice hermeneutics: the six ecojustice principles and the hermeneutics of ecological suspicion, identification and retrieval (Habel 2000b, 24–37; Earth Bible Team 2002, 38–53). *Every chapter of this book is inspired by their work.* Although their projects do not explicitly use posthumanist concepts, this book recognizes that the Earth Bible Team's ecojustice hermeneutics embraces the philosophical disavowal of anthropocentric subjectivity by claiming all beings to be coactive entities who respond to and affect one another. For example, Elaine Wainwright (2008, 132) in *Exploring Ecological Hermeneutics* uses the concept of *identification*, one of the Earth Bible Project's versions of intersectionality that "constantly expands to new areas of interdependence, creating a web of relationships that are multidimensional."[7] Wainwright intersects or identifies ecofeminism with other-than-human perspectives in her reading of Mark 14:3–9, the pouring of healing ointment narrative. By doing so, Wainwright argues that the dynamics between the woman and the alabaster jar/ointment manifest "the recognition of and participation in the play of dependence and interdependence in the web of relationships in which the other-than-human, the human, and the divine live out the unfolding gift event" (138).

Fifth, the progenitors of this book are the ecofeminists and ecowomanists. Beginning with Rosemary Radford Ruether (1996, 7), I am inspired by her invitation and challenge for a "less dogmatic and more creative" reading and writing of the Bible. Here, the dogmatic is the insistence on anthropocentric reading of the Bible. Susan Fraiman (2012, 89–115) and other ecofeminists remind me that before Derrida wrote his seminal essay, "The Animal that Therefore I Am,"[8] ecofeminists since the 1960s have

---

7. For further examples of feminist and minority ecojustice readings, see Elvey 2002, 95–107; Olajubu 2002, 108–21; and Flor 2002, 137–47.

8. Derrida's essay was published first in French in 1999. Then the essay was translated into English in 2002 with the title, "The Animal That Therefore I am (More to Follow)." In 2008, this essay and three other essays were compiled and published posthumously in *The Animal That Therefore I Am.*

been concerned with the animal question.[9] Like Fraiman, Greta Gaard has expressed her frustration on how ecofeminism's work on animals and animal studies, even on new materialism, has been overlooked (Adams and Donovan 1995, 1996; Alaimo and Hekman 2008; Barad 2007; Gaard 2011, 1993). Moreover, Carol J. Adams and Josephine Donovan's (1995, 6) work helped me see further how anthropocentrism and misogyny are two peas in a pod. These two peas are phallogocentric (hyper-masculine, reason-exclusive, anthropocentric) because they sustain the dichotomy of affect/nature/female versus reason/culture/male in which the latter is assumed to be superior. Such an assumption is precisely one of the reasons why ecofeminist scholarship has not garnered enough attention. More than ever, one must support the work of Asian ecofeminists (Kwok 2005; Oh 2011) and ecowomanists (Deckha 2012; Harris 2016; Lloyd-Paige 2010) because their intersectional activism traverse the much needed coconspiratorial, multioptic approach toward the retrieval and flourishing of all creations (humans and nonhumans).

Sixth, having lived through and with the postcolony in the Philippines, I have been challenged by Graham Huggan and Helen Tiffin's (2010, 135–38) book, *Postcolonial Ecocriticism*, to be careful from falling into the "first-things-first excuse" or the excuse of neglecting ecojustice issues because of its perceived irrelevance compared to human-related issues. Growing up in the Philippines right beside the so-called green recycling center of technology waste dumped by various countries triggered and opened my eyes to how racism evolves and manifests itself in the form of ecocide. Here in the United States, there is an illusion that the gimmick of recycling technological waste (e.g., cellphones, TVs, computers) somehow is processed through clean and humane methods. Unbeknown to many, much of this waste travels to poor countries like the Philippines where it hides from the conscionable sensibilities of consumers. And yet, for those who have to live beside these dumping grounds, we know that this is allowed and is happening because of racism that knows no borders and boundaries. Environmental racism is a form of oppression with which many (neo)colonized entities around the world and even in the

---

9. Other ecofeminists have already begun the discussion in reconfiguring the relationality between humans and nonhumans. See Adams 2015; Adams and Gruen 2014; Adams and Kemmerer 1990; Goodall 1967; Haraway 1990, 2003; Hearne 1986, 2007; and Ritvo 1989.

United States (particularly Native American tribal lands) struggle.[10] The most difficult part of environmental racism is when leaders of these poor countries have allowed such dumping to occur in their own backyard because the amount of money earned through this deal apparently helps alleviate poverty. First things first: human concerns first; nature can wait. Huggan and Tiffin (2010, 22) argue that "human liberation will never be fully achieved without challenging the historical conditions under which human societies have constructed themselves in hierarchical relation to other societies, both human and nonhuman, and without imagining new ways in which these societies, understood as being ecologically connected, can be creatively transformed." The same goes with biblical interpretation that claims to fight for the rights and empowerment of racially minoritized. We have to ask ourselves: Has our passionate concern for our welfare advertently or inadvertently neglected the welfare of the others, particularly the nonhumans? Have we fallen for the Cartesian logic in which we have participated in the solidification of human superiority at the expense of the perceived dispensability of the nonhuman other?

That is why antiracism has to intersect with antispeciesism, or at least we need to check ourselves from becoming neocolonizers of the earth. Of course, this challenge is already difficult because we are only able to respond in human ways in disavowing the Cartesian logic and the ongoing devastation of the earth. Perhaps, as Wolfe (2009, 572) argues, one of the best ways humans can participate in healing the earth is placing nonhuman studies at the heart of our human concerns. Moreover, continuing this theme of human limitation, Gayatri Spivak's (1988, 271–316) rhetorical inquiry "Can the Subaltern Speak?" reminds us that subjectivity is never (anthropocentrically) autonomous and transcendental. As Dipesh Chakrabarty (2012, 11) suggests, humans are nothing but one "geophysical force" among the various geophysical forces that compose this earth: "a purposeful biological entity with the capacity to degrade natural environment." Chakrabarty even questions the metaphysical insistence for anthropocentric ontology by arguing that humans have both human and nonhuman elements within us: "This nonhuman, force-like mode of existence of the human tells us that we are no longer simply a form of life that is endowed with a sense of ontology. Humans have a sense of ontic belong-

---

10. For more readings on the intersections of ecocriticism and Native American identity, culture, and literature, see Adamson 2001; Adamson, Evans, and Stein 2002; Dreese 2002; and Myers, 2005.

ing" (13). In other words, postcolonial ecocriticism insists that humans are part of the collective existence of various forces. Such insistence is what I sustain in my reading of select passages from the Gospel of Mark. The underlying intersectional interpretation(s) of these passages demonstrate more-than-human-centric readings of Mark that is mindful to the plight of the colonized/oppressed *ethne* as well.

Shuffle-Reading the Chapters

I invite the readers of this book to read it as Gilles Deleuze and Félix Guattari (1987) suggest their readers to read *A Thousand Plateaus*. They compare reading *A Thousand Plateaus* with listening to a music record or album (xiii–iv). Depending on the day, certain songs speak to us while others are skipped. The same goes for the chapters of *A Thousand Plateaus*. Readers might be in the mood to read a certain chapter(s) depending upon the day. As this book does not intend to have the final word, hopefully the randomness of reading it will be like listening to music according to one's mood or the ethicopolitical issues that haunt the day. In other words, it is up to the readers to decide if the finitude of each chapter ends at the last period of the chapter or continues to the next. Usually, books have trajectories that climax in the last chapter or in the conclusion. If readers would like to have more structure in reading this book, then they might begin with chapter 1 and then jump ahead to the chapter(s) of their choosing. Afterwards, they are invited to engage the concluding chapter as a way to wrap up the arguments with suggestions for further intersections.

Each chapter assembles various passages, texts, and narratives with theories, hermeneutics, or criticisms. These assemblages emerge and achieve flight in each chapter or plateau (Deleuze and Guattari 1987). The arguments of each chapter are in certain sense contained within that chapter. And yet, each chapter's argumentative intensities also overflow to other chapters. The traces of arguments left behind or picked up by the other chapters transgress the boundaries of chapter markers. The reason for such overflow is to challenge readers to find further intersections and even gaps in this book. Finding those new intersections (and gaps) hopefully encourages readers to find more ways to be creative and subversive in their ethicopolitical readings of Mark and the Bible.

This chapter offers a critical reflection, a confession of some sorts, concerning the origins of this book and those who influenced its creation by providing a guide on how to read the rest of the book à la Deleuze and Guattari's *A Thousand Plateaus*. This chapter then provides a glossary of key concepts utilized in this book. The glossary section territorializes with traces of the studies on philosophy, ecojustice, and race and ethnicity that shape the contours of this book. And yet, the chapter leaves possibilities for other connections that could reread the Gospel of Mark from other shape-forming socioethical theories, hermeneutics, or criticisms.

Chapter 2 engages the curt but bewildering Mark 1:13b: the narrative in which the Markan Jesus was with the wild beasts. This chapter works with an animality perspective that argues for (human) life-altering experience produced through the encounter with the beast(ly) or the nonhuman. Working with Derrida's discombobulation with his cat's gaze, Adams' reflection on the death of her horse (Jimmy), and Aldo Leopold's piercing encounter with the fierce green fiery eyes of a wolf he shot and killed, this chapter finds that the animal gaze/presence affectively persuades and challenges the supposed ontological uniqueness and superiority of humans (see also Bechtel, Eaton, and Harvie 2018). The relationality that is formed by being at the presence of nonhumans, as Jesus is with the wild beasts, demands responsivity. As read in this chapter, the Markan Jesus's encounter with the wild beasts causes him to struggle in his responsivity to humans (colonized *ethne*) and nonhumans alike. The Markan Jesus is described as a bestial messiah because he tries to be in solidarity with nonhumans and those that are animalized while mimicking the bestial logics of his time.

Chapter 3 approaches the empire of God with Michael Marder's work on vegetality. Instead of relegating plants to the realm of dispensability, this chapter finds in the Gospel of Mark several passages (4:1–20, 26–29, 30–32; 13:28–31) that depict plants as either teaching or demonstrating the Markan version of the empire of God. The first vegetal lesson reconfigures the empire of God as an atelic collective being that grows through multiple interactions with other actants. Second, the vegetal teaches the alterity of the empire of God. Continuing the arguments of the second lesson, the third lesson teaches us that those who are deemed inanimate or irrelevant are those that give life and direction to the Markan empire of God. Fourth, vegetal temporality teaches how to reconfigure imperial and anthropocentric time. In all of these, I acknowledge and discuss the unfortunate colonial and anthropocentric desire manifested by the Markan Jesus in 11:12–14, 20–21 (the cursing of the fig tree). Jesus's desire to curse the fig tree reflects centuries of colonial conditioning in which the colonized *ethne* are entangled to mimic the oppressors' disregard for those who are considered dispensable.

Chapter 4 rereads Mark 5:1–20 from the plight of the Sea of Galilee filled with pig carcasses. Working with Mel Y. Chen's animacies perspective and Sara Ahmed's understanding of the affect of disgust, this chapter argues that those that are considered inanimate, insensate, and immobile have affective potentialities to move and even transform organic actants. The affect produced by the disgusting pig cadaver-infested Sea of Galilee could have moved the Gerasenes to beg Jesus to move out of their region. The visual and olfactory disgust bring back for the colonized *ethne* (particularly the poor and the oppressed) memories of colonial disdain and current anger against the Roman Empire for their sacrificial machine that systematically makes those who are oppressed as killable. Unfortunately, the Markan Jesus reflects or mimics the oppressors' carnophallogocentric treatment of the dispensable ones even as he himself struggles to not do so.

Chapter 5 tackles the contentious dialogue between the Syrophoenician woman and the Markan Jesus (7:24–30) by providing another animality reading of this narrative through Ahuja's trope of the animal mask. Jesus's animalizing response to the Syrophoenician woman is a reflection of collective assemblage of enunciation stemming from centuries of animosity between the Israelites and the Syrophoenicians. The Syrophoenician woman's response is a form of animal mask, that is, a performative discourse that temporarily dons the bestial logics in order to reflect back to Jesus his animalizing rhetoric. Her animal(izing) performance wakes the Markan Jesus to the need to reconcile with other colonized *ethne* by healing each other (the daughter for the pericope) and in other decolonial ways.

The last chapter reflects upon the trajectories this book has taken. While this conclusive chapter revisits key concepts and issues that are highlighted in the book, it also addresses its limitations. By doing so, it invites readers to territorialize new assemblages with other actants, hoping that their new re-territorializations will flourish for more intersectionally ethical biblical interpretations.

A Mini-Glossary in Two Ensembles

I highly recommend reading and using this section, and perhaps even bookmarking it, as a guide for the rest of the book. The section is divided into two ensembles. The first ensemble contains concepts that are used in every chapter of the book. The second ensemble summarizes the three ecojustice-philosophical theories selectively applied in their respective chapters.

First Ensemble: Actants, Assemblage, Colonized *Ethne*, and Nonhumans

> **Actant(s):** another term for entity/ies. It acknowledges the affective capacities of all entities, including the so-called inanimate objects.

To elaborate, I follow Bruno Latour's (2004, 236; 2005, 10–11) definition of actants as "sources of affects and effects, actions and reactions, something that modifies another entity in a trial … [whose] competence is deduced from its performance and not from presumptions." This is a reaction against the anthropocentric correlation of humans as subjects and nonhumans as objects that demarcates arbitrarily the superiority and centrality of humans. To reconfigure nonhumans as actants recognizes that humans and nonhumans actually are in a network of relations mutually affecting each other: "we [humans] retain what has always been most interesting about them [nonhumans]: their daring, their experimentation, their uncertainty, their warmth, their incongruous blend of hybrids, their crazy ability to reconstitute the social bond" (Latour 1993, 142). Latour (1996, 269–81) clarifies that we humans do not grant subjectivity (or the capacity to affect) to nonhumans. Rather, we have never been the all-knowing subjects of this world.

That is why Jane Bennett (2010, 9) describes actants as "interveners" in the problematic paradigm of the subject-object dichotomy (see also Latour 2004, 75). Bennett further explains and likens the concept of actants as interveners with the Deleuzian concept of "quasi-causal operator": an operator "by virtue of its particular location in an assemblage and the fortuity of being in the right place at the right time, makes the difference, makes things happen, becomes the decisive force catalyzing an event." This paradigm shift dismantles the anthropocentric causality in which humans enact and nonhumans react. Causality and response are deconstructed from a fixation with human causality and human form of response. To approach humans and nonhuman as actants, then, places all "operators" in a fluid space, affecting and being-affected by one another in their finite assemblages.

> **(Becoming-Intersectional) Assemblage:** a fluid ensemble of actants (entities) at a certain moment in time and place. Pericope

is an assemblage. Parables, in their uniqueness as a genre, are also an assemblage.

Reading the nonhumans of Mark as actants sees the various narratives of Mark as uneven topographies or assemblages that are not centered upon Jesus but on collective actants in the form of emergent properties. Each pericope and narrative I explore in the book is taken as assemblages. The trees, the Sea of Galilee, Jesus, the Syrophoenician woman, and other actants in the Gospel of Mark are all parts of various assemblages; no one actant transcends over others (although Jesus stands out the most due to the Markan author's predilection). The assemblages formed in each pericope and across pericopes exist only because of the interactions produced by the various parts that comprise each assemblage. They are considered then as "open-ended groupings" (Bennett 2010, 24) found throughout the Markan narrative.

This Deleuzo-Guattarian concept is actually a translation of the French term *agencement*. According to Manuel DeLanda (2016, 1), *agencement* or assemblage refers "to the action of matching or fitting together a set of components (*agencer*), as well as to the result of such an action: an ensemble of parts that mesh together well." Moreover, the problem with the English translation "assemblage" is that it reflects only the second part of the definition, misconceiving the term as a product rather than a constant process of territorialization and deterritorialization or the consolidation of various parts or actants and their corresponding dissolution. After sifting through various iterations of assemblages throughout Deleuze and Guattari's corpus, DeLanda finds Deleuze's statement in *Dialogue II* the most conceptually straightforward:

> What is an assemblage? It is a multiplicity which is made up of many heterogeneous terms and which establishes liaisons, relations between them, across sexes and reigns—different natures. Thus, the assemblage's only unity is that of a co-functioning: it is a symbiosis, a "sympathy." It is never filiations which are important, but alliances, alloys; these are not successions, lines of descent, but contagions, epidemics, the wind (Deleuze and Parnet 2002, 69).[11]

---

11. For other key references on assemblage, see Deleuze and Guattari 1987, 34, 38, 67, 73, 88, 90, 97–98, 323–24, 330, 356–57, 368, 503; 1994, 36; Guattari 2011, 47, 55, 147, 188; 1996, 154–55.

This definition captures the temporary emergences of assemblages "without investing the emergent structures of power with essentialist notions of being" (Roffe and Stark 2015b, 11).

DeLanda systematically organizes Deleuze and Guattari's scattered definitions of assemblage into four main points. First, assemblages have "a fully contingent historical identity, and each of them is therefore an individual entity … that does not exist in a hierarchical ontology" (2016, 19–20). The individual in question does not signify number but its historical uniqueness (6, 13). Second, assemblages are "always composed of heterogeneous components" (20) that are not "uniform in nature or origin, and … the assemblage actively links these parts together by establishing relations between them" (2). Bennett's (2010) definition of assemblage resonates with DeLanda's second point: "assemblages are ad hoc groupings of diverse elements, of vibrant matters of all sorts. Assemblages are emerging confederations that are able to function despite the persistent presence of energies that confound them from within" (23). Third, assemblages can become components of larger assemblages (20). Fourth, assemblages "emerge from the interactions of their parts" (21). Assemblages are not ruled by a single component; rather, each emergent property is a vital force of the assemblage (24). As soon as an assemblage is formed, it immediately becomes its own source of limitations and deterritorialization because an assemblage cannot be reduced to its own parts or a part cannot transcend its own assemblage. Thus, assemblages are always in the process of dismantling and opening themselves for new formations because they have "finite life span" (24).

Since assemblages are finite and immanent, reading Mark's narratives as assemblages is actually a practice of decoding or deconstructing the givens (DeLanda 2016, 22; see also Deleuze and Guattari 1987, 322, 355). In other words, decoding in biblical interpretation dismantles the assumed fixity of identities, behaviors, and rules of engagement on what is considered good/acceptable biblical interpretation. Reading narratives of Mark as assemblages intends to decode, among other things, the assumed transcendental stranglehold of anthropocentric prejudices. This reading is not simply about forcefully retrieving or interpreting texts so as to engage with the neglected nonhumans. Rather, it is about interrogating tendencies that superimpose explicitly or implicitly anthropocentric codes on all relationalities. Reading Mark's humans and nonhumans as actants in various assemblages opens the imaginative possibilities that were once curtailed due to limitations brought about by anthropocentrism.

From an ecological perspective, the concept of assemblage resonates with the Earth Bible Team's (2000, 38–53) second ecojustice principle: the principle of interconnectedness: "Earth is a community of interconnected living things that are mutually dependent on each other for life and survival." Assemblage theory extends the spirit of the second ecojustice principle by continuing its ecojustice stance while drawing further its theoretical reach, as developed and provided by such thinkers as Deleuze and Guattari, DeLanda, and Bennett. Moreover, assemblage theory echoes Roman Catholic "geologian" Thomas Berry's "communion of subjects" (Waldau and Patton 2009, 11–14). Berry sees all nonhumans as relational subjects with their own agencies. The nonhumans are in communion with the world as they are capable of affecting and being affected by others. Although Berry does not use posthumanist concepts explicitly, his care for the earth resonates with the philosophical maneuverings argued by many theorists found in this book.

Following Berry's reconfiguration, the follow-up question then becomes: How are the actants within an assemblage in communion with each other? Among various possibilities, my understanding of assemblage echoes Stacy Alaimo's (2010, 6) term, *transcorporeality* or the way "in which the human is always intermeshed with the more-than-human world.... The substance of the human is ultimately inseparable from 'the environment.'" Transcorporeality is Alaimo's way of recognizing the entanglements of all actants materially, socially, and even affectively. These entanglements produce relationality through the movements across various forms of bodies that are "unpredictable and unwanted actions of human bodies, nonhuman creatures, ecological systems, chemical agents, and other actors" (Alaimo 2010, 2). Thus, the transcorporeality of this book is traced through transgressions of the actants in the select Markan narratives, with the guidance of animality, vegetality, and animacy perspectives.

Before I proceed further, one has to take a pause here and acknowledge the intersectional work of ecofeminists who inspire and echo the continental philosophers. One has to begin by acknowledging the monumental contribution of Kimberlé Williams Crenshaw (1989, 139–67; 1991, 1241–99) and her coining of the term intersectionality. Basically, intersectionality illuminates the system in which an oppressive discourse relies upon the existence of another oppressive discourse. It seeks to steer away from the naivete of looking at subjectivity and relations from just one identification point.

In *Neither Man nor Beast*, Adams (1994, 79) also echoes the importance of intersectionality, arguing that oppressive systems manifest as an "interlocking system of domination." To fight such complex structures is to engage them with the same level of complexity in the form of intersectionality. Additive approaches, cursorily tackling another issue as if it is an afterthought, are not enough to confront the complexity of the various oppressive systems in play because, as Crenshaw (1989, 158) states, "intersectional experience is greater than the sum of racism and sexism." Thus, reading the Gospel of Mark with the nonhumans and the plight of the colonized/bestialized people illuminates the matrix of oppression(s) haunting Mark and his context. The consilience of theories, hermeneutics, or perspectives delves into deeper questions and inquiries than one perspective of interrogation would reveal. Intersectional biblical interpretation focuses on the open-endedness of any interpretation and its necessary vulnerability to being challenged and reinterpreted constantly by another interpretation.

A critique against intersectionality is that a single system of oppression by itself is already sufficiently difficult to resolve, discuss, or master. To intersect various issues could result into haphazard or amateur understandings of all the issues, resulting in an endeavor that is useless or even detrimental to all sides. Claire Jean Kim's (2015) response to the critiques against intersectionality is her study of the tension between the Chinese exotic animal market vendors versus animal rights activists in San Francisco. In her book, *Dangerous Crossings: Race, Species, and Nature in a Multicultural Age*, Kim gathers stories, transcripts of judicial hearings, and news clippings on the tense struggle between the Chinese vendors who cried racism against the predominantly white animal rights protestors and, simultaneously, the protestors who cried speciesism against the vendors selling exotic animals. Instead of providing the solution to this struggle, Kim suggests a multioptic approach. Kim's approach, which is a simile of intersectionality, sees each intersecting optic (racism and speciesism) from within and from without through the vantage point of the other, all while holding the confluences of the optics simultaneously so as to perceive the interconnectedness of each optic (19). Mutually avowing and conflicting optics do not lead to paralysis of critique or unreflective atomization. In fact, the level of critique actually becomes more complex as the contours of critique unveil unforeseen issues hidden within single (or even double) optic interpretations (198). The conclusions brought about by Kim's multioptic approach do not seek some form of resolution for each optic. Rather, her approach actually opens the doors for further intersectional possibilities.

I am also inspired by Jasbir Puar's exposition on intersectionality. Frustrated with how intersectionality has become rigid and ironically essentializing in its definition and application, Puar argues that intersectionality has to be revisited and reinterpreted away from its current state. According to Puar, one has to reread intersectionality as having the similitude of Deleuze and Guattari's assemblage. Puar (2011) even created a portmanteau for this equation, "becoming-intersectional assemblage." This amalgamation is a response against how the categories being intersected (race, gender, class, and so on) have ironically reified the subjects they represent. If intersectionality is about pointing out the instability of identity and subjectivity, the epistemological trend to do intersectionality ironically became a signifier for certain bodies. Puar highlights Rey Chow's (2006, 53) critique against this inadvertent return to the encapsulation of subjectivity by calling it as "poststructuralist significatory incarceration." This encapsulation is formulated in the equation of difference equals identity. As this universalizing project highlight otherness, this repetition creates a fatigue in which marginalized bodies are the new centers of self-referentiality. What this means is that racially minoritized bodies have inadvertently positioned their bodies constantly as the ultimate point of referentiality when it comes to racial issues. Queer bodies are being forced to have gender and sexuality discourse as their primary or even only point of identities. As Puar (2011, 58) suggests, we need to relearn Crenshaw's understanding of intersectionality as a process in which

> Categories—race, gender, sexuality—are considered events, actions, and encounters between bodies, rather than simply entities of subjects.... Identification is a process; identity is an encounter, an event, an accident, in fact. Identities are multi-casual, multi-directional, liminal; traces aren't always self-evident.

Here, Puar finds in assemblage theory a channel to expound upon intersectionality's porous understanding of identity. Assemblage theory's attention to affect and de-privileging anthropocentric tendencies sustain the importance of "ontological irreducibility" in understanding intersectionality (62). In her book, *Terrorist Assemblages*, Puar (2007, 206) reminds her readers that

No matter how intersectional our models of subjectivity, no matter how attuned to locational politics of space, place, and scale, these formulations—these fine tunings of intersectionality, as it were, that continue to be demanded—may still limit us if they presume the automatic primacy and singularity of the disciplinary subject and its identitarian interpellation.

In other words, identity politics is left wanting if it consciously or unconsciously calcifies the ontology of the subject, leaving no room for porous transgressions of identities with the other when it is preoccupied with identity but without the political implications. The same goes with my reading of select Markan texts as (becoming-intersectional) assemblages. My reading is just one assemblage, one biblical interpretation. My take should not be calcified as the primary reading or interpretation of the pericope. To do so would incarcerate once again the fluidity of the biblical passage. Thus, I hope that Puar's argument will remind us not to calcify our interpretations of biblical passages. Such a cautionary measure will reconfigure or hopefully liberate the nonhumans and colonized *ethne* of the Gospel of Mark from anthropocentrism and animalization.

Colonized *Ethne*: a signifier for both Mark's human audience and for the human actants within the Markan narratives who are colonized by the Roman Empire.

This expression is inspired by Davina C. Lopez's monumental book, *Apostle to the Conquered: Reimagining Paul's Mission*. According to Lopez (2010, 6), outside the religious construct dependent on differentiating gentiles (*ethne*) from Jews (*Ioudaioi*), *ethne* (or *gens* in Latin, which means people, groups, ethnicities, and other variations) signifies all "peoples conquered by the Romans and incorporated into (i.e., made to serve) their territorial empire."[12] Lopez's most convincing argument is materially evident through the inscriptions on the base of a relief on the Sebasteion at Aphrodosias in southwest Turkey. In the north portico of the Sebasteion, reliefs of approximately fifty personified female representations of various colonized *ethne* stand side by side as a reminder of the penetration of the

---

12. Please note that I translate *Ioudaioi* as Judeans in general. I translated it as "Jews" here in order to replicate how it has been translated when it is limited to religious discourses.

masculine and colonial prowess of the Roman Empire. They showcase the reach of the Roman Empire by listing the names and images of these colonized *ethne*. These reliefs have bases with inscriptions and faces of their colonized *ethne* with stereotypical markers such as hairstyles and facial features. One of the inscriptions reads: "ETHNOUS IOUDAION."

In other words, in the eyes of the Roman Empire Jewish communities and other groups were colonized (and even enslaved) *ethne*. If the Romans, or the Roman Empire, are the central and most important group, the rest are mere *ethne*. I added "colonized" as the descriptive adjective to "*ethne*" because it highlights the overreach of Roman imperial ambitions in various facets of life, extending to animalization of its colonies.[13]

For this book, I add the layer of animalization in defining ethnicity. This layer emphasizes the colonial tensions undergirding relationality between various groups (not just colonizer-colonized). The mutability of ethnicity does not have to stay exclusively within the anthropomorphic realm. Nonhumans also mutate ethnicities in ways that cause their allegiances and associations to branch out even to their assemblages with lands, waters, mountains, trees, and rocks. For example, in the Gospel of Mark the Sea of Galilee is an ethnic marker of both the Galileans and the communities of the Decapolis. So too the stones of the second temple in Jerusalem encode the history and identity of the Judeans. The purple dye and the cedar trees are markers of ethnic identity for the Phoenicians. Camel-hair clothing, together with locusts and wild honey, is a metonym for John the Baptist. The cross and the fish (*ichthus*) for Christians through the ages have been metonyms for Jesus and Christianity.

The Roman Empire's animalization of their colonial subjects, or the animalization of their opponents, was a common occurrence in the ancient Mediterranean world. Aristotle apparently advised Alexander the Great to treat the colonized *ethne/gens* like ζῴοις ἢ φυτοῖς or animals and plants (Plutarch, *Alex. fort.* 6 [329b]). Caligula proclaimed himself divine while treating humans as below animals: "Having collected wild animals for one of his shows, he found butcher's meat too expensive and decided to

---

13. For more discussions on mixing of ethnicities, Roman citizenship, and the issues thereof, see David L. Balch, *Contested Ethnicities and Images: Studies in Acts and Art* (Tübingen: Mohr Siebeck, 2015), chapter 1. See also Royce M. Victor's work on colonial education of the Hellenized children during the time of Jesus in *Colonial Education and Class Formation in Early Judaism: A Postcolonial Reading* (New York: Bloomsbury T&T Clark, 2010).

feed them with [human] criminals instead" (Suetonius, *Cal.* 27). And yet, this inclination to animalize others was not solely the prerogative of the Roman Empire. The colonized and enslaved *ethne* also animalized each other by mimicking the bestial logics of the Roman Empire (more on this in chapter 3).

Of course, one could doubt or even question the possibility of knowing if many colonized persons experienced animalization or even worried about it. To assume that the characters in and the audience of the Gospel of Mark are all traumatized by colonization and animalization is an overreach. Not all colonized persons hated the Roman Empire. For example, the Jewish local elites of Jerusalem in the first century CE benefited from the empire. As Tat-siong Benny Liew (2008a, 227) suggests, the local elites are more complex in their relationality with the empire because they represent both "emancipation and oppression." This ambiguity is heightened with the Roman Empire's interest with the second temple of Jerusalem. The Roman Empire supported the Jerusalem temple not out of reverence for the sacred site but as a way to control its colony by colluding with the local oligarchs who controlled the temple (Schwartz 2001, 11–14). Perhaps the elite and those who have benefited from Roman colonization would have expressed less anger toward the colonial bestial logics because they presumed that they were not the primary target of such hatred and malignment. Nevertheless, acknowledging the psychological and physical toll that imperialism takes on both colonial and diasporic communities (wherever and whoever they may be) is not a huge leap of logic even if such suffering is unquantifiable or even denied. Moreover, this acknowledgment further responds to the suffering of *both* humans and nonhumans in their finitude, vulnerability, and passivity.

In a way, I am inviting Asian American communities to reimagine the fluidity of our identity with nonhumans. Inasmuch as the colonial discourse of animalization still haunts (Asian) minorities, this project participates in moving beyond the impasse by questioning "the discomfort zones that mark the edges of acceptable and normative practice in the guild by examining the system of exclusions" (Moore and Sherwood 2011, 130) that regulate Asian (American) biblical scholarship. I do not claim to have found *the* answer to this issue. Rather, in line with Kim's (2015, 19) argument, I approach this irresolvability not as a hindrance but as an opportunity to find pockets of resolutions and justices in this endless flow of mutual avowal among multiplicities of optics.

This invitation to reimagine our identity(ies) in the form of assemblages is a response to the "paradoxes of auto-immunitary logic" in many (Asian) postcolonial interpretations. By "auto-immunitary," Derrida (2008, 47) means an act of self-defense or self-preservation of a thing that in fact leads to that thing's self-destruction (see also 2005, 35–36, 86). There is a tendency for minority scholars to engage in auto-immunitary biblical interpretation in which the plight of the colonized or minoritized is thoroughly analyzed at the expense of (consciously or unconsciously) neglecting or sacrificing nonhumans. In this biopolitical fight for (Asian) life and identity, nonhumans are on some occasions turned into scapegoats as we minority scholars auto-immunize ourselves or (un)intentionally neglect the plight of the nonhumans by focusing too much on our subjectivity or sovereignty. The search and fight for Asian-ness should not exclude animacy to nonhumans. Instead, the task of this book is to propose the transformation of auto-immunitary biblical interpretations into community-relational and creaturely intersectional interpretations that respond to the minorities' ethicopolitical issue while fulfilling the obligation to be with and become as nonhumans.

Nonhuman(s): an umbrella term for all entities who/that are not humans.

I choose to use the term nonhuman because it questions the centrality of the human. Following Richard Grusin, humans and nonhumans have always "coevolved, coexisted, or collaborated."[14] There was never a moment in which humans became existentially different or superior than the nonhumans. The negation is a critique of anthropocentrism that haunts human-nonhuman relationality. Moreover, my preference for the term nonhuman reflects my preferential bias for continental philosophy and its proponents. Scholars in this field resonate with nonhumans over other terms, and they have worked with it for some time now.

Of course, the term nonhuman runs the risk of anthropocentrism again because it describes animals, plants, and inanimate others through negation of the human as if they could not stand on their own. Further, a definition via negation has an injurious historical legacy whereby certain

---

14. For further explanations for preferring the term "nonhuman" over nonhuman animal, nature, or other such terms, see Grusin 2015, ix–x.

minoritized groups have been defined as proximate or distant from the touted social ideal. In other words, certain bodies have been interpreted as either like or *not* like the perfect specimen. On such a scale, one is measured (and valued) depending on how much one lacks or strays from the pinnacle. In this vein, women have suffered substantially from men who insist upon reading women's bodies as lacking superior male elements. Women have been interpreted as inferior men with inverted male parts. Indeed, popular slang talks about men and women as opposite sexes as if unconsciously declaring women to be upside-down men. Even when women are not conceived as not-men, women still often find themselves defined in narrow biological terms, thereby forgetting how historical ideas of woman have been biologized. In this example, I convey the ridiculous nature of defining the majority of creation as not-something. Yet, for reasons I mentioned above, I begrudgingly maintain this term as a tentative, temporary placeholder as it appears to communicate the most transparent definition I am trying to convey.

Some ecofeminists have posited alternative terms attempting to express the spirit of the nonhuman. Such creative and generative options include "more-than-human" or "earthother" (Gaard 2017). Val Plumwood (2002) chooses the "earthother" as an umbrella term for plants, animals, inanimate objects, and even humans. According to Plumwood, these options seek to elevate the place of creatures who are not humans by bracketing them under the scope of the earth.

Posthuman is not a viable option because it seems to imply that humans are still the center of progress or change. According to Grusin (2015, ix), posthuman seems to claim

> a teleology or progress in which [humans] begin with the human and see a transformation from the human to the posthuman, after or beyond the human.... The very idea of the posthuman entails a historical development from human to something after the human, even as it invokes the imbrication of human and nonhuman in making up the posthuman turn.

In this imperfect compromise, my usage of nonhumans is not mutually exclusive with the reasons behind the use of more-than-human and earthother. Rather, I use nonhumans to embody their spirit for countering Cartesian hierarchy and for finding better ways to be in companionship with all creatures.

Second Ensemble: Animality, Vegetality, Animacy

The constellation of theories used in this book is not unique. Jeffrey Jerome Cohen's (2012, 7) editorial volume, *Animal, Vegetable, Mineral: Ethics and Objects*, for example, insists on the importance of intersecting animality studies with vegetality studies and new materialism: "the study of animals, plants, stones, tracks, stools, and other objects can lead us to important new insights about the past and present; and that they possess integrity, power, independence and vibrancy.... Human is not the world's sole meaning-maker, and never has been."

The constellation of animality, vegetality, and new materialism (in the form of animacy) is more than just a heuristic selection. The assemblage of these three theories/hermeneutics is geared toward engaging as many nonhumans in the Gospel of Mark as possible. The eclectic variety of theories employed in this book is not meant simply to chalk up points in an intellectual game. Rather, the variety signifies my desire to decolonize interpretive gatekeeping that compartmentalizes hermeneutics, criticisms, and theories. Intersecting various theories decolonizes and "reframes" (Wimbush and Liew 2002, 36) the arbitrary restrictions customarily imposed on biblical interpretation, a kind of (Foucauldian) epistemic stranglehold. Intersectional biblical interpretation does not seek allegiance to a single criticism or hermeneutics because it does not want one perspective to restrict and control the possibilities for imaginative and critical biblical interpretations. The diversity of interpretations, the infinity of interpretive assemblages and the endless blossoming of new ones, is the intent of this decolonizing epistemology.

Animality: a term that expresses the ontological fluidity of animals.

First (of the constellation of theories), no unanimously decided definition of animality studies exists. Even with the disagreements on the name of the field, however (animal studies, human-animal studies, zoocriticism, critical animal studies, posthuman animality studies, and others), all animality philosophers and activists agree that one of the core arguments of animality studies is the eradication of the Cartesian human-animal hierarchy and divide. Animality studies is generally understood as a philosophical engagement with transdisciplinary roots that seeks to work through "the question of the animal" (Calarco 2008, 6). It is indebted to ecofeminists, ecowomanists, Derrida, and other scholar-activists who have questioned the ways nonhumans have traditionally been reduced to anthropocentric essentialist taxonomies and other machinations. By doing so, animality studies seeks to be responsive to nonhumans' interruptions, hauntings, and affects.

Moore (2014, 2) insists that animality studies should never disregard the work of animal advocacy groups. Animality studies is inspired by the ecological drive to erase anthropocentric legacies. It participates in animal advocacy through philosophical and theoretical work by going against methods that delimit nonhumans to the literary realms of metaphors, tropes, and data. Nonhumans are rather viewed as material entities or living creatures who affect and influence other actants. Of course, animality studies does not claim to know animal thoughts or dare to represent nonhumans with constitutively shared characteristics based on humanist presumptions. In the end, we still assume and interpret from humanist perspectives. As Wolfe (2009, 572) argues, "it is a matter, then, of locating the animal of animal[ity] studies and its challenge to humanist modes of reading, interpretation, and critical thought not just 'out there,' among the birds and beasts, but 'in here' as well, at the heart of this thing we call human."

As I have mentioned before, my primary interlocutors for animality studies are Derrida, Deleuze, and Guattari. The drawback though of choosing Derrida is that, according to Donna Haraway (2007, 20), when he reflected on his encounter with his cat, he "failed a simple obligation of companion species; he did not become curious about what the cat might actually be doing, feeling, thinking, or perhaps making available to him in looking back at him that morning." Moore points out that Derrida seems to have anticipated such a critique because Derrida reengaged the importance of his cat's gaze:

> When I feel so naked in front of a cat, facing it, and when, meeting its gaze, I hear the cat or God ask itself, ask *me*: Is he going to call me, is he going to address me? What name is he going to call me by, this naked man, before I give him woman. (Derrida 2008, 18; Moore 2014, 7–8).

This reengagement, according to Moore, reconfigured the cat's ontology not just as the constitutive other but as the hyphenated human-nonhuman-divine, that is, divinanimality (Derrida 1987, 132). Although Derrida did not engage the nonhumans along the line of Jane Goodall or Carol J. Adams, his engagement, in all its imperfections, contributed to the dismantling of Cartesian logic.

Inasmuch as Deleuze and Guattari's various philosophical concepts are monumental, Haraway is correct in her critique of their sweeping statement against the mundane, the sentimental. Haraway points out Deleuze and Guattari's (1987, 240) discombobulating statement: "*Anyone who likes cats or dogs is a fool!*" In their desire to critique Sigmund Freud and promote the importance of becoming-animal, Deleuze and Guattari qualified the relationality between humans and animals into three groups. They prefer the demonic, pack, or affect animals who are in their multiplicity of becoming are not tied down (third group) to the classifications accorded by the State's anthropocentric taxonomy (first group), or to the individuated, Oedipal regressions of those who own pets (second group). Regarding the second group, Deleuze and Guattari critiqued those who have animal companions for their "narcissistic contemplation" or resolving their daddy and mommy issues through animal companionship (240–41). According to Deleuze and Guattari, nonhumans are freed from anthropocentrism when they are liberated from the state apparatus and human sentimentality. Miffed by their shortsightedness, Haraway (2007, 30) lambasted Deleuze and Guattari for their preoccupation with the sublime over the mundane and visceral, their "misogyny, fear of aging, incuriosity about animals, and horror at the ordinariness of flesh." Deleuze and Guattari contradicted their own concept of becoming by limiting the possibilities of relationality between nonhumans and their human companions in the interests of countering Freud's Oedipal complex. Even though Haraway's work is not based on Deleuzo-Guattarian concepts, her work grounds my interpretations by reminding me that real nonhumans should always be in my purview in understanding the multiplicity of becoming. With this in mind, I am and I seek to be haunted and guided by Haraway's mandate as I apply Deleuze and Guattari's concepts in interpreting various Markan passages.

Vegetality: a term that conveys the affective capacities of the vegetal.

Second, vegetality studies or critical plant studies argues that the vegetal entities are capable of "accessing, influencing, and being influenced by a world that does not overlap the human *Lebenswelt* but that corresponds to the vegetal modes of dwelling on and in the earth" (Marder 2013, 8). Critical plant studies does not claim to know or speak for plants. Rather, it values the life of plants by letting plants be in their own obscurity, their otherness, and their ways of existence. Chapter 4 rereads the empire of

God and its temporality through Marder's ontophytology (vegetal ontology), which means understanding the nature of existence and temporality through plants. Jeffrey T. Nealon's argument on plant biopolitics will also be utilized in the chapter. According to Nealon (2015, 107), life is "not a static or dynamic backdrop for the myriad (im)possibilities of individual lives but as the ecological territory that cuts across all strata of life … life as defined in rhizomatic territories."

If animal(ity) studies is still struggling to be accepted by mainstream academia, vegetality studies is subjected to outright ridicule or taken with a hint of skepticism at best. The relative newness of vegetality studies and its limited academic resources does not help in challenging this hostility.[15] Nealon (2015) laments the indifference shown towards plant-life and the preferential orientation of biopolitics to fleshly organisms. To counter this neglect, Nealon propounds that vegetality invites a reconfiguration of biopolitics that is vegetal, concerned with life in the territory of the emerging: "life is an interlocking assemblage of forms of processes, a series of doings, as Deleuze and Guattari insists; it is not a hidden world possessed by an individual organism" (114). Vegetality affects other actants in ways that are not organic (centered) and molarly linear (a fixed single trajectory of life), but rhizomatic (distributive) and molecularly cyclical (an endless cycle of birth, death, and rebirth), as Deleuze and Guattari (1987, 21–23) would suggest. Also, Marder (2014, xiii) in *The Philosopher's Plant* argues that "*philo-sophia*, the love of wisdom, is brought to life with the help of *phyto-philia*, the love of plants." Tracing the "intellectual herbarium" or various ways philosophers' ideas (from Plato to Luce Irigaray) are expressed through plants, Marder demonstrates that "philosophical dialogues, treatises, lectures, and meditations will grow, flourish, blossom in greater proximity to vegetable life" (xv). I, in turn, use the vegetal engagements of Marder and Nealon in reading select passages of Mark with the hope that such proximity will blossom positive vegetal engagements within the biblical studies field and contribute to the ecojustice movement.

---

15. Aside from Marder and Nealon's books, here are select academic resources on critical plant studies:
Doyle 2003; Hall 2002; Kohn 2013; Morton 2009.

Animacy: a term that animates the affective disruptions of inanimate entities.

Third, I follow Chen's (2012, 2) approach to new materialism: animacy theory. According to Chen, this theory reconfigures how matter "that is considered insensate, immobile, deathly, or otherwise 'wrong' animates cultural life in important ways." Chen's animacy theory intersects new materialism with gender and sexuality, race, ecojustice, and affect in order to "affectively disrupt and subvert the arbitrary hierarchy and ontological boundaries formed not just between humans and animals but also with those categorized as animate and as inanimate" (2).

The importance of this third approach, and what places it in the category of new materialism, is that it reconfigures the so-called inanimate objects (or as Bennett [2010, 36] describes them, "vibrant matter") as actants who have affective and generative agencies toward themselves and others.[16] New materialism embraces the embodied particularities and finitude of humans and nonhumans. The subject-object distinction is removed not by distancing from materiality but by embracing the underlying matters that brought about the dichotomy in the first place. New materialism then becomes key in further intersecting nonhumans with the experience of objectification of the colonized *ethne* in the Gospel of Mark. It resuscitates the presence of inorganic matters as vital forces that affect human characters in Mark, even Jesus and the empire of God.

---

16. This book does not engage with speculative realism or object-oriented ontology, even if they have in their own ways undermined the human-subject, nonhuman-object hierarchy. On speculative realism and object-oriented ontology, see Brassier 2007; Harman 2011; Morton 2012; and Meillassoux 2008.

2
MARKED BY THE BEAST: THE WILD BEASTS OF MARK 1:13B

Could we imagine a Jesus who could be influenced or transformed by his encounter with the wild beasts or animals (θηρία)?[1] That is, could we imagine a Jesus who cedes power to, and is genuinely moved by, the nonhuman others? Christian piety has long nurtured an image of Jesus Christ as one who moves but is never moved, who influences but is never influenced. His divinity is mightily uplifted at the expense of diminishing his humanity. Could the human Jesus have felt fear at the presence of wild beasts? Did the pitiful plight of animals move Jesus to care for those who are animalized? A far cry from the omnipotent Christ, a nonhuman reading of Mark 1:13b demands the resurgence of a more humanized Jesus due to the gaze of the wild beasts.

Mark's crucifixion narrative, especially when contrasted with those of Luke and John, has Jesus succumbing most fully to the animalizing ordeal of crucifixion: "My God, my God, why have you forsaken me?" (Mark 15:34). He does not transcend the reduction of his flesh to butchered meat, as Jesus does in Luke and John. This brings forth the question: Why did the author of the Gospel of Mark portray his Jesus with such a bestialized image? I suggest that Mark bestialized his messiah so that Mark's bestialized audience would know that their messiah is with them, that is, Jesus is also a fellow colonized person who partakes in their struggle against their animalization by the Roman Empire. Mark does this by not distancing Jesus from animals or wild beasts. Rather, Mark inaugurates

---

1. I prefer to translate θηρία as "wild beasts" over "animals" in order to emphasize the harsh context of the wilderness and to distinguish θηρία from domesticated animals/nonhumans or animals in general (ζωή).

this reconfiguration as early as possible; Mark places Jesus with the wild beasts during his preparation for ministry in the wilderness (Mark 1:13b).

Of course, Mark does not explicitly mention the details of the encounter between Jesus and the wild beasts. Could Jesus have subjugated the wild beasts? Does he have a peaceable relationship with them? The unstated details of this literary episode are, of course, unknowable, as is the inner state of this literary character. My intention, nonetheless, is to imaginatively and meaningfully fill in these narrative blanks through recourse to certain ethical discourses on animality. Another angle in interpreting Mark 1:13b comes through the experience of Derrida's encounter with his cat, Adams's life-changing reflection on the death of her horse named Jimmy, and Leopold's life-changing encounter when he saw the fierce green fiery eyes of a wolf he shot and killed. These stories highlight how humans have transformative experiences because of the gaze and presence (or absence) of nonhumans. Nonhumans have the affective capacity to shape, jolt, and even make humans question their supposed ontological uniqueness. They transgress the arbitrary anthropocentric borders of relationality and responsivity created by humans, particularly the assumption that only humans can affect the other. Applying this line of thinking to Mark 1:13b, I interpret the deliberate creation of this encounter, which is absent from its synoptic parallels in Matt 4:1–11 and Luke 4:1–13, as a way to reconfigure Jesus's messiahship early on as bestial. The Markan Jesus's struggle, however, is not always positive or in solidarity with the oppressed humans and nonhumans. As the following chapters of this book narrate, the Markan Jesus's struggle also includes his recidivism to colonial mimicry in which he uses the bestial logic of animalization on his fellow colonized *ethne*.

Tracking the Interpretations of Mark 1:13b

Even though Mark 1:13b is enigmatically short, many interpreters have imaginatively tried to make sense of this passage. As a matter of fact, the conciseness of the passage seems to bestow permission upon interpreters to come up with creative possibilities. What does the assemblage of Jesus and the wild beasts signify? What does it mean for Jesus *to be with* (ἦν μετά) the wild beasts? Richard Bauckham's (2011) ecological reading of Mark 1:13b in *Living with Other Creatures: Green Exegesis and Theology* is instrumental in laying the foundation for a nonhuman reading of the passage. Bauckham interprets Mark 1:13b as an eschatological fulfillment

2. MARKED BY THE BEAST: THE WILD BEASTS OF MARK 1:13B

of Jesus's Davidic messiahship that brings peaceable relationship with nonhumans. According to Bauckham, the passage resonates with Davidic messiahship because in Isa 11:1–9 Jesus is the "shoot that came out of the stump of Jesse" who reinstituted the peaceable relationship with all creatures (130). This peaceable relationship for Bauckham is eschatological because, aside from overcoming Satan, it hopes for a world in which humans affirm nonhumans' "independent value for themselves and for God" (131). This affirmation entails "eschatological salvation" by changing humanity's relationship with nonhumans from subjugation and domestication to peaceable companionship (131). This peaceable relationship is also relational because Bauckham describes Mark 1:13b as Mark's reconfiguration of his Jesus (or Christology) in which relationship with all of creation is a prerequisite for Jesus's messiahship and his ministry (113). Bauckham acknowledges, however, that this restoration of relationship between humans and nonhumans still has hints of human domination and forceful turning of predatory animals into vegetarians (126).

In addition to Bauckham's reading, some interpreters adhere to the new Adam typology for Mark 1:13b. The new Adam typology argues that Jesus is the new Adam who resisted the devil and restored the Edenic paradise in contrast to the Adam of Genesis who participated in disrupting this paradise. Thus, Jesus's eschatological encounter and victory over both Satan and the wild beasts represents hope for Edenic restoration with all creatures (Marcus 2000, 168–71).[2] Joel Marcus even sees the new Adam motif manifested in the portrayal of John the Baptist's garments and food, in addition to John the Baptist's traditional comparison to Elijah due to his "hairy mantle."[3] And yet, the difficulty of applying this Jesus-as-the-new-Adam motif is that Mark does not feature any garden of Eden or paradise imagery.

Another interpretive option for Mark 1:13b is to depict Jesus at odds with the wild beasts. This line of interpretation stems from the existence of ancient Jewish apocalyptic texts that represent animals or wild beasts as enemies, evil, and even demonic. These texts express fear of animals for their uncontrollability, power, and indecipherability. As William Loader (2002, 38) points out, the Testaments of the Twelve Patriarchs, in particular, depict wild beasts as part of Satan's threats to humanity. These texts

---

2. See Donahue and Harrington 2002, 38–39; Focant 2004, 70–71; Gibson 1995, 67; Marcus 2000, 168–71; Mell 1996, 161–78.

3. See comparative analysis between Jesus and Elijah in Donahue and Harrington 2002, 63.

promise the people of Israel that "the devil will flee from you; wild animals will be afraid of you, and the angels will stand by you" (T. Naph. 8.4; T. Iss. 7.7; T. Benj. 5.2).

Some scholars prefer to see the wild beasts as part of the testing of Jesus in the menacing wilderness. According to John Paul Heil (2006, 63–78), Jesus's testing corresponds to Israel's trials in the wilderness, which included hostility from wild beasts. This is also called the Jesus-Israel motif (see also Caneday 1999, 19–36). Heil marshals key biblical passages that depict the threatening presence of wild beasts against Israel (Deut 7:22; 8:15; Ezek 34:5; Ps 91:11–13). Heil's interrogation of the grammar *with the wild animals* argues that "for a peaceful subjection of the wild animals to Jesus in a restored paradise, we would expect to hear that the wild animals are *with Jesus*; but that Jesus is *with the wild animals* suggests that he is the object of their unfriendly threats just as he is the object of Satan's unfriendly testing" (2006, 65). To summarize, Ernest Best (1983, 57) interprets this passage as a holy war between Satan and wild beasts versus Jesus and the angels (see also Grässer 1986, 144–57).

But when did nonhumans decide to become enemies of Jesus? Did they ever plan to test Jesus? Nonhumans or wild beasts were never inherently enemies of humans. Humans created the conditions for such enmity. Insatiable greed, lust for power, and unfathomable indifference caused such enmity between humans and nonhumans. Moreover, to interpret this encounter as a divinely mandated subjugation or mastery over the wild beasts, following in the vein of Greco-Roman stories of heroes, perpetuates anthropocentric ventriloquism of the divine in order to manipulate the oppressed, voiceless nonhumans.[4]

These human-created conditions replicate the shackling of nonhumans into the literary where the nonhumans are sacrificed for the phallic quill pen to meet the skins of nonhumans in the form of papyrus (reed plant) or parchment (usually goat skin).[5] For example, wild beasts such as lions are turned into symbols of greatness, such as the depiction of Jesus as "the lion of Judah" in Rev 5:5. Interestingly, the same lion or other wild beasts are used as metaphors for associates of Satan or demons, threats,

---

4. John Kloppenborg (1987, 258–62) sees the similarity of Jesus's confrontation with wild animals with Greco-Roman heroes facing tests and trials before going off to adventures. Thus, the real struggle is with Satan, and the wild animals are just preparations for Jesus.

5. See Stone's (2017, 14, 21, 44) animality reading on goat skin and biblical scrolls.

and enemies of humans in general (e.g., Pss 10:9; 17:12; 22:12–13, 16, 21; 58:4–6; 91:13; 118:12; 140:3; Jos. Asen. 12.9–10; Luke 10:19; 1 Pet 5:8). The unhindered anthropocentric manipulation of wild beasts by (re)inscribing their natures for the sake of human ideological bias is one of the ways the general lack of concern for the wild beasts is expressed.

Bauckham addresses this issue by challenging biblical interpreters to retrieve the lost and abused voices of the real wild beasts in this passage. Here, Jesus is with real, living and breathing wild beasts. These wild beasts (θηρία), according to Bauckham (2011, 118–19), usually are

> wild animals in distinction from animals owned by humans, and usually to four-footed animals in distinction from bird, reptiles, and fish (Gen. 6:20; 7:20; Ps. 148:10; Hos. 2:18; 4:3 LXX; 1 Enoch 7:5; [Apoc. Mos.] 29:13; Jas. 3:7; Barn. 6:18), though snakes can be called Θηρία (Gen. 3:2 LXX; Acts 28:4–5; Hermas, *Sim.* 9:26:1, 7; Cf: Josephus, *Ant.* 17.117). However, the word can also have the more limited sense of beasts of prey or animals dangerous to humans. Though sometimes given by the context or an adjective (cf: Gen. 37:20, 32; Lev. 26:22; Job 5:22–3; Hos. 13:8 LXX; Tit. 1:12; Josephus, *Ant.* 17.120), this sense of dangerous beast of prey seems sometimes required by the word *therion* without further indication of it (e.g., Josephus, *Ant.* 2.35; Acts 11:6; Ignatius, *Eph.* 7:1; *Rom.* 4:1–2; 5:2; *Smyrn.* 4:2; Philostratus, *Vit. Apoll.* 4:38).... The word does not prohibit well-informed readers from thinking also of other animals: hyenas, jackals, caracals (the desert lynx), desert foxes, Fennec foxes, wild boars, wild asses (the onager and the Syrian wild ass), antelopes (the desert oryx and the addax), gazelles, wild goats (the Nubian ibex), porcupines, hares, Syrian hyraxes, spiny-mice, gerbils, sand-rats, and jirds.

Instead of wondering which metaphor best appropriates the wild beasts' relationality with Jesus, Bauckham suggests that they, the real wild beasts and Jesus, were simply together. Bauckham concludes this because he is calling for a more positive and hopeful cohabitation with the wild beasts without anthropocentric manipulations. He affirms the wild beasts (and all creatures in general) as "creatures who share the world with us in the community of God's creation" (132).

What remains to be said about this matter? The concept of an *assemblage* of Jesus with the wild beasts as a way to reimagine a more humanized and creaturely messiah is the jumping-off point of my own reading. From this point, I focus on the colonial animalization of the other. Instead of a peaceable relationship, the importance of this encounter is Jesus's transformation as a result of the wild beasts' gaze: the encounter with their pitiful plight caused Jesus to struggle with his own animalized past. My own reading has certain affinities with Loader's (2002, 38) interpretation of Mark 1:13b in which Jesus struggled at the presence of wild beasts not as enemies but as a voice that enhanced a sense of danger. Although Josephus critiqued the assumption that the wilderness is a place of preparation for liberation (*B.J.* 2.258–64), my interpretation finds the assemblage of wild beasts, Jesus, and the wilderness as a place of preparation for Jesus to be in tune with the reality of the animalization of both the nonhumans and the colonized *ethne*. While the image of this assemblage for Bauckham brings forth a peaceable image, for me it brings forth an image of Jesus who chose to be with the wild beasts in his preparation. He also chose to be with and become part of the colonized *ethne* who are derided with animalization. Jesus did not detach and distance himself from the wild beasts. Here, Jesus was with them/us.

In reimagining and reconfiguring this preparation scene, I tap into realistic human reactions to wild beasts or animals in which humans are either fearful or jolted to anxiety due to the inability to control the other. Did the Jesus of Mark 1:13b experience this jolt? Did his time with the wild beasts remind him of all the animalizing derision thrown at him and his fellow colonized *ethne*? Was this passage the author of Mark's mechanism of reminding his audience to remember and be comforted that their messiah is also derided and bestialized?

The Animals and the Animalized in the Greco-Roman World

The focus on this animalization is not far-fetched because the Roman Empire blurred the boundaries between humans and nonhumans through colonization-through-animalization. The colonized *ethne* lived in a world in which the sovereign state, the Roman Empire decided who lives and who dies, who are humans worthy of living and who are (non) humans unworthy of life. Applying Agamben's (1998, 120, 123) concept of biopower, Mark and his colonized *ethne* are "in politics of bare life ... [that] legitimated and necessitated total domination." Jesus and his fellow colonized *ethne* had to fight against being labeled as bestial. From the time of Jesus (and even earlier) up through today, being labeled as a wild beast or animal is an insult. According to Ingvild Saelid Gilhus (2006, 85), to be called an animal (Gk. θηρίον; Lat. *belua/bestia*), or associated with one, was to be something the Greeks and Romans (or the colonizers in general) did not want to be: Barbarians, exiles, or slaves. The Roman Empire, along with many other colonizers, used bestial logics or the systemic animalization of others in order to subdue those considering to be inferior or deserving oppression. G. B. Riddehough (1959, 201–9) provides an example of this animalization through his study of Ovid's *Metamorphosis*: "thought is what separates the human from the animal as it separates the Greek and Roman from the barbarian."

Ancient Greco-Roman authors were busy rhetorically and literally labeling foreigners, enemies, and oppressed others as beasts. Describing or associating certain groups of people with animals aided in controlling the biopolitics of superiority and the right to rule over others. According to Benjamin Isaac (2004, 213–15), animalization happened at least in three ways. First, certain groups of people were compared metaphorically with animals. Second, colonizers applied physiognomics or the arbitrary method of assigning similarities of physical and mental characteristics between certain persons and certain animals. Third, some persons were thought of as literally animals.

Expounding on the second and third ways, Semonides of Amorgos, a seventh century BCE poet, wrote iambic poems that claimed physical and psychological resemblances of ten types of women with animals and some unknown entities (Lloyd-Jones 1975, 29). Women were compared to a sow, a wicked vixen, a bitch, a stunted creature, a creature from the sea, an ashgray ass, a ferret, an offspring of a proud mare with a long mane, a monkey, and a bee. Out of these ten types, only one, the bee, was a relatively positive portrayal of women. In nine out of ten, the description of women as created by gods through animals is overtly demeaning. For example, "In the beginning god made the female mind separately. One he made from a long-bristled sow. In her house everything lies in disorder, smeared with mud, and rolls about the floor; and she herself unwashed, in clothes unlaundered, sits by a dungheap and grows fat" (Lloyd-Jones 1975, 36, 56 [ll. 1–6]). Semonides's literal bestialization of the other is nothing new. According to Hugh Lloyd-Jones, Semonides knew about the Aesopic fable tradition in which Prometheus created too many animals and not enough materials to create men. So, Prometheus created men who have human exteriors but animal interiors. Semonides probably tapped into this perspective on women and applied it to his depiction of women (Lloyd-Jones 1975, 21). Thus, this contemptuous bestialization of women reflects a culture in which women were commodified and maligned. This misogynistic culture unfortunately survived and manifested even during the time of the

New Testament writings. They survived because affect, especially derogatory ones, sticks. As (certain) Christian ethoses have survived for two millennia, so does such physiognomy. Mikeal C. Parsons (2011) in *Body and Character in Luke and Acts: The Subversion of Physiognomy in Early Christianity* expounds upon this animalization through physiognomy through his reading of the bent woman narrative (Luke 13:10–17). Here, Parsons (2011, 89) argues that her "bent" physique was perceived not only as a result of her immorality but also her laziness because she "looks/acts like" a sluggish animal. That is why Jesus had to declare after healing her that she is "a daughter of Abraham" (13:16) as a response against animalization and a transformation back to full humanity—far away from looking like an ox or a donkey.

Could these poems and narratives just be forms of light caricature or metaphorical humor and not a derisive animalization of women? To respond that these forms of comparison are just for humor is to misunderstand or fail to experience that the line between metaphorical versus literal animalization of the other is often blurred. This blurring constantly happens because there is potency in animalizing the other. Bestial logics or the animalization of the other has the capacity to oppress because of, as Christopher Peterson (2012, 7–8) argues, "its fungibility ... unceasing and seemingly illimitable production of social and political beasts." Whether the target of animalization is the colonized *ethne* or the Roman political elite, the fungibility of animalization to traverse and affect all realms of lives is a resounding reminder that the Markan Jesus and his audience probably were not exempt from receiving or hearing this ubiquitous rhetoric.

Here are other select examples of animalization by Greco-Roman authors from Isaac's comprehensive list. I chose to mention these examples here in order to demonstrate how the animalization of the other is a common rhetorical weapon used by persons of various social standings. In 353 BCE, Demosthenes recorded Euctemon calling Timocrates and his three fellow Athenians τοῖς θηρίος "as/with the wild beasts" for embezzling the goods of a merchant vessel off the Egyptian port of Naucratis (*Tim.* 24.143 [Vince]). Demosthenes also recorded Deinarchus deriding Aristogeiton and Eunomus by calling them τοιαῦτα θηρία for not paying huge sums of money to the state (*Chres.* 5.8). Also, Epichares vituperated against Theocrines for indicting his father by calling Theocrines ὦ μιαρὸν σὺ θηρίον, "you abominable beast" (*Theocr.* 49.8 [Murray]). Isaac (2004, 202) even reports that Cicero used the word *belua*, "beast," sixty-five times in his orations. In 70 BCE, Cicero spoke against Gaius Verres for persecuting Dexo of Tyndaris. Here, Cicero describes Verres's cruelty as monstrous as the savagery of wild beasts: *cum homine [enim] crudele nobis res est an cum fera atque immani belua*, "when people are cruel to us, are they either savage or inhuman beast?" (*Verr.* 2.5.109 [Greenwood]). Cicero in his philippic against Mark Antony even labels him as an *immani taetraque belua*, "monstrous and abominable beast" (*Phil.* 4.5.12 [Ker]). These examples demonstrate that animalization of one's opponent happened prominently even in (or especially in) elite circles.

Obviously, the colonized (and enslaved) *ethne* are favorite targets for animalization. Strabo states that the colonized *ethne* of the Roman Empire who lived on the mountains, particularly Kyrnos (called Corsica by the Romans), "are wilder than animals." After the Roman Empire attacked and enslaved the people of Kyrnos, the Roman soldiers marveled at the supposed "savageness and bestiality" of the inhabitants as the soldiers had difficulty selling them as slaves (*Geogr.* 5.2.7 [Roller]). In describing the Germanic and Sarmatian tribes (which includes the Peucini, Venethi, and Fenni), Tacitus in the first century CE describes two groups, the Hellusii and Oxionae, as having "the faces and visages of humans but the bodies and limbs of wild beasts" (*Agr.* 46.4 [Benario]). This bestialization of the Germanic tribes continued with Marcus Manilius. During the reign of Tiberius, Manilius in his *Astronomica* animalizes Germanic tribes as *teque feris dignam tant*, "fit only to breed with wild beasts," because he was frustrated with their traumatic defeat in which three Roman legions under Publius Quinctilius Varus lost against Arminius, the leader of the Germanic tribes, at the battle of Teutoburg (*Astr.* 4.794 [Goold]).

If the northern colonized *ethne* were animalized, the southern colonized *ethne* were not exempt. According to Isaac (2004, 202), nomads were deemed the most uncivilized and brutish because they were perceived to lack governance, domicile, and rule of law. Gaius Sallustius Crispus, a Roman aristocrat who lived in first century BCE, describes North African people in his *Bellum jugurthinum* as brutish nomads: "In the beginning Africa was inhabited by the Gaetulians and Libyans, rude and uncivilized folk, who fed like beasts on the flesh of wild animals and the fruits of the earth. They were governed neither by institutions, law, nor were they subject to anyone's rule" (*Bell. Jug.* 18.1 [Kurfess]).

Aristotle in *Nicomachean Ethics* claims that there are two kinds of humans who are bestial: "people irrational by nature and living solely by sensation, like certain remote tribes of barbarians, belong to the bestial class [ζῶντες θηριώδεις]; others who lose their reason because of disease or insanity, belong to the diseased" (*Eth. Nic.* 1149a4–7 [Rackham]). Animalization is just a metaphor for a form of disease when it is used to describe Greeks. But when it is used against non-Greeks, the metaphor turns literal. Aristotle in his *Politics* continues this us-versus-them mentality by deriding the so-called barbarians for not sharing in Greek polis system: "But anyone who lacks the capacity to share in community, or has no need to because of his self-sufficiency, is not part of the city and as a result is either a beast or a god" (*Pol.* 1253a [Rackham]). Thus, ancient Greeks treated foreigners like or as animals because of their perceived lack of civilization. Foreigners were uncivilized or bestial because they, unlike the Greeks, did not have democracy or were not (it was imagined) ruled by rationality. They were apparently ruled by feelings, passions, or bestiality (Isaac 2004, 113; see also 200). One may quickly infer that ancient Greek writers did not care about the accuracy of their assessment in describing groups of people as animals. For the Greeks, it was a political priority to place themselves as superior over others. The remedy for bestiality, according to these authors, was to become civilized like them, to become sociable like them and not like the wild and irrational *ethne* (214).

Aside from describing other groups of people as animals, Keith Bradley (2000, 110) argues that slaves were also treated like, or even assumed to be, animals by being called an *andrapodon*, "man-footed creature." Although slaves and animals were not considered as equals, Bradley argues that the masters of slaves were *inclined* to treat them as such (110). Slaves were generally viewed as subhumans (Garnsey 1996, 114). Slaves and donkeys pulled yokes together. Greco-Roman agricultural authors reflect the prevalent association of slaves with animals. For example, Cato (234–149 BCE) advises to "sell worn-out oxen, blemished cattle, blemished sheep, wool, hides, an old wagon, old tools, an old slave, a sickly slave, and whatever else is superfluous. The master should have the selling habit, not the buying habit" (*Agr.* 2.7 [Hooper]). Aside from cattle and mule, Varro (116–27 CE) discusses slaves as one of the necessary "instruments" for tilling land (*Rust.* 1.17.1 [Hooper]). Aristotle also notes slaves' animal-like utility: "the usefulness of slaves diverges little from that of animals; bodily service for the necessities of life is forthcoming from both slaves and from domestic animals alike" (*Pol.* 1254b [Rackham]; see also Gilhus 2006, 14). Even Roman laws, such as the *Lex Aquilia*, judicially designated slaves as animals in terms of financial value: "If anyone kills unlawfully a slave or a servant-girl belonging to someone else or a four-footed beast of the class of cattle, let him be condemned to pay the owner the highest value that the property had attained in the preceding year" (Justinian, *Dig.* 9.2.2 [Watson]).

Nonhumans are not always portrayed negatively or at odds with humans or used to denigrate other groups of humans. The ancient world incorporates examples of benign human-nonhuman relationships. Hellenist epigrammatists were hired to make epitaphs of pets (dolphins, cockerels, locusts, cicadas, and even ants) posing with children whereby the artifact not only suggests a high regard for nonhumans but also seems to place the value of the nonhuman on par with their human companions (Gilhus 2006, 13). Moreover, Gilhus finds the inversing of human-nonhuman hierarchy within ancient Egyptian worship of nonhumans. Many Egyptians recognized "a lack" in humans—a deficiency in humanity that was deemed less inspiring in occasional cases when compared to the uncanny nature of nonhumans. This rationale became one of the underlying logics for Egyptians to worship and attribute divinity to nonhumans (97). Ancient Egyptians and various groups who were willing to use nonhumans (e.g., bulls, cats, falcons, ibises, crocodiles) as symbols of divinity believed that nonhumans were the "dwelling place, vehicle or living image of the god" (99, 112). Porphyry even remarks that "every one of the ancients who had the good fortune to be nurtured by animal boasts not so much of his ancestors as of those [nonhumans] who reared him" (*De abst.* 3.17.1 [Clark]). In addition, Terrance Callan's 2009 article on 2 Peter marshals Jewish and Greco-Roman literatures that compare and contrast the relationality between humans and nonhumans. Callan argues that nonhumans were treated differently according to the context and the unique personalities of the humans involved. Although his article is on 2 Peter, Callan's conclusion that interspecies comparison is "nuanced and complex" applies to Mark as well (113).

Markan Jesus in the Presence of the Wild Beasts

With all of these discourses of animalization, why then would Mark depict Jesus associating with wild beasts? As discussed above, resorting to a metaphorical or allegorical reading of Mark 1:13b does not suffice, at least if one is reading for liberation, because it removes from the equation of animalization the oppressed bodies of both humans and nonhumans. Laura Hobgood-Oster (2008, 15) finds relegating animals into the symbolic as "escapist and serves to reinforce human superiority and dominance." Thus, the wild beasts who confront Jesus are real, living animals.

I argue that Mark has Jesus then in the presence of living wild beasts in order to portray Jesus as a bestial messiah. Jesus's encounter with the wild beasts is a (partial) reversal or a breaking away from the despotic naming of what is bare life—animal(ization). The presence and the gaze of the wild beasts disrupts and reconfigures the nature of the messiah for Jesus and Mark's audience. Of course, Jesus is bestial not only because of his association with the wild beasts but also because of Mark's counterintuitive narrative of Jesus. Mark did not begin his story of Jesus with a somewhat glorious royal genealogy (Matt 1:1–17), a priestly pedigree (Luke 1:5–25), or cosmic-creation overtones (John 1:1–18). Instead, Mark's Jesus begins his ministry in the wilderness. He will be baptized by a bestial prophet who roams the countryside clothed with camel's hair and a leather belt, eating locusts and wild honey (Mark 1:1–8). Itinerant and undomesticated, the Markan Jesus will meet with bestialized demon-possessed individuals (Mark 1:23–28, 32–34, 39; 3:11, 15; 4:15; 5:1–20; 6:7; 7:24–30; 9:14–29, 38–41). Jesus himself will die in a beastly way: hung up on a stake to die like an animal (15:21–37).

Further, Mark's counterintuitive narrative of his messiah is extremely piquant in 1:12: "And the Spirit [πνεῦμα] immediately drove him out [ἐκβάλλει] into the wilderness." Here, the Markan Spirit apparently has the capacity to physically displace Jesus in an instant. This capacity could be interpreted as a result of the spectral agency or actancy of the Spirit. This interesting relationship between Jesus and the Spirit thus invites us to consider a bestial Christology in relationship to a bestial pneumatology. Although Moore has focused similar reflections on the pneumatology of Luke-Acts, I apply Moore's definition of spirit or ghost to a Markan reading. Following Grace M. Cho's (2008, 40–41) work in *Haunting the Korean Diaspora: Shame, Secrecy, and the Forgotten War* and preferring to translate πνεῦμα as ghost, Moore (2017a, 99) defines it as "an assemblage composed of 'disparate elements in an environment,' not all of which are human." The Markan Spirit is indeed an assemblage of nonhuman divine material (the Spirit comes down from the heavens) and nonhuman animal material (it takes the form of a dove).

Although he focuses on Greco-Roman historical resonances and not on philosophical interpretations, Edward P. Dixon's work lists examples of immaterial and material mixing of the divine and the nonhuman. Various Greco-Roman gods and goddesses were portrayed as descending (and even ascending) in bird-like form, as textually attested, for example, in Homer's *Iliad* and Virgil's *Aeneid* (Dixon 2009, 759–80). Mark similarly likens the Spirit to a bird, specifically a dove. This dove-like Spirit is not just a metaphor or an image insulated in the spectral. Rather, the dove-like Spirit is an agent that causes the other to move materially. Hence, there seems to be some pneumatological tradition at work here that understands the animacy and agency of spirits. In a certain sense, the Spirit in Mark also impacts bodies. In 1:12 the Spirit materially drives Jesus out into the wilderness. The nonhuman Spirit infiltrates the human body of Jesus, impelling Jesus to be confronted by the gaze of still other nonhumans.

The Spirit's penetration is so forceful that the agency of Jesus seems subsumed throughout the scene. Mark does not indicate whether or not Jesus complied with the Spirit or willingly participated in his being driven out into the wilderness. Nevertheless, Mark's uses of the verb "to drive out" (ἐκβάλλω) in 1:12 "bestializes" the Markan Jesus by rendering him as one of those who are dispensable. The other occasions in which Mark uses ἐκβάλλω undergird this bestial interpretation. Such casting is linguistically reserved for expelling nonhuman demons or unclean spirits (1:34, 39; 3:15, 22, 23; 6:13; 7:26; 9:18, 28, 38; 16:9, 17), or with exercising coercion over and against someone or something (5:40; 9:47; 11:15; 12:8). Was the Spirit driving Jesus out like an unclean spirit? Which spirit is actually casting Jesus out?[6] If the Holy Ghost casts Jesus out, then why would Mark use a verb that evokes the casting out of unclean spirits? This bewildering aggressive scenario seems to have motivated Matthew and Luke to tone down their versions of the temptation narrative by changing the verb to a softer "was led up" (ἀνήχθη) in Matt 4:1 and "was led" (ἤγετο) in Luke 4:1. Scholars also mince words when it comes to this vividly forceful Markan verb. Loader (2002, 37), for example, paraphrases the event as "the Spirit is compelling." Other scholars also tiptoe around the aggressiveness of the Spirit's action with technical verb tense discussion and resonances with other passages.[7]

Such circuitous approaches to the text reflect hesitancy to argue for the possibility that the Markan Jesus is not only the mover but also the one who is moved by the other. In other words, to understand the Markan Jesus

---

6. Mark mentions spirit in three ways: (1) "Holy Spirit" in 1:8; 3:29; 13:11. (2) "Spirit" in 1:10, 12; 2:8; 8:12; 12:36; 14:38. (3) "unclean spirits" in 1:23, 26, 27; 3:11, 30; 5:2, 8, 13; 6:7; 7:25; 9:17, 20, 25.

7. See Gundry 1993, 54; Donahue and Harrington 2002, 65; van Iersel 1998, 102; Kernaghan 2007, 39; and Moloney, 2002, 38. For Hebrew Bible resonances of being physically displaced by the "spirit," see 1 Kgs 18:12; 2 Kgs 2:16; Ezek 8:3.

as bestialized is to understand that Mark seeks to reconfigure his messiah in a way that avoids any transcendental guarantee of being uninfluenced and physically unmoved by the other. One of the defining features of the messiah for Mark is the possibility that he may be moved, thrown out, and even nailed to a cross in order to redefine relationality in the empire of God. Could it be that the Markan Jesus's ministry begins with a sort of God-Spirit forsakenness, a bookend to the experience and feeling of forsakenness at his death (15:34)? Could it be then that the persistent theme of secrecy in Mark, coupled with the systemic failure to understand, is ultimately about the difficulty of accepting Mark's message that his messiah is bestial? Are the disciples and the crowds in Mark possessed by the phallic desire for the messiah to be the infiltrator of bodies, the one who impels, rather than the one who is penetrated?

As introduced earlier, the disruptive gaze of the wild beasts on the Markan Jesus finds its constellation of resonances with the respective encounters of Derrida, Adams, and Leopold with nonhumans. Derrida's encounter with his cat is now a famous tale that has reconfigured animality theory. After feeling ashamed of his nakedness in front of his cat, Derrida (2008, 4) questioned his own reflex of shame: "Whence this malaise?" Why do humans feel ashamed of being naked in front of nonhumans? Why do nonhumans not feel ashamed as well? Through this experience, Derrida felt the "gaze of a seer" upon him: his cat's challenge against the anthropocentric logic of the shamefulness of nakedness. According to Derrida, anthropocentrism created the border between human versus nonhuman where what is proper for humans is to be clothed, and what is proper for nonhumans is to be unclothed. Derrida calls this impropriety of shame he felt from his cat *animalséance* (4). This *animalséance* made Derrida question his feelings of shame and his unjustifiable feeling of superiority over nonhumans. It also impelled him to *responsivity* toward animals. This responsivity is not asking whether animals can speak or not (logocentrism). Rather, it demands the recognition of finitude and mortality of all creations: "the possibility of sharing this nonpower, the possibility of this impossibility, the anguish of this vulnerability, and the vulnerability of this anguish" (28).

Adams has also experienced a life-changing encounter with a nonhuman. After returning from Yale Divinity School in 1973, Adams heard from her distressed neighbor that someone had just shot one of Adams's horses. Adams frantically ran through the pasture and found her beloved horse, Jimmy, lying dead. That night, Adams was utterly distraught over the dead body of her beloved nonhuman companion. And yet, on her dinner table, she had a hamburger. Then and there she realized that "the invisible became visible: I became aware of how I objectified others and what it means to make animals into meat" (Adams 1994, 163).[8] Her encounter with two corpses, one in her pasture and the other on her table, disrupted Adams in almost every possible way. She became conscientious in her actions and decisions. The traumatic experience of that night became an impetus for her to become a feminist vegetarian a year later, to dedicate her life to fighting against the objectification and animalization of the other, and to participate in decolonizing epistemologies in which the consumption of the weak is no longer institutionally sanctioned.

Leopold also had a life-altering experience when he killed a wolf in the wild. In "Thinking Like a Mountain," Leopold (1950) recounts this traumatic event. While he was eating lunch with his friend on a high rim rock, they saw below on the riverbank a half-dozen wolves wagging their tails and playfully mauling each other. Up to this point, Leopold never interrogated his involvement in hunting wolves. He had understood his actions as having a positive impact on other nonhumans (deer in particular). In effect, he thought that he was saving them from these predatory nonhumans. Without any hesitation, he and his friends killed the wolves. The distance from his target spared him from viscerally feeling the impact of his gun. But after descending upon the riverbank where the wolves were lying, drenched in their blood, Leopold saw the fierce green eyes of the wolves slowly extinguishing. The dying gaze of the wolves changed Leopold. At that moment, he realized that "neither the wolf nor the mountain agreed with such a view" (129–30). Leopold realized that the death of the deer at the fangs of wolves might be gruesome to watch for humans, but for the trees and the deer themselves it was a needed part of the circle of life. The decreased wolf population corresponded with the exponential increase in the number of deer. This phenomenon, in general, leads to extreme defoliation, which in return depletes food sources for the deer. This lack of food leads to their death by starvation. As Leopold noticed, "perhaps with better cause, for while a buck pulled down by wolves can be replaced in two or three years, a range pulled down by too many deer may fail of replacement in as many decades" (132). The wolves'

---

8. Adams (2015, 11–12) also relives this traumatic event in her *The Sexual Politics of Meat*.

gaze prompted Leopold to reexamine his own anthropocentric biopolitical tendencies to determine which nonhumans deserve to live, and which ones deserve to die.

On a personal note, I myself struggle in the presence of nonhumans not in the sense of fear and cowardice but in the sense of awe at their indecipherable gaze. Growing up in the rural places of the Philippines, I was with nonhuman animals (dogs, cats, chickens, snakes, bats, spiders, frogs, Asian water monitors) most of my life. Constant proximity with various nonhumans would or should have made me feel comfortable with nonhumans. And yet, I am still uneasy around them. Perhaps because in the Philippines, nonhumans are often marked as hosts of diseases. I am still amazed at humans who have no qualms with touching nonhumans (particularly dogs), petting them especially when they are stray or wild. No matter how adorable and friendly they are, I am still hesitant to the point that I wait for their permission to be petted. Mostly, I never do. The indecipherability of their gaze makes me question my desire to be with, domesticate, and even pet them in the first place. How do I know if the nonhuman wants my presence at all? What cues do I read as an invitation into a new relationality?

Instead of confining the wild beasts to the cages of metaphor and other literary devices, my reading releases them in their material selves. Could then the Markan Jesus of Mark 1:13b also has experienced a life-changing moment because of his encounter with the wild beasts? Could the gaze of the wild beasts reconfigure the assemblage between Jesus, the other colonized *ethne*, and the wild beasts? Instead of remaining in the stratum of oppressive animalizing discourse, Mark depicts his Jesus among the wild beasts in order to associate Jesus with their finitude or dispensability, and as such with the colonized *ethne* who are subjected to the bestial logics of the Roman Empire. Mark did not have his Jesus prepare his ministry through recourse to prominent teachers and orators who constantly profess their (human) superiority over others. Mark did not distance his Jesus from the animalized other, treated like the wild beasts, in order to be more like the Greeks and Romans. Mark has his Jesus prepare for ministry by being exposed in (and embraced by) the wilderness with the uncontrollable yet ultimately vulnerable animal gaze. In other words, Jesus was with the lowest of the low, those that are deemed not worthy of life.

Even in the face of bestial logics, Mark chose to depict his Jesus with the wild beasts so as to let their gaze teach, disrupt, and remind Mark's audience of the struggles of all of those who are oppressed. The nonhuman lesson reminds us that nonhumans are the firstborns, the first occupants of the planet, the masters, and the subjects: "who was born first, before the names? Which one saw the other come to this place, so long ago? Who will have been the first occupant, and therefore the master? Who [is] the subject? Who has remained the despot, for so long now?" (Derrida 2008, 18).

My reading of the Gospel of Mark seeks to participate in disrupting the "Great Chain of Being" cosmology (Chen 2012, 233). This cosmology believes that there is a divinely mandated hierarchy in this world. At the top is, of course, gods and goddesses, followed by angels, demons, and demi-gods, then by humans, and at the bottom are nonhumans. The wild beasts of Mark are "divinanimals" because they are actants who transgress the borders of the divine, human, and animal (Derrida 2008, 132). This transgression, according to Moore (2011, 88–89), suggests that nonhumans are "ontological threats" to the Markan Jesus or the "Son of Humanity." The Cartesian inspired pristine division between humans and nonhumans, which has infiltrated even the critical reading of the Gospel of Mark, is being threatened so as to reconfigure Mark's Son of Humanity to become not just divine but also human and an ontologically affected nonhuman (his destiny is to be butchered, after all), an interstitial being who overlaps in his animality, divinity, and humanity.

Greco-Roman gods and goddesses were known to be represented as, associated with, and accompanied by animals. Gilhus (2006, 112) argues that the connection between gods, goddesses, and nonhumans has to do with the "prevalence of the agricultural societies, dependence on animals, and the belief that the animal contributed to the concept of the divine." This avowal of animality, however, does not completely eradicate the humanist tendency for anthropocentric disavowal of nonhumans. Peterson (2012, 2) asks: "To what extent are both racist and antiracist discourses predicated on a shared repudiation of animality? How might we comprehend animality in non-pejorative terms?" Peggy Kamuf (2005, 14) would reiterate Peterson's argument as "disavowal of disavowal." We are haunted by the desire to relinquish all forms of exclusionary and hierarchical logics; yet we also realize our incapacity to fulfill such desires totally because we have conflicting perspectives regarding the good and the parameters for differences. Peterson (2012, 16) calls for a "weaker or lesser disavowal of difference" that resonates with Derrida's (1995b, 71) "lesser violence." Since we are stuck in between valuing differences and policing discourses of exclusion, this ambivalence should lead us to the embrace of humility. This embrace acknowledges the impossibility of unconditional hospitality and total inclusion. Thus, perhaps we are invited to embrace the inescapability of this dilemma but not the excusability of the situation.

In all these matters, Jesus is still haunted by what Peterson (2012, 19) would term "the *stain* or the unavoidable tendency for discrimination that marks all social relations."[9] In the Markan stories of the Gerasenes and their pigs (Mark 5:1–20), the Syrophoenician woman (7:24–30), and the trees (11:12–14, 20–21), Jesus seems to relapse into anthropocentrism. Following Derrida, we might say that Jesus was stained with the desire for beastly sovereignty. In *The Beast and the Sovereign* (*Bête et le Souverain*), Derrida delves into the irony of the homophony of the French words *et* and *est* in which similar-sounding words produce quite dissimilar meanings. According to Derrida (2009, 18), the sovereigns or those who view themselves above the law look down upon beasts (*bêtes*) or those that are assumed to be ignorant of human laws. And yet, the stupidity (*betise*) of the sovereigns is that they mimic the "lawlessness" of those they abhor: "my fault, my failing, evil, or illness, the defect from which I suffer well, it would first be necessary to take into account perhaps, a kind of contagion of *bêtise*, a mimeticism of *bêtise*" (158). Kings and emperors during the time of Jesus were the sovereigns who existed without, above, and outside the law like the beasts they maligned. Jesus on the one hand, fought against this sovereignty that animalizes the colonized ones. And yet, on the other, as I show in the ensuing chapters, Jesus mimics this sovereignty against the Gerasenes and their pigs (Mark 5:1–20), the Syrophoenician woman (7:24–30), and the trees (11:12–14, 20–21).

This ambivalence reflects how ingrained bestial logics are in the psyche of those who are animalized. Derrida (2005, 35–36, 86) would call this the auto-immunitary nature of democracy. According to Derrida, auto-immunity can be explained through the irony embedded in the concept of democracy. The irony is that democracy must allow room for those who are against democracy even if such a compromise destabilizes its intention. This inevitability reflects the impossibility of a perfect concept or idea. Nevertheless, its vulnerability in its imperfection allows for relationality to open for change and nonidealization. The Markan Jesus fights for the dispossessed while inadvertently allowing for their (both human and nonhuman) destruction. His auto-immunization is his struggle as colonized *ethne* to care for all. Jesus's promise for "liberation to come" in the

---

9. The concept of stain is derived from Philip Roth's (2001) work.

Derridean sense aims to bring the empire of God into this world through "a despairing messianicity or a messianicity in despair" (86) manifested on the cross and in the empty tomb. The Markan Jesus's messiahship seems to be an act of despair from the perspective of anthropocentrism but represents a hopeful liberating ambivalence for those who see this Jesus as bestial, with the wild beasts, particularly for those who are animalized.

3
VEGETAL LESSONS: HOW MARK'S PLANTS TEACH US ABOUT GOD'S EMPIRE

> They tried to bury us but they did not know we were seeds.
> —A Mexican Proverb

The title of this chapter is inspired by Kelly Oliver's (2009) book, *Animal Lessons: How They Teach Us to Be Human*.[1] Oliver's work challenges not only anthropocentric philosophical discourses but also those with posthumanist bent to show more concern for actual, real and living nonhumans by avowing human dependency on animal pedagogy or on how nonhumans teach us to be humans (5). Oliver asserts that human-nonhuman kinship should be based on a sustainable ethics that learns the indebtedness of humans to nonhumans even if this learning process constantly demands further negotiations. Oliver's sustainable ethics is based on two premises. First, Oliver extends the list of teachers to whom humans should learn from to the earth. That is, Oliver seeks an earth pedagogy. Second, Oliver finds Derrida's hyperbolic ethics to be a paradigm for her sustainable ethics because it constantly challenges the limits of ethical considerations (305–6). Derrida's hyperbolic ethics (i.e., hospitality, gift, and forgiveness) is a form of ethics that constantly engages the borders that fix laws, mores, norms, customs, and others regulating forces, even if this engagement seems to be difficult and out of reach (see Derrida 2000, 25, 75; 2001, 25–60; 2005, 148–49). For example, this demand for constant vigilance transgresses the laws of hospitality. For a host to be truly

---

1. I am indebted to Stephen D. Moore for cultivating vegetal reading of biblical texts. See Moore 2017a, 107–26.

hospitable the rules that divide host and guest should be blurred, the fluidity of subjectivity in which the eater or the provider also becomes the eaten or the provided and vice versa. However, Derrida does not claim that hyperbolic ethics is pure and absolute. As Oliver (2009, 116) points out, it is more like "a virus invading a host." In other words, this ethics is paradoxical in its hyperbole or unconditional nature. This ethics needs the conditional to articulate its absoluteness: "Only an unconditional hospitality can give meaning and practical rationality to a concept of hospitality. Unconditional hospitality exceeds juridical, political, or economic calculation. But no thing and no one happens or arrives without it" (Derrida 2005, 149).

Heeding Oliver's call to learn from the earth, this chapter expands and reconfigures this kinship and sustainable ethics to plants. If hyperbolic ethics seeks to push the limits of acceptability and the figures who establish the bounds, this chapter pushes the limits of ethical consideration to plants as teachers who reconfigure the boundaries of (sustainable) ethics. Instead of depicting the empire of God and its temporality only through human figures or human temporality, the author of Mark invites the possibility that humans could learn from plants. These select vegetal lessons are narrated in Mark 4:1–20 (parable of the sower and the seed), 4:26–29 (parable of the growing seed), 4:30–32 (parable of the mustard seed), and 13:28–31 (lesson of the fig tree). And yet, this kinship is not always rosy. Mark 11:12–14, 20–21 (Jesus curses the fig tree) reflects anthropocentric biopolitics rooted in Mark's (or Jesus's) struggle to break free from relegating plants to the nonliving, expendable commodities.

Mark models the empire of God on plants or the expendable ones who are at the bottom of the great chain of being. Why would Mark, who is busy depicting his messiah and empire as authority-driven, link them with those who are perceived to be dispensable? This chapter argues that Mark's decision to use plants and their vegetal lessons in illustrating the empire of God could be because they reflect the quotidian needs and struggles of the colonized people. The vegetal discourse resonates with William R. Herzog's understanding of parable within the agrarian milieu. Inspired by Paulo Freire (1973), Herzog (1994, 3) argues that parables are "not earthly stories with heavenly meanings but earthly stories with heavy meanings, weighted down by an awareness of the workings of exploitation in the world of their hearers." Parables speak not only about the role of the divine in the daily lives of the people; they "decode" or problematize the givens (21). The parables interrogate the shackles of socioeconomic oppression and political exploitation by the dominant (73).[2] In the same vein, Mark interrogates these shackles, among many other ways, through a vegetal approach in which those that/who are relegated to the dispensable actually define the messianic and the empire/kin(g)-dom of the divine.

Defining Vegetality

On the one side, when the word *vegetal(ity)* is used in English-speaking modern contexts, it unfortunately connotes passivity, inactivity, and sedentariness. This interpretation stems ultimately from many ancient Greco-Roman philosophical and literary works that relegate plants into lifeless matter. With the ancients' preoccupation with soul and flourishing, the finitude and inevitable recurring decay of plants did not correspond to their search for the transcendental. In Plato's *Phaedrus*, Socrates confesses to his conversation partner Phaedrus: φιλομαθὴς γάρ εἰμι· τὰ μὲν χωρία καὶ τὰ δένδρα οὐδέν μ' ἐθέλει διδάσκειν, οἱ δ' ἐν τῷ ἄστει ἄνθρωποι "I am fond of learning. Now the country places and the trees won't teach me anything, and the people in the city do" (*Phaedr.* 230d [Emlyn-Jones]). In *De Anima*, Aristotle unleashes his violence against plants by dismissing their actancy due to their lack of movement: "plants seem to live without sharing in locomotion or in perception" (*An.* 410b [Hett]). Aristotle also describes plants as apparently "deprived of eyes"—an ableist metaphor for insufficiency in general (*Metaph.* 1022b24 [Tredenick and Armstrong]). (Pseudo-)Aristotle (or Nicolaus of Damascus) in *De plantis* intensifies Aristotle's trajectory in describing plants as incomplete (ἀτελὲς πρᾶγμα) and lifeless: "But the plant does not belong to the class which has no soul, because there is some part of the soul [μέρος ψυχῆς] in it, but the plant is not a living [ζῷον] creature because there is no feeling in it" (*Plant.* 816a35–40; 816b5–10 [Hett]).

On the other side, the etymology of vegetal(ity) (Lat. *vegetabilis*) actually means "growing or flourishing." The verb form, *vegetare*, is defined as "to animate" or "to enliven." Tapping into this etymology, Michael Marder (2014, xvi) reveals the hypocrisy of these ancient philosophers who relegated the vegetal to the lowest rank of relevancy when, as a matter of fact, plant life nourished them physically and philosophically. Nevertheless, Marder highlights a philosopher and botanist who swam against this

---

2. See 1994, 53–73 for Herzog's analysis of the agrarian systems and their corresponding oppressive structures against the peasants.

current: Theophrastus. Born in 370 BCE at Eresos in Lesbos, Theophrastus was one of Plato's students, who after Plato's death led the Lyceum and managed Plato's library. During his tenure, the Lyceum had amazing gardens with flowers and plants from all over the known world. This access to local and foreign plants enabled Theophrastus to systematically observe and classify various plants (Locy 1925, 35). In *Enquiry into Plants*, Theophrastus contradicted Aristotle's argument in *Historia animalium* that plants are inferior to animals. Theophrastus asserts that plants actually are not the same and may even be superior to animals because they "have the power of growth in all [their] parts, inasmuch as [they have] life in all [their] parts" (*Hist. plant.* 1.3–4 [Hort]). In other words, if an animal's life begins and ends with their heartbeat, a plant's life is decentralized. Plants can simultaneously have some parts that are dead and other parts that are growing. The multiplicities of life sources in plants make them incomparable to animals. Thus, following and building upon Theophrastus's perspective on vegetality, this chapter expounds upon the vegetal hermeneutics that plants are actants that have the capacity to affect others as they grow, reproduce, and even decay.

Apparently, to argue with and for plants is an uphill climb since it stands on speculative grounds. My response to this assumption is to follow Anna Tsing's definition of landscape. For Tsing (2004, 173–74), landscape is a "configuration of humans and nonhumans in their material ... as well as 'social' (created within human projects) and 'natural' (outside of human control; populated by nonhuman species) [aspect]." Tsing's concept of landscape resonates with the Deleuzo-Guattarian concept of assemblage. These landscapes have "gaps" or "conceptual spaces and real places into which powerful demarcations do not travel well" (175). Vegetal reading of the Bible questions the demarcations of what counts as speculative or otherwise. It questions the demarcations because it does not follow the rigid reason-centric, human-logos based, and unaffected (especially by the nonhumans) reading of the Bible. Rather, it approaches biblical narratives as landscapes with gaps here and there. In other words, to embrace the vegetal and the rest of the nonhumans reconfigures and reimagines our relationality with the all of creation. This is decolonial because it does not succumb to the bestial logics that demand us as animalized others to disavow the nonhumans in order to claim full humanity. Instead, to embrace the vegetal is an invitation to shift the episteme not just of reading the Bible but also of our perception and understanding of ourselves, the nonhumans, and the divine.

Marderian Vegetality

Building upon these gaps of possibilities for actancy or liveliness for animalized humans and nonhumans, this chapter works primarily with Marder's (2013) ecojustice, philosophical exposition on vegetality.[3] The vegetal lessons found in Mark teach his audience that plants are actants who are capable of influencing and challenging the colonized *ethne* in reimagining the empire of God and its temporality. As they are unpacked, Mark's vegetal lessons teach that the empire of God is first an atelic (or open-ended, incomplete, and infinitely changing) collective being that grows through the multiplicities of interactions with various actants (e.g., sun, water, air, bees). Second, the vegetal teaches alterity of being and becoming by abandoning the familiar human terrain of encroachment and colonization of nonhumans. Third, it teaches that those who are deemed irrelevant are ironically those who give life. Fourth, vegetal temporality reconfigures imperial and anthropocentric time.

The novelty of applying vegetality in reading the Gospel of Mark requires several caveats. First, encountering plants should not entail fetishizing their otherness (Marder 2013, 3). Vegetality is not about saying that plants have feelings, rationality, personhood, or any other human attributes. I myself am not claiming to know the esoteric knowledge and discourse of plants. Botanists and other scientists might have better knowledge of the workings of plants, but vegetality insists that inasmuch as knowing plants is important, the form of this process of knowing should fall under the auspices of respect. Thus, in this chapter, Marderian[4] vegetality is inspired by the findings of botanists while keeping a healthy sense of alterity regarding the things unknown about plants.

In addition, this chapter pays homage to applied scientists such as Janine Benyus for promulgating biomimicry, the science that studies nature as a model and inspiration for human problems and designs, such as leaves inspiring solar cells, whale fins inspiring wind turbine blades, spider silk inspiring thread materials, prairies teaching how to grow food, finding cures like the chimpanzee, conducting business like a redwood forest, and other mimicries. Biomimicry is not about exploit-

---

3. For other resources that echo Marder's work, see Chamovitz 2013; Halle 2002; Irigaray and Marder 2016; Laist 2013; Pollan 2002; and Vieira 2016.

4. An adjective justified by the fact that Marder's work on vegetality has been seminal for the emerging field of critical plant studies/plant theory.

ing nature but about learning from nature's 3.8 billion years of expertise (Benyus 1997, 2–3). Biomimicry questions centuries of anthropocentric science that prevented nature from becoming our mentor or teacher. The neglect of our nonhuman teacher has created inventions detrimental to humans and nonhumans alike, even depleting ecological resources to the point of extinction. Benyus invites people from all fields to walk into the forest again in order to learn from nonhumans. This willingness to learn from nonhumans, as Benyus states and with which I agree, requires a certain combination of "brains, humility, and spirituality" (9). Thus, this chapter mimics Benyus's spirit in approaching the vegetal in the Gospel of Mark.

Second, vegetality requires the emancipation of plants from the greenhouses of Linnaean taxonomy (Blunt 2001) and the anthropocentric limitation of plants to the stratum of literary devices such as metaphors, analogies, and other expressions (Nealon 2016, 88–89). Expounding upon Luce Irigaray's work, Marder (2014, 220) critiques the unhindered and unabashed reduction of plants into the literary. Deleuze and Guattari might have championed rhizomes, subterranean plants that shoot their roots through their nodes in multiple ways, as the ultimate image of thought for the multiplicities of all actants and assemblages. And yet, Deleuze and Guattari (1987, 19–20) ironically reappropriated trees and rhizomes in the form of a straw man (or straw plant) fallacy. They chose the image of trees as the symbol for the hierarchical, genealogical, centralized, phallic, and even transcendental. Moreover, Yii-Jan Lin (2016, 169, 171) rightfully cautions the use of rhizome, or at least the Deleuzian way of doing so, for its "innate, living force" that could fixate reading of the Bible back to biological determinism. As Deleuze and Guattari (1987, 20–21, 25) questionably describe rhizomes as having their own rigidity, despotism, and hierarchy in their immanence, they even categorize trees as the phallic objects of reproduction who are stuck in their endless growth and filiation: "external reproduction as image-tree and internal reproduction as tree-structure." Trees are apparently to be shunned because they do not fit the poststructuralist philosophical mold of multiplicities, finitude, and autonomy. This categorization superimposes phallogocentrism upon trees so that the vegetal is once again sacrificed for human linguistic consumption. Thus, it calls us to ask the question: Do we really have to signify the tree as phallic? Are rhizomes deterministic in their crawl for vegetal regeneration? Rhizomes creep, falter, regenerate, and then falter again—a cycle of vegetality. They channel but never innately claim any form of "source" or origin of life. Their horizontality is without linearity of intention. Trees are not phallic; anthropocentrism is.

I also follow Marder's critique of this anthropocentric correlation. Instead of trying to detach the signification of trees from the phallic by creating an unintentional binary division, Marder channels Derrida's deconstruction and finds a solution to the issue by unraveling from within by adding the prefix "phyto" to phallogocentrism: phytophallogocentrism. Phallogocentrism prefers and privileges masculine or patriarchal speech, logos, or manifestations. Marder (2014, 208) adds the vegetal (phyto) to this erectile structure in order to collapse the structures of metaphysics or the transcendental signified and phallic: "the flower deflowers (dehiscence) itself at the peak of blossoming, and *logos* interrupts its own monologue in the middle of addressing itself to itself. Internally decentered, phytophallogocentrism falls apart into multiple outgrowths." Vegetality is a reminder of finitude and decay especially for the phallic (and those who espouse phallogocentrism), a reminder that nothing stays erect or transcends the transgressive nature of relationality.

Third, the limitation of Marderian vegetality is that it primarily intersects with Western ontology and ethics. Marder explains that his decision to limit his work to Western ontology is due to the need to repair the damage it has caused. This chapter's primary engagement with Western philosophy is due relatedly to the fact that many biblical interpretations have been too enmeshed in or rely solely on Western philosophy. Nevertheless, it is my hope that future vegetal interpretations of Mark will engage non-Western philosophies.

First Vegetal Lesson

Nature does not hurry, yet everything is accomplished.
—Lao Tzu

The empire of God may have been initiated by humans scattering seed on the ground, but it did not grow by their hands. In Mark 4:1–20, the parable of the sower and the seeds, the four different seeds sown represent the gospel, and the different grounds or soils represent how various humans received the call to discipleship. A vegetal reading of this passage reveals that although a sower might have scattered seeds in various areas, the human actant (the sower) did not control the seeds' growth or their corresponding demise. The nonhuman actants that surrounded the seeds determined their fate. The vegetal atelic collective dependency of plants and seeds teaches a lesson in reconfiguring the nature of discipleship and the empire of God.

Reading Mark 4:1–20 from an anthropocentric perspective tends to focus on deciphering the four grounds that have received the seeds with certain characters or groups of people in Mark.[5] The ensuing issue that arises from such deciphering is its preoccupation with anthropocentric concerns (i.e., who understands the gospel or not) that caricatures the nonhumans as the enemies who prevent humans from understanding the word or the teachings of Jesus. A vegetal reading of this parable invites the reader to closely read the text while gardening or farming, to be where the parable happened in order to embody, see, and feel the parable. Some interpreters have metaphorically (perhaps even literally) brought Mark to a garden or farm in order to understand the passage. Joachim Jeremias narrates that the farmers are cognizant of the situation that some seeds fell on soil inhospitable for vegetal growth. So Jeremias (1972, 11–12) imagines that the sowers would come back and plow the field. The loss, then, would be minimal, making the parable financially and agriculturally sensible. Countering this optimistic reading of the parable, Marcus (1997, 258) argues that the parable is not just simply about the falling of the seeds but also their eventual growth or even their lack thereof. The parable narrates four times that the sower did not come back to plow the seeds. Thus, the parable emphasizes the tendency for the seeds to be lost more than the fruitfulness of a few. Barbara Reid (1999, 94) echoes Marcus's work by providing two possible scenarios. If the sower is a peasant farmer, then the parable reflects a "sloppy and wasteful manner of sowing."[6] But if the sower is a tenant farmer or a day laborer, "their reaction would be sympathetic. They would know all too well the amount of seed and effort that is

---

5. Mary Ann Tolbert (1989, 153–75) relates the four grounds to four groups: the ground along the path with the scribes, the Pharisees, the Herodians, and the Jerusalem Jews; the rocky ground with the disciples and those who are healed; the thorny ground with the rich man (Mark 10:17–22); and the good earth with those who are healed as a result of their faith (e.g., the woman with the excessive blood flow, 5:25–34).

6. Like Marcus, Reid (1999, 94 n. 9) mentions that "there is some debate whether the custom was to plow after sowing, as this parable envisions," with some texts referring to plowing *before* sowing (Isa 28:24–6; Jer 4:3; Ezek 36:9; Gos. Thom. 20; Pliny the Elder, *Nat.* 18.176) and others speaking of plowing *after* sowing (Jub. 11.11; m. Shabb. 7:2; b. Shabb. 73a–b).

expended that never bears fruit because of the difficult conditions" (94). In a certain sense, Reid's concern on the "difficult conditions" resonates with William Herzog's (2012, 197) reading of the parable as a "hidden transcript" (using the expression from Scott 1990, x–xiii) or "a critique of power spoken behind the back of the dominant and that is typically expressed openly—albeit in disguised form." Working with the *campesinos* in Solentiname, Herzog (2012, 196) finds in the parable hidden transcripts or "the struggle to appropriate symbols (a bountiful harvest), identify causes, and assess blame (birds, thorns, and rocks are more than they seem)." In other words, parables such as this could be imagined as using the people's (i.e., Galilean farmers') daily discourse to instigate conversations that critique the oppressors. For those who garden or farm, this parable would easily generate conversations that lead to insider talk—a hidden transcript necessary in avoiding the colonizers' gaze.

My take on this hidden transcript, my vegetal reading, is that one has to question this whole anthropocentric assessment that blames the birds, thorns, and rocks. That is, a gardener or farmer knows that nonhumans are the actants that move the seeds to various grounds. After the sower broadcasts the seeds and before the seeds were taken by birds or somewhat grow, a close vegetal reading of this parable probes and acknowledges the obvious relationality and actancy not only of the birds, thorns, rocks, and seeds, but also of other nonhuman actants. Although he does not designate his work as vegetal or ecological, George Nnaemeka Oranekwu's (2006, 247–48) interpretive retelling of the parable from the perspective of traditional Igbo culture highlights the importance of the actancy of nonhumans particularly in between the timing of the seeds being sown and their growth:

> Listen! Imagine, a certain Sower who after due preparations, went to his large farm and sowed many seeds. Later after he had finished sowing, there was a heavy storm and his farm was over-flooded with water. The flood carried many seeds away and they died. Some seeds were left on the surface of the earth and they were eaten up by the birds and some were gone too. Some, which survived the great flood and the birds of the air, germinated and grew up. But due to extreme heat of the sun after the flood, they died off without bearing any fruit. But the rest that survived all bore fruits: some thirty, some sixty, and some a hundredfold.

Oranekwu acknowledges the inevitable vicissitudes of the farmer: "He experiences flood, he sees the birds of the air every day, the excruciating heat of the sun forms part of his daily life experiences" (248). This acknowledgment is the first vegetal lesson: nonhumans are the "farmers" of the land. Their vegetal ways exemplify the vegetal empire of God.

To elaborate, while recognizing the role of the Roman Empire and the actancy of humans in the reception of the word and the formation of the empire of God, a vegetal reading of Mark 4:1–20 reveals the hidden transcripts of the nonhumans in seed transmission and plant formation. Aside from the birds, rocks, and thorns explicitly mentioned in the parable, wind, water (in the form of flood or rain), animals, insects, and other nonhumans could have moved those seeds from wherever they were first thrown by the sower. The parable does not say that the sower plowed the seeds or worked on the land after sowing the seeds. Connecting this parable with the other vegetal parables that follow it (4:26–29 [parable of the growing seed] and 4:30–32 [parable of the mustard seed]), I suggest that the absence of human interference and the primacy of nonhuman actancy is the key in understanding 4:1–20.

In terms of discipleship, highlighting the presence and actancy of the nonhumans disrupts the oppressive exercise of stereotyping certain groups of persons to certain types of soil. For example, a vegetal reading of the parable of the sower and the seeds mitigates anti-Semitic interpretations of Mark 4:1–20. The facile equation of Jewish leaders with the seeds fallen on the path and eaten by Satan (4:4, 15) has been a harmful interpretation with a violent legacy.[7] A vegetal reading allows for an interpretation in which the seed-ground interaction territorializes with signification but is always open for deterritorialization and reterritorialization with any person or group. While anthropocentrism tries to molarize or fix the signification of these four seed-ground interactions, a vegetal reading instead takes a step back and admonishes the audience of Mark that no one is always the good soil or the thorny ground. As Mary Ann Tolbert (1989, 163) argues, "the seed and the good earth ... must combine to bring the kingdom in power" thereby yielding "a *typology of disclosure and interaction* rather than conversion and dominance"; every person and community who seeks and follows the word of Jesus will be in one of the four seed-ground interactions in one moment and in another seed-ground interaction on a different occasion, depending upon their willingness to learn the vegetal message of the word/seed/empire of God. The

---

7. Terence J. Keegan (1994, 501–18) emphasizes that even within the Jewish leadership, there is much complexity and varied responses to Jesus's words and actions.

fluidity and precariously humbling nature of their place or soil as followers of Jesus testifies to and teaches the unpredictability of the reception of the word and the nature of the empire of God. This unpredictability is due to the active presence of the nonhumans who teach humans to be humble and revisit our supposed clear understanding of the divine and the empire of God. Perhaps Mark portrays the ignorance or inability of the disciples to follow Jesus because of their anthropocentric tendency not to learn the vegetal nature of disciples and the empire of God.[8] On the other hand, the woman with an alabaster jar (14:3–9) understood this vegetal lesson because she prepared Jesus for his burial by reconnecting him with the soil, that is, with his vegetal lessons he had been preaching all along. Jesus proclaims that she should be remembered (14:9) because she has formed an assemblage between Jesus and the nonhumans (alabaster). She should be remembered not just for her actions but also for her willingness to acknowledge the actancy of the nonhumans in the identity of the messiah and the empire of God.

In the same vein, Mark 4:26–29 narrates a parable in which Jesus equates the empire of God with the growth of seeds into fully ripe plants without human interference. The soil produces grain: first the stalk, then the head, and then the full kernel. Only after the grain ripens do humans enter the process of harvesting. A nonhuman reading of this text perceives the earth as the actant who cultivated the seeds. In Gen 1:11–12, the earth brought forth vegetation—it was a cocreator with the divine:

> Then God said, "Let the earth put forth vegetation: plants yielding seed, and fruit trees of every kind on earth that bear fruit with the seed in it." And it was so. The earth brought forth vegetation: plants yielding seed of every kind, and trees of every kind bearing fruit with the seed in it. And God said that it was good. (NRSVue)

Genesis and Mark did not explicitly mention or elaborate upon the composition of the earth, but one could surmise that the earth was comprised of an assemblage of interactions and exposures of the seed with sun, soil, air, water (through rain or other ways), microbes, worms, and other nonhuman actants. Thus, a Marderian reading of Mark 4:26–29 would argue that the vegetal empire of God was not produced by one (human) cause.

---

8. Mark portrays the disciples as failing to understand Jesus and his mission. See 4:13, 35–41; 6:45–52; 8:17–21; 10:35–41.

Rather, the causalities of the growth of the seeds are dispersed throughout the internalities and externalities that surround the seed and the potential within the seed body itself. To be vegetal is to be "heteronomous or spatially and temporally dependent upon others for growth" (Marder 2013, 67). Thus, Mark 4:26–29 teaches that the vegetal empire of God does not grow solely by human hands. Humans might have inserted themselves once in a while, but this empire grows and produces because of the other.

The vegetal empire of God's heteronomy (Marder's term for spatial and temporal dependence upon others) implies that it is a "collective being or a body of non-totalizing assemblage of multiplicities, an inherently political space of conviviality" (Marder 2013, 85). No part or organ of a plant dominates or is dominated by the whole. A plant grows due to the collective exposure of each organ to its surrounding elements. The more they are oriented towards the other (in particular, the sun), the more they become alive (150). This act of reaching out reflects a space of political conviviality. In *The Philosopher's Plant*, Marder (2014, 222) reformulates this space as "vegetal fidelity" or a plant's faithfulness to its milieu. A plant's growth is "loyal or honest" to its environment: the kind of water, the amount of sunshine, the nutrients found in the soil, and other such factors. Mark's empire of God requires this political conviviality or alliance with fellow colonized *ethne*. Colonized *ethne* are fellow actants who coexist in this oppressive milieu. They feed and help each other grow (see esp. Mark 10:42–45). Vegetality is about being attentive to others in this alliance to cosurvive and cofight the Roman Empire's sly divide and conquer scheme. As Richard A. Horsley (2001, 27–51) puts it, Mark is a story of the submerged and subjected agrarian village communities who are in alliance through their Israelite traditions and fight against Rome-designated rulers who oppress the daily lives of their communities. And yet, as the following chapters show, sometimes this reaching out to the other turns into a devouring of the other.

I partially agree with Marder's (2013, 68) understanding of plants as atelic: open-ended, incomplete, and infinitely changing since they are not "sovereignly self-determined [for their own ends] and that [they] do not assert themselves over and against their environment." Inasmuch as this statement tries to depict plants as maintaining a constant state of magnanimity, ecologically speaking, this is overstated. Strangler figs cover the host tree and kill it eventually. Kudzu plants also kill its host, which it needs for support. Venus flytraps and sundews gain nutrients by imbibing other nonhumans. Vines encroach upon their environment. In other words, vegetality does not imply passivity, unmitigated generosity, or codependency. Rather, vegetality reimagines the empire of God organically growing in its responsiveness to the other. This organic growth means openness to decay and even death (see esp. Mark 8:34–35). Contra colonial-capitalist desire for the perfect fruit without blemish or discoloration, the organic empire of God is faithful to its unavoidable bumps and bruises, bite marks from nonhumans, and eventual rotting. Mark's empire of God might be harvested in the end by humans, but the grains organically grow without initial human interference. This empire, unlike the Roman Empire, accepts the inevitability of their vulnerability—to depend on, grow alongside, and decay with the other.

Where would God fit in all of these green blueprints? A vegetal reading does not negate the presence of God. In fact, God is one of the actants who affect the growth, decay, and rebirth of plants. God's immanent presence cocreates with the earth and all creatures, since we are animated through God's breath and through the *adamah*, the humus, the soil. Vegetality is a way to see the divine in all entities (panentheism), especially in the vegetal, while it finds and emphasizes in the ontology of plants a way to learn also about the divine.

A contemporary Jewish celebration called Tu B'Shevat (fifteenth of the month of Shevat), also known as the Jewish New Year for Trees, balances the privileged place of the divine in human affairs by seeing in trees a way to be in harmony with the world and with one's religiosity. Tu B'Shevat commemorates the "Torah of Trees," which includes Orlah and Neta Reva'i (letting plants and the lands lay fallow for three years and tithed on the fourth; Lev 19:23–25; 26:3–4), Maaser Ani (the third tithing in which the produce is given to the poor; Deut 14:28), and Maaser Sheni (the second tithing in which the produce is brought to Jerusalem and eaten there in the presence of God; Deut 22:22–27) (Parsons 2016). Instituted by the kabbalists of Safed in the sixteenth century CE, many contemporary Jewish communities observe Tu B'Shevat seder in which various fruits and nuts are eaten with four cups of wine. This seder comes from the belief that trees symbolize the "tree of life, which carries divine goodness and blessings into the world" (Eisenberg 2004, 252–54; see also Steinberg 2007). Responsible and respectful consumption of the gifts provided by the trees through the seder ritual is to participate in liberating the divine energy out of their shells, renewing life into the world (Eisenberg 2004, 252). Here, humans participate in the flow of positive, life-giving energy between the divine and the vegetal. In the same vein, could one see in Mark 4:26–29 a harmonic eco-divine play at work in growing this empire?

Second Vegetal Lesson

The second vegetal lesson invites a relinquishing of the anthropocentric assumption that to fully know the nature of the empire of God is possible. The irony of Mark 4:26–29 is that its audience, the Galilean farmers and many of the colonized *ethne* in general, probably knew how plants organically grow. They presumably understood the seasons, farming techniques, and the stages of plant growth. And yet, Mark 4:26–29 does not invite them to till the land. Pheme Perkins (1994–2004, 8:577) alludes to this secretive growth of the seeds as "a warning about the suddenness of the coming Judgment." Expounding upon Perkins's interpretation with the intersection of a nonhuman and colonized *ethne* perspective, the suddenness seems to be less that of the coming judgment (or end of the world) and more so of the sudden detachment from controlling the growth of the empire of God. For the colonized *ethne* who barely have any control over their lives due to the dictates of the Roman Empire, predicting the coming and the nature of the empire of God probably signified hope and an expression of catharsis. And yet, Mark 4:26–29 invites a relinquishing, a pause that decolonizes and prevents oneself from falling into traps of carnophallogocentrism.

Marder (2013, 9) asserts that vegetality invites an approach to plants from a standpoint of "obscurity" or alterity according to Nealon's definition. Nealon's alterity affirms the difference of the Other but not due to an inability to understand or totalize the Other. Alterity refuses to associate with plants on the basis of the (im)possibility of finding similarities or sameness. Plants are producers of effects and affects on various matters. Vegetal alterity in Mark then teaches us to abandon anthropocentric assumptions that humans are the only ones who affect others.

This standpoint is needed more than ever as humans have been trying to control and manipulate nonhumans for human ends (e.g., pesticides, monocropping, genetic manipulation, industrial food production, ecosystem destruction and clearing). Vegetality is about watching and learning from the flourishing, decaying, and regeneration of plants according to their world, time, and space. By describing the manner of growth with the adjective in adverbial form "by itself" (αὐτομάτη) in Mark 4:28a, the narrative harkens back to Lev 25:5 and 11 in the Septuagint where "growing by itself" depicts the untilled growth that happens during the Sabbatical and Jubilee years (Donahue and Harrington 2002, 151). Leviticus 25:6–7 commands that humans should receive whatever the earth produces for them on that year: there is to be no human interference or anthropocentric tilling of the land. The Sabbatical year is a period in which the current assemblages based on human consumption of the land are dismantled in order to make space for new nonhuman assemblages to emerge. This emergence or letting the land go fallow teaches a vegetal reminder on how suffocating human involvement has become for nonhumans. Before it is too late, the cyclical reminder that occurs every seven years teaches humans again and again how to coexist with nonhumans in obscurity or respectful alterity. Vegetality teaches how nonhumans cultivate the land and grow seeds on their own terms.

Alterity does not mean complete avoidance of eating plants literally and symbolically. Rather, as Marder (2013, 185) argues, it asks the question: How am I to eat ethically? To eat ethically resonates with Derrida's (1995a, 278–80) call "to eat well" (*bien manger*) or to unhinge plants from the sacrificial structure of the killable. To eat ethically is to form rhizomatic relations with plants even as we eat them. Rhizomatic relations with plants consider them not as static entities or dispensable ones but as actants with multiplicities of becomings or possibilities to affect the other. It reflects plants' iterability and heterogeneity in life, death, and regeneration. Simply put, respectful alterity means deploring commodification of plants into "storehouses of calories" (Marder 2013, 185). This commodification limits the *telos* or the end (goal or purpose) of plants to human consumption. Such limitation drives plants "to ontological exhaustion" (184) when vegetality is supposed to be atelic or open-ended, incomplete, and infinitely changing.

An example of eating plants well is at the Last Supper event in Mark 14:22–25. Here, Jesus mimics the generosity or unconditional hospitality of plants toward the other. As plants (grains and grapes) are processed into bread and wine to be consumed for the nourishment of the other, the actancy of these nonhumans enabled Jesus to commemorate his body and blood to be symbols of rhizomatic connections for all who consume him. Interestingly, Marder (2013, 33) critiques the Eucharist because it "appropriated the bodies of plants, processed them into food, and then ventriloquized them as something they are not (voice of Reason and that of Revelation), thereby ceasing their existence as plants." Marder's argument seems harsh. I argue that making bread and wine for ecologically justifiable and sustainable means and ends can find a place in the realm of eating well. In any case, the assemblage of Jesus with the processed nonhumans creates a positive transformative emergence that continues to be felt and repeated even today. Again, it is a matter of relegating nonhumans not as the dispensable ones but as the remembered ones who are raised up before the communal meal for all to see, who are commemorated for their gifts of life to all who partake.

The Monsanto Jesus

Before going any further, one has to engage, difficult as it may seem, that Mark has his Messiah struggling with the vegetality of his own message. Mark narrates Jesus in Mark 11:12–14, 20–21 as someone who struggles with the alterity of the vegetal. Jesus's humanity cannot fully shun the colonial and anthropocentric desire to interfere, manipulate, and commodify plants. After Jesus left Bethany, he became hungry. Seeing a fig tree from a distance, Jesus went to it and found no fruit because it was not the season for figs. Nevertheless, Jesus cursed the fig tree to never bear fruit ever again. This narrative has become the quintessential story of banishing vegetality into the category of expendable commodities.

The frustration displayed by Jesus in this narrative as he cursed the fig tree is not an isolated, accidental emotion. His anger reflects the centuries of abuse suffered by the colonized *ethne* and their fig trees. Figs were one of the staple foods of the colonized *ethne* and nonhumans in the Judean and Galilean regions. The fig is also a tree that produces fruit precariously. Newly planted fig trees will not produce fruit until the fourth or fifth year. Even healthy, mature fig trees will not bear fruit if the environment is excessively hot or cold or if they are over-plucked or over-pruned (Palmer 2016). Luke 13:6–9 narrates the difficulties of growing fig trees. And yet figs were important because they were the food of the masses. According to m. Ketub. 5:8, Jewish husbands were required to provide their wives with (among many other things) a measure of dried or pressed figs for their sustenance. Moreover, figs symbolically represented Israel's relationship with God (Jer 8:13; Hos 9:10; Mic 7:1). Furthermore, fig trees were associated with peace and safety for the Israelites (Mic 4:4; Zech 3:10; 1 Macc 14:12; see Hunzinger 1971, 751–59).

The interference of the Romans and their colluding local elites, according to Douglas E. Oakman (1993, 261), forcefully deprioritized figs in order to concentrate on plants such as olives, grapes, and wheat that were more profitable for the Roman Empire. This is, in modern parlance, monocropping. Moreover, Oakman evinces that the reason for the absence of figs in Mark 11:12–14 was because "the Jerusalem elite took all figs to the storehouse or to the local market, their policies resulted in an 'artificial famine' of such staples. Consequently, nothing was left for the peasant family or hungry passerby" (261–62). This colonial food hoarding (an early form of oppressive agrocapitalism) withered the customs of colonized *ethne* and the vivacity of figs as actants. Wendy Cotter (1986, 64) mentions Pliny the Elder's observation: "The fig tree is also the only tree whose leaf forms later than its fruit" (see also Pliny the Elder, *Nat.* 16.49 [Rackham]). Following Pliny's observation and assuming that the fig tree of Mark 11:12–14 was in its fruit bearing years (even though 11:13d says that it was not in season yet), the lack of fruit could signify either Jesus's unfortunate late arrival because others had already harvested the fruit or a reflection upon the dire situation of the colonized *ethne* where they had to fight for scraps such as the fruit of a random fig tree.

Thus, the difficulty of pinpointing the timeframe of Mark 11:12–14, 20–21 is due to the recurring oppressive interventions of the Roman Empire and their local collaborators with the lives of the colonized *ethne* and their (fig) trees.[9] The unfortunate repercussion to these malevolent entanglements with the oppressors is that Jesus became one of those who mimicked the oppressive imperial temporality that demanded un-vegetal ripeness or the commodification of plant time. Instead of respecting the alterity of plant life and reproduction, Jesus was bewildered at the incongruence of a fig tree that was not at his beck and call.

---

9. This is Oakman's (1993, 315–27) fuller exposition on the dating of the pericope: "Because of the imagined botanical difficulties, the dating of the 'cursing' episode has long been discussed. Is this event to be associated with Jesus' entry into Jerusalem during the Feast of Tabernacles in the fall (see Nineham, 1963, 293)? In this case, Jesus would be seeking fruit roughly in the period September to October, before the leaves drop off for the winter (November). The fruit on the new wood, representing the major part of the fig harvest for the year, would be available at this time. Jewish peasants did not pick all of the fruit at once, since it was not all ripe at once (Hamel 1990, 10). The other dating option is to place the Cursing episode in the spring before Passover. Here the leaves would be just on the tree (appearing at the end of March). The early fruit, ready by late May, would hardly be ripe, although some fruit from the previous season might be on the tree. Mark's comment has often been taken to imply such a date, if καιρός ("the season") means the late-summer fig harvest. Otherwise, Mark's comment can be referred to the June harvest of the early figs (on old wood)."

Could the cursing of Jesus have been directed not against the fig tree but against the Jerusalem temple (Telford 1980; 1991; Belo 1981, 180; Myers 1988, 299; William 1982, 235–39) or the Roman Empire (Weissenrieder 2010; 2013)? Is it possible that the effect of Jesus's frustration is directed toward and limited only to the Jerusalem temple and the Roman Empire? This containment is impossible because Jesus's curse withered the fig tree. The curse may have portended or looked back at the destruction of the Jerusalem temple, but it did not destroy the temple, much less the Roman Empire. The Roman Empire still stood mighty and even flourished during the time of Mark. Here, one has to question again the intent to trivialize the plight of the fig tree under the aegis of the literary and the symbolic. To argue that it is not really about the fig tree undermines the penetrating reach of human *logos* into the material bodies of nonhumans. I discussed in chapter 3 how the nonhuman reading of the Bible is wary of excusing the use and abuse of nonhumans through metaphors, allegories, and other literary devices. Metaphors penetrate borders and boundaries. They leak and contaminate their contents to real, living nonhumans. When contamination happens, it is hard to wash away the derogatory cursing remarks that have already seeped into the tissue of the nonhumans.

The cursing of the fig tree incident implicitly demonstrates human interference through a biopolitics that designates plants as bare life. Did Mark 4:26–29 seek to illustrate the empire of God void of human interference because humans have been imagining and implementing the growth of this empire in ways detrimental to nonhumans (and humans), as in Mark 11:12–14, 20–21? One can only surmise. Nonetheless, a way to not interfere is to follow Nealon's vegetal biopolitics, which preliminarily admonishes us to pay "close attention to the power effects rendered by the myriad practices by which we do in fact differentiate ourselves from other forms of life, and what forms of violence those practices inevitably inflict" (2015, 13). One of the most significant forms of violence incurred against vegetality is to exhaust it of life.

An Organic Remedy

Nealon's vegetal biopolitics challenges the definition of life, which has been based so far on living organisms. Life belongs to all kingdoms, to begrudgingly use the Linnaean taxonomy. Vegetality sees all actants to be in the plane of "ecological territory that cuts across all strata of life as we have known it, life as primarily defined rhizomatic territories, which is to say by the practices of emergence and transformation" (Nealon 1998, 107). Deleuze and Guattari (1987, 242) call this "interkingdoms." Vegetal biopolitics is a response to Wolfe's (2012, 56) call in which "race and species must ... give way to their own deconstruction in favor of a more highly differentiated thinking of life in relation to biopower." That differentiated thinking of life deterritorializes life from the stratum that resembles humans or animals and reterritorializes life into the plane of emergences or actancies. If life is to cause actancy, then plants are living or with life. Hence Mark's vegetal empire of God admonishes to see (and not interfere with) the life-producing capacity of the vegetal in cocreating the empire of God.

Of course, if vegetal biopolitics is about understanding life as affective emergences, then the question remains on which parameters is life extended or designated. In other words, if life is defined as having the capacity to affect others, does that definition have ethical limits? Do anthrax, cancer cells, and other harmful toxins and carcinogens deserve to have or be called life? Roberto Esposito (2008, 188) argues in *Bios: Biopolitics and Philosophy* that "as the human body lives in an infinite series of relations with the bodies of others, so the internal regulation will be subject to continuous variations." The regulations or parameters do not have to follow the extreme logic of all or nothing. Esposito proposes that attributing the value of life to a certain entity is never a one-time event. Vegetal biopolitics is an ongoing process, deconstructed continuously, in order to prevent stagnation and fascist outlooks on life. The challenge then, according to Nealon (2015, 117), "is to account as fully as possible for various forms of violence, not to renounce the violence of choice or life altogether (as if that were even possible). ... Undecidability complicates decision; it doesn't make decision impossible." Anthrax does not belong to the realm of life or life-giving for now, but future technologies might come to a different conclusion and find life in this toxin.

This life is expressed, according to Marder (2013, 102), in "the nonsynchronicity, the asymmetry, and the non-contemporaneity of human and vegetal temporalities and that release the time of plants back to the contingency of the other." This nonsynchronicity, asymmetry, and noncontemporaneity could also be called vegetal play. Derived from post-Kantian aesthetic philosophy, vegetal play liberates plants from the anthropocentric formula for cost-profit efficiency, that is, the business model based on the least possible cost in order to make the highest profit possible. Mark 4:26–29 exemplifies vegetal play because the land grows not at the pace, space, and time of humans. The plants and their surrounding milieu create the production through their play and interactions. As plants grow toward the sun (light) and in reverse sink deeper into the soil (darkness), the vegetal empire of God is ubiquitous but hidden, knowable but obscure, void of human manipulation but invites humans back as its ripeness comes into fruition (Marder 2013, 177). Vegetality plays to resist what has always been. Vegetality teaches that difficulties and uncontrollability are the hallmarks of both the empire of God and life as the colonized *ethne*. Their messianic revolution is and will be excessive, transgressive, unexpected, and even death-bound.

Third Vegetal Lesson

The third vegetal lesson reminds us that those who are deemed irrelevant are those who give life. Mark 4:30–32 narrates the empire of God with two hyperbolic claims. The first claim assumes that the mustard seed is the smallest (μικρότερον) seed in the ground. For those who were farmers among the audience of Mark, this would have been a baffling claim because they would have been aware of other seeds similar in size to the mustard seed.[10] The second claim describes and imputes greatness (μεῖζον) to the size of the mustard shrub when it only grows up to six (Donahue and Harrington 2002, 151) or ten feet (Funk 1973, 5). Rather than just dismissing the author of Mark as ignorant of plant and seed sizes, a nonhuman reading of Mark 4:30–32 sees these ironic and hyperbolic claims as evidence of the affective aftermath experienced through receiving and learning vegetal generosity. The vegetal empire of God teaches us that those who are deemed most insignificant are the ones who are the most generous and the defining image of this empire. This argument stems from Moore's book, *Empire and Apocalypse* (2006, 36–44), which highlights how Mark uplifts liminal, countercultural, seemingly insignificant figures such as the child (παιδίον), servant (δίακονος), and slave (δοῦλος) as models for emulation (see Mark 9:35–37; 10:13–16, 42–45; cf. 13:34).

Some commentators have already mentioned the comic irony (Donahue and Harrington 2002, 152) or the "light-hearted burlesque" (Funk 1973, 7) of Mark 4:30–32 in describing the empire of God as a small mus-

---

10. There are other seeds known to exist in the Levant that were of somewhat similar size to the mustard seed during the time in which Mark was written, including the bramble, mint, and mulberry seeds. See Bauckham 2011, 67.

tard shrub. They have argued that great trees are used to describe empires, including in the Hebrew Scriptures. Ezekiel 17:22–23 prophesies using the cedar tree to describe the fruition of the empire of Israel:

> Thus says the Lord God: I will take a sprig from the lofty top of a cedar; I will set it out. I will break off a tender one from the topmost of its young twigs; I myself will plant it on a high and lofty mountain. On the mountain height of Israel I will plant it, in order that it may produce boughs and bear fruit, and become a noble cedar. Under it every kind of bird will live; in the shade of its branches will nest winged creatures of every kind. (NRSVue)

Ezekiel 31:1–9 compares the empire of Assyria with the cedar tree of Lebanon as well. Daniel 4:20–22 depicts Nebuchadnezzar and his empire with a great tree. These passages, like Mark 4:30–32, illustrate how animals come under the trees' shade and dwell in their branches.

The irony is that the mustard shrub is not as great as the trees mentioned above. Matthew 13:31–32 and Luke 13:18–19 probably knew about the tradition of comparing empires with great trees because they revised Mark's shrub (λαχάνων) into a tree (δένδρον). Moreover, the burlesque or absurd quality of this passage is only accentuated by the fact that it neglects to mention that mustard shrubs do not have leaves all year around because they are only in bloom during the summer. Robert W. Funk (1973, 5) contends that this change of description is a theological move because it tries to conform to the "prophetic and apocalyptic tradition" that tends to magnify the actual size of a mature mustard plant. Perkins (1994–2004, 8:578) also sees the use of the mustard shrub as a way of emphasizing divine providence.

Instead of imagining the empire of God as a great tree with all the nations under its shade or rule, Mark presents an empire that hyperbolically lives for the other. Considering that the mustard shrub is incapable of providing leaves for shade and nesting for the birds and animals all throughout the year, the lesson of the mustard shrub in Mark is that the colonized *ethne* should not expect the empire of God to follow the prescribed image of a towering cedar-like empire: the biggest, most powerful, most self-serving colonial mechanism. Mark chose the mustard shrub as an image for the empire of God in order to accustom the colonized *ethne* to a different way of becoming in this empire of God. The customary prerogative of an empire, which is to conquer all, is reversed. This empire of God gives to all hyperbolically. In other words, the statement of Mark

4:32, "so that the birds of the air can make nests in its shade," exemplifies vegetal generosity.

Vegetal generosity translates into plants' orientation for the other in their embodied finitude. To argue that "plants are oriented for the other" does not claim to know the intentions and purposes of plants. But it does not go to the other side in asserting that plants do not have "a self to which [they] could return nor a fixed, determinate goal or purpose that [they] should fulfill" (Marder 2013, 153). If the vegetal could dictate its own so-called self or its self-imposed purpose (assuming that we, humans, could actually figure it out, let alone overlook the imposition of anthropocentric prerogatives) and if its dictations are something that could be learned by humans like me, then I could learn generosity from plants by living in that liminal obscurity.

This generosity is not just an act of giving; it is an act of teaching or coaching others to do the same. The content of its teaching is on the unconditional and democratic nature of generosity: "the non-economic generosity of plant-soul, giving itself without reserve to everything and everyone that lives" (Marder 2013, 52). Plants' growth, reproduction, decay, and regeneration are contingent upon their fluid, immanent, and dispersed relationality with the other (12–13, 152). In every year and season, plants expose their vegetal bodies for the other. Even in their death, their potentialities are never exhausted. Their dehiscence and decay become the seeds and nutrients for new life. Just like animals, plants blur the demarcations of life and death (53). Even if living trees are turned into snags by forest fungi, these wildlife trees are the specters of liminal existence as they become living homes of animals and other new sprouts. If vegetal life and generosity is not about naive vitalism, then the empire of God should not be imagined by the colonized *ethne* as naively self-serving. Rather, the vegetal empire of God is with and for others with all of their corresponding decay and regeneration.

Vegetal generosity's orientation for the other does not condone abuse, especially of plant life. The gift of vegetal generosity might be inexhaustible, but a way vegetality counters abuse is by demonstrating how nonhumans interact with each other. Mark 4:26–29 has already shown the reason why nonhumans can show a better image of the empire of God than humans: birds can nest and eat the fruit of the tree every year and every season without killing or exhausting the whole tree. Mark 4:30–32 teaches us the importance of restraint, as no one nonhuman dominates the shades and the branches of the shrubs. The only way vegetal generosity is abused is when humans intervene abusively: over-plucking, deforestation, and forceful commodification of vegetal production and time.

Hence, the vegetal empire of God is atelic or open-ended in its being-for-the-other. Like plants, the vegetal empire of God is "inappropriable, both in us and outside of us, just as the life it bestows upon 'all living creatures' cannot belong to any one of them once and for all" (Marder 2013, 46). The mustard shrub forms rhizomes and assemblages with birds, wind, twigs, and other actants. The wisdom in this vegetal assemblage teaches the colonized *ethne* that they cannot belong unto themselves only. The vegetal empire of God is for all. In effect vegetality, celebrated in the Markan Son of Humanity's mustard seed parable and his other vegetal teachings, constitutes a model for the Son of Humanity himself whose destiny it is "not to be served but to serve and to give his life … for many" (Mark 10:45).

Fourth Vegetal Lesson

Vegetal temporality reconfigures imperial time by reattaching temporality to the material bodies of the nonhumans and the colonized *ethne* and by detaching these same bodies from anthropocentric linearity based on human obsession with efficiency and control. These deterritorializations and reterritorializations are based on Marder's (2013, 94) understanding of vegetal temporality or ontophytology, the ontology of plants. If vegetal temporality finds this reconfigured time in the being and spatiality of plants, then Mark's parable of the fig tree manifests the reconfigured temporality of the empire of God as the branches becoming tender and putting forth leaves.

For the colonized and enslaved *ethne*, wars, famines, persecutions, and other forms of suffering listed in Mark 13 were not events waiting for them in the future; they were experiencing or had experienced one or more of these sufferings in their lifetime because of the Roman Empire and other oppressors (such as the local elites). Mark 13:32–37 then cannot be read only as a metaphor or futuristic forecast but must also be read as a description of present and past reality that resonated with the colonized *ethne*, the majority of Mark's audience, and the tenant farmers and enslaved who worked in the fields. Mark 13 would have been an affirmation of their suffering and an affirmation of the nature of their vindication. They suspected that their vindication will not happen in one event or by one self-professed savior. Years had gone by. Several self-proclaimed saviors (Mark 13:21–22) had arrived but the expected messianic revolution did not come to fruition. Waves of rebellions arose but they all subsided as fast as they emerged. In this context, Mark 13:28 affirms the expectations and struggles of the hearers by offering a vegetal temporality: an embodied time oriented toward others, heterogeneous in its finitude for growth and decay, and regenerating season after season as a promise for a future based on the traces of the past's decay.

Arguing for a reading of Mark 13 as a concurrent apocalyptic discourse for the hearers of Mark, I follow Donahue and Harrington's (2002, 379) definition of apocalyptic discourse as "the literature of the dispossessed." "This generation" in Mark 13:30 could be interpreted as a metaphorical generation that covers a multitude of lifetimes or a cipher reference for modern day apocalyptists. However, for both the audience of Mark and for those who are suffering or dispossessed here and now, the invocation of "this generation" is probably felt viscerally in the present. Working with the Earth Bible principles, Keith D. Dyer cautions against associating Mark 13's eschatological images with twenty-first-century apocalyptic imaginations promulgated by biblicist doomsayers and those who use this narrative as an excuse to not care for the earth by blaming the divine necessity clause in which God apparently wills the destruction to happen (δεῖ γενέσθαι, "this must take place"; see 13:7).[11] From a vegetal temporality perspective, this divine necessity clause is a retelling of the painful past by the first century CE colonized *ethne* in which they are trying to make sense of why God has not intervened and why their plight has not yet improved.

Even with years of disappointment, Mark still promises the coming of this vindication through the growth pattern of fig trees (13:28). Mark is not alone in his fascination with the image, seasonality, growth, and even the decay of fig trees. Many Jewish prophets used the image of the fig tree for various reasons (McNicol 1984, 200). Some prophets used the barrenness of the fig tree as a symbol for prophetic judgment against Israel (Hos 2:12; Joel 1:7, 12; Hag 2:19; Jer 3:13). Fig trees in full bloom have also been used as a symbol for the promise of reconciliation between God and

---

11. Dyer (2002, 38–53) is working primarily with the first principle (the universe, Earth, and all its components have intrinsic worth and value), second principle (Earth is a community of interconnected living things that are mutually dependent on each other for life and survival), and fourth principle (the universe, Earth, and all its components are part of a dynamic cosmic design within which each piece has a place in the overall goal of that design).

Israel (Joel 2:22; Zech 3:10). As J. Lyle Story (89, 92) argues, the fig tree is chosen not just because of its connection with the Jerusalem temple and the messianic age but also because of its dramatic life cycle in which "it casts its leaves, so that the bare spiky twigs which give it an appearance of being utterly dead, make it possible to watch the return of the rising sap with special clearness."

Story's point on the dramatic life cycle of fig trees is fertile ground for a vegetal reading of Mark 13. As fig trees tender their branches and bring forth leaves almost every summer, the temporality of the fig tree reflects the timing of the vindication: seasonally expected but precariously actualized. Expounding upon the nature of the fig trees through the lens of Marder's ontophytology, fig trees or plants in general are precarious because they do not follow the singular linearity of time dictated by human vitality, since death ends all potentialities for humans. Vegetal temporality, however, begins with death or negative futurity. As seeds germinate through their burial in the earth, as flowers blossom by withering away their buds, and as seeds are produced through dehiscence, these negative vegetal phenomena open the ground for actualization of latent vegetal potentialities.

These moments of "non-fruition and non-accomplishment" (Marder 2013, 98) are the initial manifestations of vegetal temporality. Plants are temporally heterogeneous in their infinite lives and deaths because the various parts of plants seasonally totalize (like a tree that is in season for fruit bearing). The withering of leaves does not portend to the demise of the whole plant. The leaves' finitude is premised by the hope of regeneration in due time. The same goes for the time of vindication for the colonized *ethne*. This vindication, the coming of the empire of God, will happen irregularly and imperfectly. Sufferings will still haunt this generation and the next. The Roman Empire's regime will not immediately dissipate. But the hope is that as branches will grow tender and bring forth leaves, the vindication for the colonized *ethne* will regenerate season after season. Even in its death or failure, the demise of a vindication will become the seed for the next.

Another complexity illustrated by the fig tree of Mark 13:28 is that its growth, its potentialities, are not self-dependent. The maturation or potentiality of the branches to become tender and bring forth leaves are contingent upon the other: sun, rain, minerals, and other nonhumans (Marder 2013, 100–101). As mentioned before, this dependency reflects a plant's non-synchronicity with itself. Depending upon the exposure (or the lack thereof) to externalities, various parts of plants grow differently.

Even on the same tree, some branches become tender and some do not. Some leaves grow better than others. This nonsynchronicity is not due to lack or excess like humans' experience when they get sick. The heterogeneity of temporality within each plant allows for multiplicities of growth and decay simultaneously. In other words, each part or organ of the plant has potentially infinite growth patterns (and infinite potentialities for decay as well) because they grow based on their exposure to various externalities. This potentiality is expressed well through the iterability of leaves:[12] "an ephemeral register for the inscription of vegetal time as the time of repetition, a register not archived but periodically lost and renewed, such that these losses and renewals themselves make up the temporal, temporalizing trace imprinted on it" (Marder 2013, 114). Leaves teach us a lesson on the ephemeral nature of the empire of God. Branches might be intact but leaves fall and spring back to life in their alterity.

In addition, Manuela Infante's one-person play, "Estado Vegetal," is a vivid, visceral, and eye-opening performance that echoes Marder's exposition on leaves. As Infante (2010, n.p.) states:

> What would it be like to grow without returning to the center, without every regrouping, always moving outwards? Never being able to close oneself upon oneself, never reaching the full circle of "This is I." To be, to grow, always, further out. So that, that thing called I is only the memory of a seed. To be oneself, to be just one-self, is only a seasonal event. They tried to tell us all this, to cover the whole world with their varied words, but all they managed to say was: leaf. Always the same lead. It's not possible to escape planthood by means of plants. Nor to escape humanity by human means.

Applying this lesson to the colonized *ethne*, the vindication they awaited was not self-dependent. Rather, this vindication depended upon the assemblage of various *ethne*, angels, nonhumans, and other actants (see Mark 13:27). To say that summer is near does not always equate with branches becoming tender and leaves sprouting. In reality, some fig trees' branches will not become tender and bring forth leaves again. The colonized *ethne*

---

12. According to Derrida (1988, 119), iterability "does not signify simply ... repeatability of the same, but rather alterability of this same idealized in the singularity of the event.... There is no idealization without (identificatory) iterability; but for the same reason, for the reasons of (altering) iterability there is no idealization that keeps itself pure safe from all contamination."

knew this because they had experienced firsthand the unpredictability of vegetal growth and also how the colonizers destroy or commodify vegetal temporality for their own imperial purposes.

Mark 13:24–25 further expresses this irregularity and unpredictability with celestial interruptions.[13] Dyer (2002, 52) interprets this passage with a pre-Copernican lens and argues that the heavenly bodies represent human leadership: "they would be understood as the realignment of temporal powers in the East after the fall of Jerusalem and the establishment of the House of Flavian in Rome." Donahue and Harrington (2002, 374) point to the demise of the "elemental spirits of the world" (στοιχεῖα τοῦ κόσμου) who are also known to rule the world (see Gal 4:3; Col 2:8, 20; 2 Pet 3:10, 12). These cosmic portents also resonate with the theophanic narratives of the Hebrew Scriptures (Isa 13:10; 34:4; Ezek 32:7–8; Joel 2:10–11, 31; 3:4, 15; Amos 8:9; Hag 2:6, 21). Instead of limiting interpretive possibilities to anthropocentric concerns, a vegetal reading of Mark 13:24–25 argues that these celestial interruptions are common nonhuman phenomena. The sun darkens (solar eclipse; Mark 13:24b). The moon loses its light once in a while (new moon; 13:24c). The stars fall (shooting stars; 13:25a). Storms shake the heavens (13:25b). All of these "heavenly powers" disrupt the supposed regularity of human cosmology.

These interruptions echo the interruptions of plants. In explaining the interruptions of plants in their growth and decay (expansions and contractions), Marder finds Johann Wolfgang Goethe's theory of the metamorphosis of plants helpful: "the organ that expanded on the stem as a leaf, assuming a variety of forms, is the same organ that now contracts in the calyx, expands again in the petal, contracts in the reproductive apparatus, only to expand finally as the fruit" (Goethe 2009, 100; see Marder 2013, 110). These interruptions reflect the traces of finitude in the ostensibly infinite lives of plants. The same applies to the vindication of the colonized *ethne*. The vegetal empire of God expands and contracts like plants. Vegetal temporality maps an oscillating matrix of relationality (expansions and contractions) that interrupts the supposed obvious and predictable human timeline of the coming of the empire of God. By following the time of the plants, the vegetal teaches that death and decay are integral parts of this coming because through them new offshoots of hope spring forth.

---

13. "But in those days, after that suffering, the sun will be darkened, and the moon will not give its light, and the stars will be falling from heaven, and the powers in the heavens will be shaken."

Branches becoming tender and putting forth leaves is a statement of hope for a precarious future. "To be awake" (Mark 13:37) is not about waiting for that one moment that will bring the world to its end. As Dyer (2002, 54) argues, it is to be in "existential alertness and faithful action." In vegetal terms, it is to know that this existential vindication will come in faithful multiplicity, in various iterations, and in the expectation of its finitude while waiting for the other to germinate it again into fruition. New regenerations will sprout with the traces of the past cycles of life. Marder (2013, 112) finds hope in the *ex-scription* (using Jean Luc-Nancy's word) of time in the accretion of vegetal "rings" on the bodies of plants. When tree trunks are cut diagonally, one can see the age of trees by counting the concentric rings that manifest the number of seasons and the kinds of climate the trees have endured. These rings, the plants' *ex-scriptions*, are bodily reminder for the colonized *ethne* that their vindication is already happening within them. Year after year, their struggle to survive as manifested through the wearing and scarring of their skins, the withering of their hair, and the decay of their bodily organs promise that their future will bud with new life this coming summer or the next.

4
AND SAY THE SEA OF GALILEE RESPONDED?

In March 2013, sixteen thousand dead pigs were found floating and decomposing in the tributaries of the Huangpu River in Shanghai. A forty-eight-year-old fisherwoman described the Jiapingtang River, a tributary adjacent to her home, as "inky black, covered in a slick of lime green algae, and it smells like a blocked drain" while "at [her] feet a dead piglet bobs on the river's surface, bouncing against the shore" (Davidson 2013). These rivers, once used for fishing, swimming, and drinking, had become the dumping ground for contaminated carcasses. This incident generated scrutiny in national and international media: negligence and greed through lack of environmental concerns compounded by the illegal market meat trade. A sudden high demand for pork in the 1980s converted Jiaxing, a former fishing village, into one of the biggest producers of pork in the world. The current infrastructure, however, could not support the surge. Inadequate production channels caused some farmers to resort to illegal market meat trading, selling diseased meat to usually unaware buyers. When law enforcement cracked down on this illegality, some farmers resorted to discarding their dead pigs in the river.

Images of this catastrophe caught national attention through China Central Television (CCTV) and Weibo (China's social media program). International news outlets reported these violations as well. The BBC coverage posted an image in which sanitation workers in orange vests and blue protective suits used wooden sticks to pick up dead pigs (Sudworth 2013). CNN reported that the Shanghai residents drinking the water flowing from the Huangpu River had already been skeptical of the quality of the water (Park and Zhang 2013). For these locals who were immediately impacted by this catastrophe, the effect of visual evidence confirming their fears induced utter disbelief. Their water came from the same source as where pig carcasses were floating! The Shanghai residents were further infuriated when the government leaders told them that the water from these tributaries was safe to drink. This led many of the residents to voice their complaints to social media: "Since apparently, the water has not been contaminated, big leaders, please go ahead and have the first drink," one local quipped (Park and Zhang 2013).

Mark 5:1–20 and its afterlives reek of disgust. I cannot help but smell the resonance of Mark 5:1–20 with the affect produced by the tragedy of Huangpu River. Imagine the stench of thousands of large animals decomposing, the stench of their bobbing and bouncing carcasses hitting against the shore, contaminating the relatively small, enclosed Sea of Galilee that was supposed to provide drinking water and food for its adjacent towns. The Roman Empire's imposition on the city of Gerasa to produce pork mirrors the sudden influx of pork factories into the town of Jiaxing. The collusion of the local elites with the Roman Empire anticipates the lack of infrastructural concern for the people of Jiaxing and Shanghai by the local Chinese government. The anger of the pig herders (βόσκοντες) and the Gerasenes against Jesus, and their plea for him to leave their town, mirror the fury and disgust of the fisherpersons and the residents of Shanghai.

The Gerasenes exhort (παρακαλεῖν) Jesus to leave their region in Mark 5:16–17. Why did they do so? Was it the loss and the potential further loss to their business (i.e., the death of pigs) due to the presence of Jesus? Were they afraid of possible imperial reprisals against them because the food supply of the Roman legion was eliminated? The text does not explicitly say. Taking our cue from the fury of the fisherpersons and other residents of Shanghai, should we surmise that the anger and plea of the pig herders and Gerasenes was occasioned particularly by the grotesque pollution of their primary water source? The affect of disgust created by seeing the gruesome spectacle of thousands of pigs in the Sea of Galilee, and the realization that their water and food (fish) from the Sea of Galilee would always be affected by the hauntings of these pigs' cadavers, likely traumatized the Gerasenes. This disgust compels the Gerasenes to implore Jesus to leave.

Although I invoke the affect of disgust to compare Mark 5:1–20 and the plight of Jiaxing and its tributaries, Mark 5:1–20 does not literally say that the Gerasenes, or Jesus for that matter, were disgusted. This chapter follows Moore's (2017b, 287–310) method of affective close reading as modeled in his rereading the Gospel of John.[1] This form of close reading

---

1. Moore cites Brinkema 2014, xiv, 37–39.

requires an imaginative leap in which contemporary affective encounters guide the possibilities for reading texts that could be channels for affective resonances. I am not crudely implying that sniffing the pages of your New Testament book will detect repulsive odors similar to rotting pig cadavers. Rather, as Moore (2017b, 297) points out, the disgust of Mark 5:1–20 fumes out from the "absences, elisions, ruptures, gaps, and points of contradiction" that have characterized previous scholarly interpretations of the pericope, interpretations oddly oblivious to the two thousand pig carcasses dumped in the Sea of Galilee at the pericope's end and left to rot there as Jesus and his disciples leave the scene. If Mark 5:1–20 is understood as an affective encounter by living actants, both human and nonhuman, then this chapter invites a rereading of Mark 5:1–20 that smells and sees the what ifs of the gaps hidden between verses and words, fuming out affective and visceral possibilities of interpretation.

This affective and visceral nonhuman reading of the Bible resonates with ecojustice hermeneutics. As mentioned in the introductory chapter, ecojustice hermeneutics acknowledges the affective responsivity/actancy of those who are deemed inanimate. The earth is imaginatively portrayed to have an enduring voice that witnesses to the vicissitudes of time. There is no literary evidence to support the explicit voice of the earth. And yet, ecojustice hermeneutics affectively find through the materiality of real-world issues (such as factory farming, genetic modification, mountaintop mining, and other environmentally harmful activities), the hidden gaps through which some aspects of the voice of the earth can be retrieved. Following this line of approach, this chapter builds upon ecojustice hermeneutics by intersecting the affect of disgust with Chen's animacies theory for a nonhuman reading of Mark 5:1–20. Chen's (2012, 2) animacies reconfigure the Sea of Galilee as an actant who exercises its affective potentialities even if it is assumed to be "insensate, immobile, deathly, or otherwise 'wrong.'" The Sea of Galilee, now saturated with rotting pig flesh, animates disgust and potentially moves human actants into decisive actions, even if it is considered inanimately toxic.

This chapter also borrows its title from Derrida's essay, "And Say the Animal Responded?" This is a rebuttal against Jacques Lacan's (2008, 121–22) "The Subversion of the Subject" in which animals are singularized through the Cartesian logic of relegating nonhumans as creatures capable not of response but only of reaction: "the animal has neither unconscious nor language, nor the other, except as an effect of the human order, that is by contagion, appropriation, domestication." Derrida argues that Lacan characterizes the nonhuman as incapable of "pretending or *erasing its traces*, unable to become a subject or subject of the signifier" (120). Derrida does not argue, however, in favor of attributing certain human capacities (e.g., speech, reason, mourning) to nonhumans. Rather, his argument questions the supposed *"pure, rigorous, indivisible"* nature of humans (135). Derrida complicates the distinction and instills the *différance* between response and reaction, acknowledging the multiplicity of human and nonhuman responses. This chapter's reading of the nonhumans of Mark sees them as actants who respond but not according to anthropocentric expectations of expression. How they respond, among many other ways, is through affect. The Sea of Galilee tells *their* story, their response to Jesus and other humans, through disgust.

A Legion of Scholars on Mark 5:1–20

Ecojustice interpreters have already called out the schadenfreude of the anthropocentric readings of Mark 5:1–20 in which sacrificing the pigs is a nonissue or simply a joyous symbolic victory over the Roman Empire. Annika Spalde and Pelle Strindlund (2012) have traced various trends of Christian interpretations of Mark 5:1–20 throughout history that either see Jesus as a callous person toward the pigs, use the narrative as a justification for abusing nonhumans, or highlight the imperial backdrop of the narrative. Finding these works insufficient because nonhumans are still relegated as property, Spalde and Strindlund reread Mark 5:1–20 with an ecojustice lens. Borrowing from Andrew Linzey (2000, 40), they conclude that nonhumans should be recognized to have "theos-rights" to live in harmony with others in their God-given purpose. Humans are then called to serve and "expand a dominion of love to all creatures" (Spalde and Strindlund 2012, 113).

Interpretations of the pericope throughout the years have been anthropocentric (intentionally or not) and void even of imperial presence (Sugirtharajah 2002, 91–92).[2] Some have interpreted the passage from a colonial-mission perspective, in which the placement of the narrative outside of Jewish territory (i.e., Gerasa) supposedly indicates the proto-spreading of the gospel to gentile or pagan territories, which by extension includes

---

2. See the following for mainstream interpretations of Mark 5:1–20: Aus 2003; Craghan 1968, 528–29; Derrett 1979, 3; and Gundry 1993, 260–61.

Asian, African, and South American nations (Staley 2006). Others have used social-scientific methods and Western psychological theories to analyze the demon possession and healing of the Gerasene (Hollenbach 1981, 572; McGann 1985, 71–80; Newheart 2004; Robbins 1999). A third approach, especially prominent among African biblical interpreters, has been to vernacularize the passage and focus upon its correlation with African belief systems regarding supernatural powers (Avotri 2000).

As early as 1920, Mary Baird was one of the first scholars to associate the legion of Mark 5:1–20 with imperial, military connotations. Baird referenced the tenth Roman legion that was garrisoned in Palestine during the time of Jesus. Baird (1920, 189) was unequivocal in her argument that "there is no example in Hellenistic Greek of this word [legion] being used with other than a definite *military* connotation.… Therefore, it would appear in the N.T. contexts the word should be interpreted *literally*." A century has passed, and yet there is still a legion of scholars of Mark 5:1–20 that prefers to live within the confines of theological (meaning Christian dogmatic) and nonimperial perspectives. Mark 5:1–20 is apparently one of the *crux interpreta* of Mark because it does not conform to the usual glorified view of Jesus (Haenchen 1968, 160). That is why R. S. Sugirtharajah has called for more imperial, liberation, and postcolonial readings of the narrative. Interestingly, there has been no shortage of responses to Sugirtharajah's call (Dormandy 2000, 335; Garroway 2009, 60; Ched Myers 1988, 194; Calpino 2008, 15–23).

Moore (2006, 31) has refrained from reducing the Markan narrative simply as a matter of "Jesus bumping Caesar off the throne." Moore posits an ambivalent stance entailed in the Markan Jesus's mimicry of the Roman Empire's colonial methods. The Markan Jesus may have allegorically overthrown a legion of the Roman Empire by drowning the pigs with the demons called legion in the Sea of Galilee. Nevertheless, the Markan Jesus mimics the imperial model of colonization when he commands the Gerasene who was possessed previously to spread Jesus's imperial victory to the colonies. This command entails a reiteration of a colonial takeover story in which a region (Gerasa) is cleansed of vestiges (here symbolized by pigs) of the old regime. This postcolonial reading questions the supposed liberating reading of Mark 5:1–20. Is it truly liberating when the process of liberation mimics the oppressive methods of the colonizers (the expendability and recolonization of the weak and oppressed)?

As a missionary and missionary kid myself, I know and have experienced firsthand the neocolonial tendency to mimic the (former) colonizers' methods particularly in using the Bible as a colonial weapon. A couple of centuries ago, Christian missionaries came into our ancestral lands and colonized us by using the Bible. According to George Alexander Chadwick, nonwhite persons were apparently the Gerasenes, "mixed race, place where the shadow of sin has fallen, and direst wretchedness" (from Leander 2013, 96). They even used biological determinism and racism (Georges Cuvier) to justify why nonwhite people and women in general were more susceptible to demon possession. With all of these racist statements and having been converted to Christianity under oppressive conditions, one would assume that the colonized would shun colonial technologies. However, history shows that twentieth and twenty-first-century Asian missionaries have mimicked their former colonizers' oppressive methods by perceiving themselves as the new "divine ambassadors" who will cleanse the heathens of their sins (97).

Turning to the intersection of postcolonialism and masculinity studies, Warren Carter's 2015 article (139–55) revisited the term *legion* in its military connotation and the demon's unusual request to enter the pigs. Carter employed empire-critical and hegemonic masculinity perspectives in reading Mark 5:1–20. Carter, on the one hand, depicts Jesus as a hyper-masculine figure who tames the "out-of-control, demonic, militaristic, effeminate Roman Empire" (145). Jesus subdues or penetrates into submission the legion or the premier army that symbolically represent the Roman Empire by commanding the demon to penetrate the pigs (or boar, the symbol of the tenth legion of the Roman Empire). According to Carter, this sexual language of penetration has a long pedigree. Aristophanes, in particular, pejoratively referred to female genitalia as pigs or piglets.[3] Since the Roman legion is like or symbolized by a pig or boar, then Mark 5:1–20 demonstrates the victory of Jesus over the Roman Empire and its legion by the penetration of the phallic demons into the Roman Empire's (female) genitalia.

On the other hand, Carter expounds upon the ambivalence of Jesus's hyper-masculinity. Following Colleen Conway, Carter (2015, 155) argues that any celebration would be precipitous because ten chapters later Jesus became the "emasculated victim" at the cross (see Conway 2008, 100–106). Jesus's hyper-masculinity in Mark 5:1–20 imitated the *venationes* or the

---

3. Carter found these references that describe female genitalia as pigs or piglets: James Adams 1990, 82; Dover 1972, 63–65; Ewans 2012; Henderson 1975, 1998, 153–55; and Sommerstein 1980, 194–95.

mass killing or subjugation of animals in front of an audience. This spectacle of subjugated animals contributed to the "normative Roman identity" as conquerors of the world, the triumph of the civilized over the barbaric other (Carter 2015, 149). The request of legion to be "sent into the pigs" in Mark 5:1–20 similarly reenacts this imperial control over the animals and the land that sustains them. And yet, ironically the Markan Jesus himself became the spectacle, a subjugated colonized *ethne*, who was crucified and subjected to an animalizing death because he tried to disrupt the imperial normativity. If Mark 5:1–20 poses Jesus as a symbolic hyper-masculine penetrator of the Roman Empire and its legion, the Roman Empire returns the favor by penetrating Jesus as well with nails in his hands and feet (see Mark 15:24).

This chapter's affective animacy reading of Mark 5:1–20 finds Carter's postcolonially ambivalent narration of the penetrating and penetrated Jesus as an important conversation partner because Carter brings out the lived realities of the colonized *ethne*. Moore (2006, 27) argues that Mark 5:1–20 should be read as a "national allegory," a colonized person (the demoniac) standing allegorically for the history of an entire group or nation.[4] Expounding upon Moore's argument, the disgust felt by the Gerasenes with the affect produced by the Sea of Galilee and the dead pigs in Mark 5:1–20 represents the history of bestial logics or the objectification of the other experienced by the colonized *ethne* and the nonhumans under the Roman imperial colonizers' gaze. It is one thing to say that the Sea of Galilee is disgusting because it is filled with pig cadavers; it is another to say that the colonized *ethne* feel the disgust viscerally as the dead pigs mirrored the dispensability of their lives, their livelihood, and of their hope for a new empire of God. The death of the pigs is not a joyous symbolic destruction of the Roman Empire. Rather, their death becomes the necroactant, the death driving entities who push the other to dispensability or killable. This reminds the colonized humans and nonhumans of their shared emasculation under the Roman Empire.

The death drive of Mark 5:1–20 echoes the escalating ecological crisis happening in almost every corner of the planet today. The gloomy tone of interpretation of the present chapter echoes various ecojustice interpretations of Mark 5:1–20 where scholars are at a loss on how to retrieve this

---

4. For more detailed explanation of national allegories, see Aijaz Ahmad 1987, 3–25; Jameson 1986, 65–88; and Samuel 2007, 1–16.

narrative. Responding to the need to care for the earth, Bauckham's (2011, 98) ecological or green reading of Mark 5:1–20 begrudgingly resorts to the grey area or the lesser evil argument to explain Jesus's action to let demons kill the pigs. This argument reflects the first-things-first approach—it is better to save one human over thousands of pigs—in which none of the choices are redeemable. Bauckham interprets Mark 5:1–20 this way because he acknowledges that the "peaceable kingdom of God" does not come into fruition in perfect form (77). Bauckham finds hope in but cannot fully commit to Michael Northcott's (1996, 224) image of Jesus as "one who lives in supreme harmony with the natural order." David Rhoads (2004, 67) also acknowledges that the list of "egregious examples of disparaging attitudes toward nature in the New Testament include the drowning of the 2,000 pigs in the Sea of Galilee." Loader designates this passage as one of the irretrievable passages that blatantly espouse destruction of the earth. For Loader (2002, 41), Mark 5:1–20 treats the pigs as "collateral damage" in the war against the Roman Empire and the evil powers.

Kendra Haloviak Valentine's 2017 essay, "Liberating Legion: An Ecocritical, Postcolonial Reading of Mark 5:1–20," revisits the pericope by focusing on the violence done to the fields of Gerasa and its corresponding neglect of the plight of the poor. Using Mary Douglas's groundbreaking work, *Purity and Danger* (1966), Valentine (2017, 209) redefines the concept of "unclean" for Mark 5:1–20 as the "hazardous and dangerous use of the fields for ecologically unsustainable purposes. Valentine reimagines this violence or unsustainable use of the land (χώρα) in Mark 5:1–20 by emphasizing how the Roman Empire transformed fields meant for the cultivation of plant crops ("allocation" economy) into grazing lands for the pigs that were consumed by the Roman legion ("extraction" economy).[5] This cooptation of land catered directly to and benefited solely the Roman Empire and their rich local collaborators because first century CE pig husbandry required vast amounts of land, time, and resources (i.e., grain and water) before any form of benefit could be garnered. This luxury husbandry was not geared toward providing sustenance for the poor since pig husbandry negatively correlates to the food provision of the poor: the more pigs were fed with grain (and other basic sustenance), the less food the poor had left for themselves. The field should have been cultivated for crops because such utilization could provide food more easily for the

---

5. Valentine quotes Boer 2015 passim. See also Marvin Harris 1974 passim.

masses. Instead, the fields that should have been producing such food were coopted into lands for the rich and their pigs. That is why, according to Valentine (2017, 201), Mark 5:1–20 is a narrative of protest against this displacement. Mark 5:1–20 protests against the unclean oppression of the poor and the land. Jesus's healing of the demoniac thus represents a symbol of threat to the Roman Empire's power structure and its rich local collaborators because it signified the expulsion of the pig husbandry and its corresponding violence against the land and the people (200, 208).

Affected by the Sea of Galilee

While Valentine ecocritically and postcolonially reimagines the fields and its relations with the poor, local elites, and the Roman Empire, this chapter finds solace in the affective actancy of the Sea of Galilee in influencing Markan interpretations. Many Markan scholars would not say that the Sea of Galilee affected them to interpret in certain ways. But they would agree that the author of Mark's frequent use of the Sea of Galilee affected their perception in understanding the metanarrative of the Gospel of Mark. For example, most Markan scholars would agree that the Sea of Galilee is the geographical focal point for the first half of the gospel (Malbon 1984, 363; see also Malbon 1986). Jesus called his disciples (1:16, 19, 20), taught, and healed the crowds by the sea (2:13; 3:7; 4:1; 8:13–21). Jesus also traversed the Sea of Galilee by both floating and walking on the water's surface (6:45–56) in order to meet with various colonized *ethne* (4:35; 5:1, 21; 6:45, 53; 8:10, 13). Moreover, Elizabeth Struthers Malbon (1984, 377) asserts that the Sea of Galilee "makes known the Jesus of Mark as both Jesus from Nazareth of Galilee (1:9) and Jesus Christ the Son of God (1:1; 1:11; 3:11; 9:7; 15:39)."

The relatively small size of the Sea of Galilee seems to not hinder its affective potentialities and narrative role in Mark's Gospel. The Sea has a total length of thirteen miles (21 km) and is seven miles (11 km) wide in its widest points with depths of about 130 to 148 feet depending upon the season.[6] From a hill one can see the entire lake. From the slopes above Tel Hum (Capernaum), and almost anywhere along the eastern shore, it is totally visible and arguably underwhelming.

---

6. Due to climate change, these figures are bound to fluctuate. See Encyclopedia Britannica, "Sea of Galilee | Lake, Israel | Britannica.com," https://www.britannica.com/place/Sea-of-Galilee.

The importance of the Sea of Galilee in Mark 5:1–20 is further evinced by how the author used it as a focal space for the narrative, even if the author seems to be geographically challenged when it comes to determining the distances of towns in relations to it. Mark claims that Jesus crossed the Sea of Galilee to Gerasa. This is impossible because Gerasa (Jerash) is about 42 miles or 67.6 kilometers from the Sea of Galilee. According to the description of the environment in the pericope, the only possible place that Mark 5:1–20 could have happened is in Kersa or Kursi because of its steep slopes and proximity to the Sea of Galilee. Eric Francis Fox Bishop (1951, 399) even narrates a story about the steep slopes of Kersa as it resonates with the way the pigs drowned: "The steep place at Kersa slopes down at once to a depth of 49 feet and a short distance further out gives the sounding of 102 feet. A motor boat bound for the Jewish colony of ain Geb on the eastern side and somewhat overloaded turned right over and most of the passengers who could not swim, were drowned." No wonder its moniker is *al Ghuweir*, or "the little sunken dip" (399).

Encounters with the Sea of Galilee produced different names according to various groups of people (or colonized *ethne*): Lake/Sea of Kinneret (Num 34:11; Josh 12:3; 13:27; contemporary Jewish Israeli citizens call the lake by this name), Gennesaret (Luke 5:1), and Tiberias (John 6:1; 21:1) or Bahr Tabariyeh (the name used by modern Arab-speaking persons). Mark used the name θάλασσαν τῆς Γαλιλαίας, "the Sea of Galilee," even if it is inaccurate (cf. Luke 5:1, 2; 8:22, 23, 33, which call it lake or λίμνη) because it alludes to the places (i.e., the land of Zebulun and Naphtali, by the way of the sea, and beyond the Jordan) that will be honored and will see the light according to Isaiah's prophecy (Isa 9:1; see also Matt 4:12b–16; Notley 2009, 187). Instead of Gennesaret or Tiberius, Mark chose Galilee since it symbolically stands as a place-name that ascribes prophetic significance and affective resonance to the lake and its region for the Markan Jesus and his empire of God.

Another Story of Tehomicide?

Still, the enduring approach in dealing with nonhuman actants, such as the Sea of Galilee, is to consider them as background objects for anthropocentric ends. For many biblical interpretations, the cumulative anthropocentric perspective on the Sea of Galilee is that it is apparently a "place of chaos and destruction" (Rhoads, Dewey, and Michie 2012, 70). Following Cotter (1999, 131–63), the stilling of storms is a common motif in narratives on Greco-Roman Olympian pantheon deities (Poseidon and Aphrodite), regional deities (Dioscuri, Samothrace deities, Isis, Serapis, the Jewish deity), and even humans or heroes (Orpheus, Pythagoreans, Apollonius of Tyana, and Julius Caesar). Many of these narratives impose agency on bodies of water as capable of reacting to the chants, prayers, or commands of these divine and human entities. The motif is also found in biblical literature. Psalm 148:7 imbues the cosmic sea creatures and ocean depths with the capacity to speak so that they can praise God (see also Ps 104:7). Job 38:8–11 anthropomorphizes the sea as a newly born baby wrapped in garments and obedient to God's imposed limitations. These traditions of anthropomorphizing relegate the sea into the service of divine and human desires. In Mark 4:35–41, the Sea of Galilee is implicitly imbued with the linguistic capacity to understand human language because the narrative depicts Jesus commanding the Sea of Galilee into submission through human words. The narrative never questions the seemingly natural recurring pattern of shallow lakes having huge waves during storms.[7] Moreover, the narrative does not respect the alterity of the Sea of Galilee. Instead, the Sea of Galilee is anthropomorphized as an untamed beast meant to be subdued in order to elevate the human protagonist. In Nah 1:4, the prophet states that God's rebuke and anger have the power to dry the seas and rivers. The prophet does not say which specific bodies of water. Nevertheless, the point is that Nahum chose to describe God as someone willing to destroy bodies of water just to teach or reprimand humans.

Another example is Rev 8:8–11, in which "something like a great mountain, burning with fire," is "thrown into the sea." Subsequently, "a third of the sea [becomes] blood" and "a third of the living creatures in the sea [die]," and "a third of the rivers and … springs of water" become "wormwood," all at God's behest. In Rev 16:3–4 and 12, God finishes the job, causing the entire sea to become "like the blood of a corpse" so that

---

7. According to Shelley Wachsmann (1995, 121): "There is a daily order to the winds during the summer and fall around the Sea of Galilee. In the winter months, the weather system is more chaotic, and the winds have a tendency to shift, blowing first from one direction and then the other. It is also during the winter that the *sharkia* [strong winter easterly wind in the region of Israel; from p. 397 of Wachsmann] comes howling down the Golan Heights to stir up the Kinneret, raising waives that pound the western side of the lake. *Sharkias* come at a frequency of about once every two weeks and generally last for about three days."

"every living thing in [it dies]," and the rivers and springs of water also become blood, and the waters of "the great river Euphrates" become "dried up." Not surprisingly in Revelation's "new creation," then, "the sea [is] no more" (21:1). These passages describe a divinity who subjugates or destroys inanimate objects to prove a point (Faricy 1982, 42–48). From another angle, one could argue that human authors ventriloquize the mouth of the divine in order to project their intent in a more authoritative way. One could argue that these passages are all just metaphors, and should be taken with a grain of salt. And yet, in Mark 4:35–41, the calming of the Sea of Galilee by Jesus is not a metaphor. The narrative was not written as a parable or an analogy in a teaching event. The taming of the Sea of Galilee is in line with healing narratives that are arguably presented as historical. In a similar vein, Ps 107:23–29 asserts that God controls the sea literally. Job 38:8 and 11 even depict God as setting the boundaries of various "real" bodies of water.

Moreover, for Mark, bodies of water are apparently dumping sites for various other bodies. Mark 5:1–20 already demonstrated this destructive practice of disposing of abject bodies in the Sea of Galilee. Mark 9:42 turns an unspecified sea into a death zone for those who cause "the children" to stumble. They are to be thrown into it with a large millstone around their neck, sentenced to the sea of death. Further, Mark 11:23 tells the followers of Jesus that they could destroy a natural ocean habitat (throw a mountain into the sea) if they choose or have faith to do so. The ease with which the Sea (of Galilee) is disposed of or destroyed is due to an anthropocentric tradition of labeling or connoting sea(s) as chaos, threat, and danger in opposition to land that symbolizes order, promise, and security (Malbon 1984, 376). This ecocidal tradition is reflected in Mark's decision to use θάλασσα "sea" instead of λίμνη "lake," even if λίμνη is the more accurate descriptor for the Sea/Lake of Galilee. Malbon (1984, 364) argues that Mark chose θάλασσα because it has a richer connotation that flows from the Hebrew Scriptures. The so-called richness though, as shown above, is concerned with depicting the threatening nature of the sea, representing it as being at enmity with both God and human beings.

Catherine Keller describes this negative signification of the sea as tehomophobia or fear of the abyss of the primordial waters of creation. She also questions the orthodox Christian belief of *creatio ex nihilo*. Keller (2003, 12) prefers tehomophilia, an alternative or third space, that sees the sea/*tehom* as "the topos of the Deep ... as primal chaos [that] precedes and gives rise to the generative tensions of order and disorder, form and formlessness … in which the strange inter-fluences of creatures—in ecology, predation, genetic, cultures—crisscross the abyss of differences." Keller poetically expresses that in *creatio ex profundis*, in the matrix of possibilities, there could be "radical interrelation" between humans and nonhumans (160–61). Keller's reading of Mark 4:35–41 sees Jesus's annoyance not with the sea but with the tehomophobic disciples who do not have the courage to "activate" or do the gospel themselves (214).

Is Mark 5:1–20 then a story of tehomicide? The Sea of Galilee is interpellated (i.e., forcefully given an identity) as a living monster that needs to be tamed. Often, however, people living in ancient Israel and across the Mediterranean world would have demonized the Mediterranean Sea. Communities throughout history gave the Mediterranean Sea various *noms de guerre* due to its relative vastness and consequent perils. In the Hebrew Scriptures, for example, it is both "the Great Sea" (הים הגדול; see Num 34:6–7; Josh 1:4, 9:1; 15:47; Ezek 47:10, 15, 20) and "the Sea of the Philistines" (Exod 23:31). In addition, the Mediterranean Sea is associated with the Roman Empire when the "Beast of the Sea" of Rev 13 is discussed. Compared to the Great Sea, the Sea of Galilee—actually a mere lake—does not exude threat on a cosmic scale.

And yet, the Sea of Galilee of Mark 4:35–41 and 5:1–20 is not exempt from being interpellated as a threatening monster that, on the one hand, needs taming and, on the other hand, is capable of dissolving into oblivion the bodies of all that are dumped in it. No matter their size, this interpellation proves that the Sea of Galilee was definitely conceived by Mark and his tradition as a force that needed to be suppressed. Hence, following the Earth Bible Project's principle of voice (Earth is a subject capable of raising its voice in celebration and against injustice), the voice that needs to be *reretrieved* in Mark 5:1–20 is the voice of the Sea of Galilee.

Animating the Aqueous Voice

Norman C. Habel (2008, 8), reflecting on Gen 1:26–28, created an imaginary voice of the Earth in the first-person in order to convey his ecological reading through the principle of voice. Following Habel, I read the Sea of Galilee not as a threatening monster but as an affective actant who has the capacity to, as Chen (2012, 3) would say, "revise biopolitical spheres" or reconfigure the assemblage hierarchy in Mark 5:1–20. That is, the disgust felt viscerally through the dead pig carcasses in the Sea of Galilee becomes the animating, powerful actant that drives Jesus away from the region of

Gerasa, staging a reversal and placing Jesus as the affected in this particular animacy hierarchy.

Chen (2012, 2) explains that animacy theory challenges the confinement of animacy with humans. Animacy theory argues that those who are "considered insensate, immobile, deathly, or otherwise 'wrong' animate cultural life in important ways." This reconfiguration of animacies is not a new phenomenon. Before theorists expounded the actancy of the inanimate, one could already glean the wisdom of (critical) novelists who wrote on the affective actancy of all entities. For example, in *Postcolonial Ecocriticism* (2010), Graham Huggan and Helen Tiffin's analysis of Amitav Ghosh's novel, *The Hungry Tide* (2005), bespeaks of the agency of water and storm as actants who redefine relationalities. For this chapter, this novel's generous engagement with the actancy of the nonhumans echo Mark 5:1–20.

To summarize Ghosh's novel, the protagonists are Piya, a female metropolitan scientist who wants to research the dolphins, and Fokir, an illiterate fisherman whom Piya hires because he is knowledgeable about the rivers that engulf the islands. Their relationship represents the clash of two worlds: the conservation of nonhumans versus the preservation of human lives by killing tigers. *The Hungry Tide* is based on the bloody tension of the 1970s between the West Bengal government and the World Wildlife Fund (WWF), on the one hand, and the refugees of the Marichjhapi islands (Sundarbans), on the other. The former wanted to protect the wildlife animals in the islands of Marichjhapi, particularly the Bengal tigers, from extinction. The latter were refugees who were displaced due to the break-up of East and West Pakistan and took residence in the islands. The former wanted to remove the refugees in order to conserve the islands for the nonhumans. The latter were trying to establish a space to live to the point that they had encroached upon the spaces of the nonhumans. The government officials and WWF enforced harsh and even deadly measures to expel the refugees who stood their ground. The refugees, however, resorted to killing the Bengal tigers because of the constant confrontation. The novel reaches its climax when a storm caused havoc on the islands, killing Fokir as he protects Piya. Through this storm, Ghosh's philosophical narrative unfolds. Here Ghosh signifies the storm, the waters, and the wind as the agents who displaced the binaries, the divisions, and the tensions brewing in the islands. Huggan and Tiffin (2010, 191) conclude that agency (or, for the present chapter, actancy) does not reside with those who have "essentialist, anthropocentric capacities to effect change. Rather, agents [or actants] are those who effect change itself." The storm blows away the impasse between the two groups. When houses were blown away into the rivers, animals were stranded by debris, government officials' boats were torn into pieces, and Fokir sacrificed himself for Piya, the storm's actancy dispelled the two groups' contempt for each other.

Echoing the storm's actancy, Mark 5:1–20 should be read, like *The Hungry Tide*, with an acute awareness of the actancy of the Sea of Galilee. In particular, the affective assemblage of the Sea of Galilee with the pig cadavers should be allowed to transgress the anthropocentric wall of textual bias. Usually, sensorial approach to text is dismissed just because one is untrained or prohibited to acknowledge that liberating and decolonizing reading of the Bible includes the affect and the senses. Unfortunately, some liberating and decolonizing readings of the Bible have followed the logocentricism even if they did not intend to do so. But if one permits oneself to tap into the affect, to one's senses, then one could engage the revelatory joy and excitement of noticing how the nonhumans are animating or have animacy even in an ancient text. To liberate and decolonize is to liberate one's affect and feelings imprisoned within the carnophallogocentric prison. It is to decolonize the binary of reason versus emotion, as ecofeminists and ecowomanists would say. In other words, one sees and smells how the Sea of Galilee with the pig cadavers animate the Gerasenes to drive Jesus out of their region. The inanimate necro-actant forcefully animates human actants (both Jesus and the Gerasenes) who, according to anthropocentrism, were supposed to be the only source of animacy. In the overall narrative of Mark, no nonhuman determines Jesus's movements quite as decisively as the Sea of Galilee replete with pig cadavers. In other words, an affective nonhuman reading of Mark 5:1–20 demonstrates how the anthropocentric animacy hierarchy is challenged by none other than the dead or deadly ones.

The goal though is not simply that of reversing the hierarchy of animacy. Rather, the goal is to expose affective assemblages into the realm of "insurgent vulnerability" (Alaimo 2016, 94). This chapter exposes readers and listeners of the Gospel of Mark to our permeability to the toxins of anthropocentrism, environmental neglect, and neocolonial tendencies. By realizing our exposure to these toxins, the hope is to see that inanimate necro-actants are fellow sites of and sources for ethicopolitical engagements. Their actancies, no matter how delegitimized they are by anthropocentrism, arouse and impel us to action. What are seemingly inanimate entities animate, affect, and move the supposedly animating subjects

(Jesus and his disciples) into action. Could we also imagine listeners of Mark, both ancient and contemporary, being affectively impelled to action by listening to the plight of the Sea of Galilee?

The animacy of the wind and the water is documented as well in Mark 4:35–41. The passage begins with Jesus rebuking and commanding the wind and the Sea of Galilee to be quiet (σιώπα) and silent (πεφίμωσο): "Peace! Be still!" (v. 39). The narrative reports the wind and the Sea of Galilee were able to "listen and follow" Jesus because the "wind ceased, and there was a dead calm" (v. 40b). After witnessing this animacy, the disciples of Jesus were afraid greatly (φόβον μέγαν), and said to one another, "who then is this, that even the wind and the sea obey [ὑπακούει] him?" (v. 41). Here, the disciples were not afraid or in awe because the wind and the Sea of Galilee obeyed him. Rather, they were utterly afraid or in awe because of the authority of Jesus over the wind and the sea. In other words, the disciples did not question the animacy of the wind and the sea; they lived in a world that considered their animacies as givens. As Mark describes how the disciples of Jesus fail to understand Jesus throughout the narrative, here once again their doubt is not on the animacy of the wind and the sea but on Jesus's messianic identity and capacities.

The Disgust That Moved the Markan Jesus

Just as Moore (2017b, passim) traces the vestiges of putrefaction of Jesus and Lazarus's bodies through the Gospel of John, finding the affect of disgust in Mark 5:1–20 requires a step back to the beginning stages of decay and is haunted by the ensuing putrefaction as it becomes rot to be ingested by humans and nonhumans alike. This disgust could also be expressed through Chen's queering of toxicity. Chen troubles the subject-object binary by narrating the unfettered transgressions of toxicity, particularly how it is ingested by humans through mouth, skin, nose, and other means. This is due to the animacy of toxicity in which it "fails over and again to privilege rationality's favorite partner, the *human* subject, rather defaulting to chairs, couches, and other sexual orientations" (Chen 2012, 209, 221). The sovereign and those who are disgusted with the other are already contaminated as the disgusting Sea of Galilee has already slipped and leaked into their bodies. The assumed rationality of the Gerasenes has failed them in their willingness to challenge the sovereignty of Jesus (by asking him to leave), even though he is the one with the unquestionable power over demons and probably even over the Gerasenes. The sovereign Jesus himself could not overcome the animacy of toxicity, and so is obliged to leave even after demonstrating his prowess. The putrefaction of the pig cadavers in the Sea of Galilee, the promise of its unnerving animacy through disgust, rattles the nerves of those who self-designated themselves as being above the inanimate.

If disgust, according to Sara Ahmed (2014, 87), is a "contact zone in which it clings to that which is near," then the disgust of pig carcasses floating in the Sea of Galilee clung to the skin of Jesus. He reeked with an imperial stench. The stench reminded the Gerasenes of the Roman Empire's disgusting colonialism that forced them to produce pork for the Roman army. And yet, the Gerasenes are pulled into the ambivalent feeling, the other side of disgust, in which they are also disgusted by their loss of income, their profitable collusion with the Roman Empire. Ahmed describes disgust as ambivalent because it involves "desire for, or an attraction towards, the very objects that are felt to be repellent" (84). As Ahmed suggests, we push away objects that disgust us while being simultaneously pulled us toward these objects, making us do "double-takes" on what is disgusting (84).

Elaborating on this ambivalence, on the one hand, the Gerasenes probably abhorred the *Legio Decima Fretensis*, the tenth Roman legion (with the emblem of a boar), which was stationed in Galilee during the Jewish revolt. Paul Winter (1974, 181) focuses on how the Latin *legio* is used in Mark 5:9 instead of a Greek or Aramaic words for troops or a great horde: "The use of the Latin word constitutes a direct verbal thrust against the occupation-forces in Jewish lands."[8]

On the other hand, there were also Gerasenes who benefited from this arrangement. The local elites and the merchants in particular benefited due to their privileged positions to negotiate with the occupying Roman legion. Herman Waetjen (1989, 116) mentions the value of having the legion army stationed in or near Gerasa because they protected the "lucrative trade routes to both southern Arabia and India." In view of the Parthian threat, it would seem that a Roman presence would have to be stationed in Gerasa in order to guard both the frontier and the eastern and southern trade routes. Perhaps the *strategos*—the military general placed over the free cities of what had once been Coele-Syria by the Romans

---

8. See also Burdon 2004, 149–67; Crossan 1991, 314–88; Horsley 1998, 2003, 100–108; Juel 1994; Marcus 2000, 341–53.

under Pompey, as Josephus indicates in *Ant.* 14.74–76—may have resided in Gerasa (Kraeling 1938, 34).

These contradictory impulses do not resolve themselves. They linger and impose upon our memories. As William Ian Miller (1997, x) argues: "even as the disgusting repels, it does so without also capturing our attention." Killing off the pigs was a counterimperial move because it disrupted the food supply of the imperial army. Nevertheless, it caused both massive financial loss, instigating the ire of the Roman Empire, and significant destruction to the supply of water and fish for the Gerasenes.

The disgust-in-ambivalence toward the Roman Empire is also manifested through the bestial and vegetal messiah, the Markan Jesus. Simon Samuel (2007, 127) pictures the Markan Jesus subduing the legion or the Roman Empire surreptitiously. And yet, Jesus also became the "new Caesar who can cross the stormy sea and conquer the enemy." As mentioned above, Moore (2006, 26) finds the Gospel of Mark to be a ripe location for postcolonial reading because it deals with land, occupation, liberation, and destruction. The Markan Jesus might have allegorically overthrown a legion of the Roman Empire. Nevertheless, the Markan Jesus also began his colonial gospel by commanding the Gerasene demoniac to spread his victory (Anderson 1976, 146–51).

This is the quagmire of the Markan messiah: he is on the one hand proclaiming a different way of being and becoming, and yet on the other hand he mimics the colonial logic of totalitarian method. Adding to Moore's (2011, 90–91) Markan Jesus, who is a hyphen between the divine and the animal, Jesus is also a hyphen between the colonized and the neocolonizer. As Jesus was trying to help his fellow colonized *ethne* (epitomized by the Gerasene demoniac), he also succumbed to the lure of manifesting his carnivorous virility by killing thousands of pigs and subduing the Sea of Galilee by dumping the pig carcasses in it. According to Derrida (1995a, 280), carnivorous virility is the pursuit of a subject to be installed as the virile figure by sacrificing others. Jesus inadvertently sought absolute sovereignty by sacrificing the flesh of others. This schema of subjugation or sacrificial structure privileges the adult male over women, children, and nonhumans. Moreover, this sacrificial system, as Yvonne Sherwood (2014, 251) asserts, is based on the clear cut "division between god, human, animal, and inorganic matter." Hence, a virile man, the *chef d'Etat*, or head of state, is described as potent and carnivorous: he devours women through his phallocentrism, and eats the flesh of nonhumans as signs of his prowess and sovereignty (Derrida 1995a, 281). The Markan Jesus seems to be imitating this carnivorous virility in Mark 5:1–20. He tried to showcase his virility by commanding demons, destroying pigs in the thousands, and sending his new subject to spread his gospel. The Markan Jesus imitated emperors who treated the colonized *ethne* and nonhumans as killable.

And yet, the Markan Jesus's virility is thwarted by something that is more affectively intense than his exorcism. In verse 17, the colonized and enslaved *ethne* of Gerasa came and saw what Jesus did: healed the Gerasene demoniac and killed thousands of pigs, driving them into the Sea of Galilee. The Gerasenes who begged Jesus to leave because the death of the pigs in the Sea of Galilee created a new assemblage that "delimited and re-zoned the areas of proximity that are discomforting versus acceptable" (Brinkema 2014, 131). Seeing the massacre of these pigs, seeing the closeness of mass death, a specter that had been kept at bay due to their collusion with the Roman Empire, caused visceral repulsion at the decay and the ensuing stench emanating both from the pig carcasses and the subservience of Gerasa and many other colonized *ethne*. What were once considered forsaken, forgotten, and outside were now too close and inside. The death of the pigs and the massive contamination of their source of water and food caused the Gerasenes to gag upon the disgusting thought that the empire was once a thing of allure to them while being simultaneously revolted for allowing themselves to be enslaved.

Rachel Carson (1991, xiii), in her updated preface to her book *The Sea around Us*, discusses how the dumping of radioactive waste in the sea will be catastrophic because the toxins are widely distributed not only by water but also through the movements of living creatures. The same goes with the pigs' parts floating and drowning in the Sea of Galilee. No matter how energetically the Gerasenes might have immediately removed the pig cadavers from the Sea of Galilee, some parts of those pigs would have transcorporeally been transmitted and digested into the bodies of fish, stones, and other nonhumans. Fish who are supposedly benign have now incorporated the particles of decay and disgust into their bodies. Like how the Shanghai residents were repulsed with the idea that their waters were contaminated by rotting pink blobs, the thought of imbibing contaminated pig-water and eating fish that ate dead carcasses would likely have churned the stomachs of the Galileans, the Judeans (particularly those devout Jews who followed kashrut), the Gerasenes, the Roman soldiers, and everyone else who would have enjoyed the bounties of the Sea of Galilee.

The rotting Sea of Galilee inserts itself in relational ontology/ies in which no one is essentially uncontaminated, superior, or clean. If to feel disgusted with something or someone translates to a feeling of revulsion over the inferiority or "belowness" of the other, Ahmed (2014, 88) argues that "given the fact that the one who is disgusted is the one who feels disgust, then the position of 'aboveness' is maintained only at the cost of a certain vulnerability." For Mark, then, the Roman Empire, the one that views itself as above and the one that is disgusted with the other, expressing that disgust through bestialization, itself feels disgusted by the other at the risk of being contaminated by its porosity, at its fluid borders, by feeling disgusted with itself for feeling the disgust.

Feeling disgusted and simultaneously feeling numb over environmental destruction persists today. The Sea of Galilee is still being polluted today by industrial waste and illegal fishing (Ashkenazi 2007; see also Basofin 2012). Up to the time of my writing this book, Flint, Michigan's water crisis of 2014, after years of struggle, has still not yet been resolved. The disgust of political inefficacy has continuously caused severe health risks to humans and nonhumans in Flint, including the possibility of being affected by legionnaire's disease (Roy 2016). Nonetheless, the (contaminated) waters animated or instigated ethicopolitical measures through their affective production of disgust. The revulsion of these waters might have been distant for those who do not live in the Sea of Galilee or in Flint, Michigan. Yet, the transcorporeality of water, or the thought that my water could also be contaminated one way or another, probably made the listeners of Mark (in my imagination of them, anyway) and the viewers of the daily news feel the disgust more viscerally and proximately because disgust bends spatiality as it affects even those who are not contiguous to the disgusted.

To draw further wisdom from recent headlines, in the historic standoff against the Dakota Access Pipeline, water has also become the bearer of memory and teacher of invaluable lessons (for Gaard's recounting of this event, see 2017, 183–86). Many Native American tribes, most notably the Standing Rock Sioux tribe, gathered at the Standing Rock Indian Reservation in North Dakota to protest against the construction of a massive crude oil pipeline that would lay along the Missouri River, the Cannon River, and their tributaries as well as through sacred Indian lands. One of the protestors or protectors was grandmother Faith Spotted Eagle. As she was narrating the miraculous birth of a baby girl named *Mni Wiconi* or "Water is Life" in Oceti Sakowin camp, which is located north of the Cannon River, she also talked about the animacy of water. For the grandmother, "water ... also has memory. When people speak or sing to it during a ceremony, it is believed that the water holds on to what it hears and can later share what it learns. So, when a group of women gathers on the river bank next to the crowded main camp and they hold up tobacco offerings while singing prayers, the water is listening" (Ravitz 2016).

The No Dakota Access Pipeline protest (NoDAPL) is a fight for the preservation of sacred space because, among many reasons, water and land are the ancestors, the spirits, the guiding actants who listen, speak, and teach all who traverse, drink, and live in them. Water and land are brothers, sisters, fathers, and mothers. What seem to be inanimate from the perspective of unquenchable corporate greed are the actants who animate the indigenous spirits, affecting people from around the world to come to the protest line, catching the fire of environmental awareness in social media, and rekindling the disgust against the degradation of nature.

On December 5, 2017, I was able to participate in the clergy call to protest with the Standing Rock Sioux tribe against the Dakota Access Pipeline. Thousands of clergy from around the United States (and even from other countries) gathered by heeding the call to protect the sacred waters and lands. December 5 was the last day before we were supposed to be removed from the campsite. We stood together, side by side, chanting for a miracle from ten in the morning until two in the afternoon. Around 2:30 p.m., Chief Archibald arrived at the camp and brought the good news that the Corps of Engineers would not enforce evacuation of the campsite. We were extremely jubilant that day. Together, we were an affective assemblage who rejoiced for our temporary victory over unhinged corporate greed. That day, the call of the sacred waters and lands moved the hearts and minds of many people around the world to respect the sacredness of nonhumans, no matter how short lived it was.[9] Unlike the hyper-masculine response of Jesus against the legion, we chose the path of the water, of our mother healer, who taught us to protect the other and to cleanse ourselves from unhinged corporate greed and US imperial colonization. If December 5 was Mark 5:1–20, we would not have killed the pigs. We would have provided the demon possessed with healing waters. We would have invited the nonhumans and the Gerasenes to (re)build a

---

9. The work of Native American scholars on the intersectionality of race, ethnicity, and nonhuman concerns deserves much more engagement than I have given it here. See Adamson 2001; Harrod 2000; Kimmerer 2013; Savoy 2015; and too many more to mention here.

community together against the Roman legion colonizing and enslaving our land, water, and even the spirits.

5
THE ANIMAL MASKS OF THE SYROPHOENICIAN WOMAN AND THE MARKAN JESUS

The contentious and yet temporally short-lived assemblage composed of Jesus and an unnamed Syrophoenician woman (Mark 7:24–30) reeks of colonial angst. Syrophoenicians and Galileans/Judeans had tense relations throughout their long colonial history. If Jesus and the Syrophoenician woman stand as "national allegories" for their respective groups (Moore 2006, 27), Jesus's derisive remark in Mark 7:27 that the Syrophoenician woman was a dog (κυναρίος) echoes the tense infighting among the colonized *ethne*. Mark 7:24–30 stokes further bewilderment by having the Syrophoenician woman respond to Jesus's animalizing jab with a groveling response. All she wanted was for Jesus to heal her daughter. Instead, the dialogue taps into the deeply rooted animosity spawning the children versus dog, us versus them, "fight for scraps" colonial insider dialogue that the author of Mark assumed the listeners of his gospel would understand. This internecine feud was stirred up by the long history of colonial meddling in the economic, social, and even psychological lives of the colonized *ethne*. Jesus's unfounded fear that his healing power is insufficient to be shared with the Syrophoenician's daughter stems from decades (or even centuries) of deprivation or the idea thereof instilled on the oppressed.

Various interpreters have already expressed their frustration with Jesus's un-Jesus-like response to the Syrophoenician woman. Scholars have described the scandalous words of Jesus as: peirastic irony, that is, a form of verbal challenge in order to test the opponent's response (see Camery-Hoggatt 1992, 149–51; and Iverson 2007, 51–52); a test to demonstrate her faith as paradigmatic (Marcus 2000, 468; Aquino and McLemore 1993, 412); and a symbolic struggle and desire for a gentile mission (Guelich 1989, 386–89).[1] I am wary and cognizant of the possibility of falling into the trap of inadvertently labeling the side of Jesus or (ancient) Jewishness as patriarchal colonizers, in line with Amy-Jill Levine's caution about such ways of reading.[2] Whether the Syrophoenician woman is a rich, well-educated, and urban (well-integrated) Hellenist or a poor widowed or divorced woman (Beavis 1988, 6; Hurtado 1983, 115; Rhoads 1994, 343–75; Ringe 2001, 86, 89; and Theissen 1991, 70–71), I am not essentializing her as the ultimate symbol of victimhood versus Jesus as the patriarchal colonizer who represents the Jewish people. A postcolonially ambivalent stance acknowledges the critical interpretations of Mark 7:24–30 expressed by (Asian) feminist and postcolonial interpreters while being sensitive to Levine's concern of (un)intentionally stereotyping negatively the Jewish community as a whole.[3]

In other words, neither Jesus nor the Syrophoenician woman were untainted by the influences of their colonial circumstances. Jesus's bestial logics designed to animalize her as inferior was expected. Her preliminary response felt like she would also fall and follow the bestial logics of the colonized. And yet, her ensuing response, her animal-making (as explained below), disrupted the internalized, pathetic narration of two colonized bodies performing and ventriloquizing the bestial logics of their time. She resisted by embracing their animalization, painful as it may seem. She taught Jesus that the way forward is not animosity or isolation, reactions the colonizers would expect. Rather, she embraces all of herself, all of Jesus, and her daughter—all of their animalization and enslavement to hate the other. She does so by putting on a mask of self-revelatory technique that candidly shows that we are all animals and animalized.

---

1. Theissen (1991, 62–63) summarized the various interpretations on Mark 7:24–30 in three groups: biographical, paradigmatic, and salvation-historical.

2. See Levine's (2004, 91–99) warning against postcolonialism's inadvertent anti-Judaism as it tries to resist colonialism. Further reflecting upon Levine's point, see Sun 2010, 381–94; Sugirtharajah 2002, 13–15; and Leander 2013, 109–15.

3. For more postcolonial or feminist reading of this narrative or of Matthew, see Bae 2004, 390–403; Choi 2015, 85–108; Laura Donaldson 2005; Dube 2000, 162–77; Guardiola-Sáenz 1997, 69–81; Kinukawa 1994, 2004; Kwok 1995; Nelavala, 2009; Schüssler Fiorenza 1992; Tolbert 1992; and Wainwright 2001.

Collectively Enunciating the Colonized Assemblages

Jesus's utterance in Mark 7:27, "let the children be fed first, for it is not fair to take the children's food and throw it to the dogs," is not just his direct statement. It is an expression of a (Deleuzo-Guattarian) collective assemblage of enunciation. If an assemblage, as discussed previously, is composed of actants, then one way these actants link and become a community or organization is through "the enforceable social commitments created by the enunciation of speech acts" (Delanda 2016, 55; see Deleuze and Guattari 1987, 88). A collective assemblage of enunciation is "based on particular space and time and in relation to a machinic assemblage" (Eugene Holland 2013, 78) or an automated way of processing our surroundings. These expressions or enunciations, however, do not reside in an individual. In their utterance, "there is no subject, but always collective agents; and in what the utterance speaks of, there are no objects, but machinic states" (Deleuze and Parnet 2002, 71). Applying this to Mark 7:24–30, Jesus's verbal jab at the Syrophoenician woman cannot be reduced to one individual's scathing remark against another. Rather, Jesus's statement, following Eugene W. Holland's (2013, 96) understanding of collective assemblage of enunciation, is derived from a collective "unconscious ... composed of very diverse kinds of elements, including libidinal, social, and technical machines."

For Mark 7:24–30, the machinic states, operating independently of the volition of any given individual, are the colonial histories of pain and infighting between the colonized *ethne*. Their enmity is expressed through machinic formulations such as applying bestial logics to one another. These machinic formulations in many cases are blurted out automatically or without compunction. In other words, speech acts stereotyping or labeling the other are unreasonable and yet easily uttered because they are automated in the psyches of those whose communities have been enunciating them for generations. The questionable utterances in Mark 7:24–30 are mechanical releases of frustration that spring from visceral, libidinal, social, and especially colonial trauma that haunt the actants. One's expression is never an isolated incident. Statements such as Mark 7:27 are "derivatives" (E. Holland 2013, 78) of the collective or the de-territorialized expressions that haunt the present by going "beyond the individual" (Guattari 1995, 8–9). Thus, the formation of a collective assemblage of enunciation is "the redundant complex of the act and the statement that necessarily accomplishes it" (Deleuze and Guattari 1987,

80). That is why a statement is "order-words," because it not only relays information, it also commands and seeks obedience in its redundancy. The point is to see that a collective assemblage of enunciation emerges from "group phenomena, social assemblages, and technological apparatuses" (Young, Genosko, and Watson 2013, 70). In other words, expressions even by an individual are already expressions that have been repeated before by others in their unconscious derivations. Statements are less about who said them and more about the performativity and the deep-seated coloniality of the statements.

To say that the speaker is not fully responsible for the originality of a statement does not negate the affect and effect of the said statement. The bodies of the actants may not have changed immediately, but the speaker or the spoken undergoes an "incorporeal transformation" (Deleuze and Guattari 1987, 80–81) because of the utterance. Deleuze and Guattari use the example of a judge pronouncing a sentence. The person who receives a criminal verdict goes through an incorporeal transformation. The body of the person does not change, but how this person is now expressed or enunciated, that is, as a "criminal," changes due to the sentencing. However, the signification of a criminal relies upon its repetitive expressions within its particular collective assemblage of enunciation. For a more affective example, Donald Trump's slogan, "Make America Great Again," changed the persona of Trump from a real estate mogul and reality show entertainer to the leader of the so-called silent majority. Trump's corporeality was not changed by the statement, nor did the statement change Trump's body literally. Nevertheless, Trump's political ingenuity was in the "non-totalizable intensive multiplicity" of his statement and its capacity to resonate with many of his supporters according to their context (Guattari 2011, 55).

The unconscious that gave rise to the socioethical and colonial-technical machines of the Markan Jesus and his statement in Mark 7:24–30 is the history of and the concurrent animosity between two colonized peoples. In discussing and tracing the importance of the geographical boundaries of the Markan narrative, Jeffrey W. Aernie (2014, 193) argues that "the abusive distinction developed between the children and the dogs with respect to the appropriate distribution of bread in Jesus' statement in Mk 7:27 may stem at least in part from the inherent socioeconomic and political situation that plagued the region." The ensuing effect of this tension between the colonized peoples is to desire or mimic the imperial animalization of the other. Following Samuel's (2007, 85) reading of Mark 7:24–

30, Jesus stands in a liminal space of "double vision, i.e., with the vision of the colonized and colonists, and speak with a forked tongue, speaking as the dominant and the dominated." He is the product of "the dynamics of transcultural (consensual and conflictual) hybridity" (85). Where Samuel diagnoses Jesus's harsh statement as "the problem of approximation or Jesus approximating a colonist posture" (85), I see Jesus's statement as his colonial mimicry of carnophallogocentrism (or his colonized toxic masculinity). While Samuel suggests the Syrophoenician woman's response is an expression of "liberative dynamics of reiteration (woman repeating the words of Jesus)" (85), this chapter argues that her response reexpresses this liberative stance through an animal mask.

Ambivalent Animosity between the Colonized *Ethne*

Before delving into defining a few key philosophical terms, a history on the ambivalent relationship between the Israelites and the Syrians and/or Phoenicians is necessary here. Some scholars propound that these groups are enmeshed even at their (etymological) origins. This etymological entanglement is suggested by the fact that the Greek word φοῖνιξ is derived from the Akkadian word *kinahhu*, "purple." This Akkadian word, according to those scholars, is apparently the basis also for the Hebrew root letters for Canaanite: *k-n-n* (see Bryce 2014, 112–13; Herm 1975; Luz 2001, 338; and Moscati 1968, 1989). Gerhard Herm (1975, 25) supports this argument by stating that the Phoenicians usually referred to themselves as Canaanites even at the time of Alexander the Great's conquering of Tyre. Furthermore, the Septuagint translates Canaan in a few places as Φοινίσσης (see Exod 6:15; 16:35; Josh 5:1, 12). However, some scholars find this etymological connection accidental. Sabatino Moscati (1989, 24) argues that the term Canaan included, but was not solely, the name for the Phoenicians (see also Speiser 1936, 121–26). Genesis 10:15 mentions that Canaan was the father of the Sidonians as well. Claims of a Canaanite-Phoenician connection have to be taken with a grain of salt because of the "complete loss of Phoenician literature and the difficulties of archaeological research, due to the fact that the most important ancient sites are covered by modern buildings" (Moscati 1968, 38). And yet, this did not stop Matthew from describing the Syrophoenician woman of Mark as a Canaanite. As Moore (2017a, 63) argues, perhaps in the minds of Matthew and his audience, Canaan(ites) still represented or connoted "an unerased remnant, a polluted people … whose name connotes idolatry and hence abomination." This negative connotation expressed through collective assemblage of enunciation has affectively entangled the Syrophoenicians and Canaanites. In one sense, Matthew's portrayal of the Canaanite woman as a representative of Canaan(ites) is dubious as best. In another, the affective tension carried by the hatred of these two groups blurred the distinctiveness of these two groups of people as manifested through Matthew and Mark's renditions of this narrative. Thus, most information about Phoenicia, Syria, and its regions are at the mercy of other groups or writers' written accounts about them. For example, Homer describes the Phoenicians in the *Odyssey* as rogues and deceivers (*Od.* 14.287–91 [McCrone]). And yet, Homer sings a different tune in the *Iliad* where he describes the Phoenicians as great merchants (*Il.* 23.743 [Murray]; see Herm 1975, 162, 167). In any case, scholars today would agree that the Phoenicians and their neighbors were among the best seafaring peoples and merchants of their time.

Another biblical claim somewhat agreed upon by scholars is that the Phoenicians or the Syrians were influential in the region of Levant as early as the tenth century BCE (Peckham 1992, 5:349–57). Their influence endured through the period of Israelite monarchy. Of course, some scholars would argue that one could push this date back further to Genesis (Gen 10:19a: "and the borders of Canaan reached from Sidon toward Gerar as far as Gaza"). According to the Hebrew Scriptures, Israel and Phoenicia were in trade relations, albeit skewed ones (Knauf 1991, 168). First Kings 5 demonstrates that there was an on-going treaty between Solomon and Hiram, the king of Tyre. Solomon's decision to build the Jerusalem temple led him to seal a deal with Hiram. Due to Israel's lack of skilled labor and valuable goods to build the temple, Solomon depended upon the Phoenicians (see Donner 1982). The Phoenicians supplied Solomon with cedar and juniper logs (1 Kgs 5:8), gold (9:11, 14), and skilled labor (7:13–14). Solomon paid Hiram an annual tribute of wheat and olive oil (5:11–12) and even territories, although Hiram did not find them useful (9:10–14).

Whether or not the details of these exchanges and the names of those who were conscripted to forced labor in 1 Kgs 5 and 9 are reliable, for Ernst Axel Knauf (1991, 168) this kind of trade reminds one of the unfair trade relations between first world and majority world countries today, Israel in this instance being the majority world. The Phoenicians were portrayed to be the rich, technologically advanced gateway region for world trade. If the Israelites were primarily farmers and shepherds, the Phoenicians were depicted as cosmopolitan citizens who ran advanced commerce and technologically advanced economy. Although it is a prophecy against Tyre, Ezek 26–27 sums up well the mercantile success and grandeur of Tyre (and probably several other Phoenician cities), which lasted until the sixth century BCE (see also Zech 9:3). According Ezek 27:17, Judah and Israel were also part of the nations who were desperate to trade with Tyrians and Phoenicians in exchange for wheat, honey, olive oil, and balm.

The skewed relationship between the two groups escalated into a tense one when Solomon followed Ashtoreth, the goddess of the Sidonians, due to his Sidonian wife (1 Kgs 11:5, 33; 2 Kgs 23:13). Solomon's descendant, Rehoboam, also assimilated to the Phoenician religiosity by building asherah poles on "every high hill and under every spreading tree" (1 Kgs 14:22–23). Abijah, the successor of Rehoboam and king of Judah, also followed his father's assimilation of Sidonian or Phoenician deities (1 Kgs 15:3). The northern kingdom of Israel was no exception. As a matter of fact, the incursion of Phoenician religiosity was at its height through the marriage alliance between Jezebel, the daughter of Ethbaal (the king of the Sidonians), and Ahab, the son of Omri (the king of Israel). Ahab not only married Jezebel but also built an altar and a temple for Baal in Samaria and an asherah pole as well (1 Kgs 16:32–33).

The key story of contention between these nations is, in fact, the story of Jezebel. Since there is no historical account from Jezebel's perspective, the authors of the books of Kings have to be taken with a bit of suspicion in their negative assessments of her. First, she apparently plotted the murder of Naboth in order to usurp his vineyard for Ahab (1 Kgs 21:1–17). After hearing about this conspiracy, Elijah curses Jezebel to be devoured by dogs at the wall of Jezreel (21:23). Second, Jezebel convinces Ahab to fall into idolatry (21:25–26). Third, Jehu describes Jezebel as a harlot who was also into witchcraft (2 Kgs 9:22). Last, Jezebel is portrayed as deserving a gruesome death: thrown down from a window, her blood is spattered on the wall, her body trampled by horses, and her cadaver eaten by dogs (9:32–37). Athalya Brenner-Idan (1985, 28) argues that Jezebel is demonized in 1 and 2 Kings because the authors of these texts were proponents of Jehu and repulsed by Israel's tendency to assimilate with foreign deities (2 Kgs 10:18–31). The attack on Jezebel reflects the religiopolitical tension between the ruling parties in Israel: Jezebel versus Elijah and Jehu. That is why the authors of 1 and 2 Kings, who side with Jehu, consistently denigrate and even suppress or exaggerate Jezebel's roles in these narratives.

First and Second Kings have other narratives that portray disapproval of assimilation with Phoenician deities. Asa expelled male shrine prostitutes and removed all idols from Judah. He even deposed his grandmother, Maakah, from her position as queen mother because she made an image of Asherah for worship (1 Kgs 15:12–14). Jehu massacred Ahab's seventy sons and all of the priests, prophets, and servants of Baal (2 Kgs 10:1–27). Furthermore, Jehu even eliminated worship of Baal (2 Kgs 10:28), a ruling which led him to be described as one of the few kings of Israel who had done "right in the eyes of the Lord" (10:30). Although exactly when the Phoenicians were colonized is unclear, these narratives further stoked the strife between these colonized peoples.

And yet, the Israelites, Judeans, Tyrians, and Sidonians were bonded by the same experience of colonialism under Nebuchadnezzar, king of Babylon. According to Jer 27:3, Jeremiah's prophecy was not just against Judah; it included Tyre and Sidon. Alongside their enemies, Jeremiah prophesied that the Israelites and Judeans would carry the yoke of subjugation together with the Tyrians and Sidonians (27:1–7). They would be taken to Babylon together until the day the Lord decided to bring them back (27:22).

It was not until the defeat of the Neo-Babylonian Empire by the Persians under Cyrus the Great that the exiles were given the chance to repatriate to their homelands. Those who returned in batches were not just the Judeans and Israelites; it also included Tyrians and Sidonians. When the Judean returnees decided to rebuild the Jerusalem temple, once again they sought the assistance of the Tyrians and Sidonians: "Then they gave money to the masons and carpenters, and gave food and drink and olive oil to the people of Sidon and Tyre, so that they would bring cedar logs by sea from Lebanon to Joppa, as authorized by Cyrus king of Persia" (Ezra 3:7).

However, this alliance was short-lived. Nehemiah began an exclusivist politics in Judah. He started to impose regulations that created borders dividing the Judeans from the neighboring nations. For example, Nehemiah disapproved of the resident Tyrians selling fish and all kinds of merchandise in Jerusalem during Sabbath (Neh 13:16). Alongside the Tyrians, Nehemiah reproached the Jewish nobles of Judah for not keeping the Sabbath (13:17–18). Nehemiah even physically reprimanded certain persons by pulling their hair and beating them because they married foreigners (13:23–27; see also Ezra 9–10). Their marriages were considered so egregious because they recalled Solomon's marriages with foreign women, which were assumed to be the sinful reason for his downfall. It also goes without saying that Jezebel and Ahab's marriage still lingered on the minds of those who had seen the results of unhindered assimilation with the Phoenicians and Syrians.

And then came the Romans. Mark 7:24–30 attests that Jesus met a Greek (Ἑλληνίς) woman from Syria-Phoenicia. During the time Mark was written, Syria and Phoenicia were also under the Roman Empire (see Pliny the Elder, *Nat.* 5.17–19 [Rackham]).[4] Syria had become a province of Rome in 64 BCE with Antioch as its political center. The cities of Syria barely fought Pompey's annexation of the region. According to Appian of Alexandria, "the Romans, without fighting, came into possession of Cilicia, inland Syria and Coele Syria, Phoenicia, Palestine, and all the other countries bearing the Syrian name from the Euphrates to Egypt and the sea" (*Hist. rom.* 11.50 [White]). The primary reason for the lack of opposition was trade. Syria became the primary hub for global trading. The Orontes River functioned as a conduit for transimperial commerce coming from the East (e.g., China, India) into the Mediterranean. Juvenal the satirist laments the so-called pollution of Rome with exotic goods: "The dregs of Orontes have (now) been flushed into Father Tiber" (*Sat.* 3.62–63 [Rudd]).

Delineating the exact boundaries of Syria is difficult because, as Kevin Butcher (2003, 10) argues, "ancient sources themselves fail to provide any clear guidelines to follow." The composition of "Syria" or the hyphenation of the name of a certain region as "Syro-" during the Roman Empire signifies that the term *Syrian* for the Romans was less of a cultural or ethnic designation and more of a "shorthand for things and people inhabiting the Syrian region" (10). Whether or not there was a political identity called Syrian before the Romans came to the region is not a concern for the empire. What was more pressing for the Roman Empire was the functionality of using the term Syrian as a way to effectively rule a region for taxation, governance under a governor, and adherence to the imperial cult (79).

---

4. According to Trevor Bryce (2014, 5), the etymology of Syria probably comes from a "variant of 'Assyria,' the Bronze and Iron Age kingdom based in northern Mesopotamia. In its ancient context, 'Syria' is used by many scholars in a broad geographical sense to cover a conglomerate of lands extending southwards from south-eastern Anatolia to Arabia, through the Amuq plain of modern Turkey, the modern country of Syria west of the Euphrates, and the territories of Israel, Palestine, Lebanon, and Jordan, and eastwards from the Mediterranean littoral to the western fringes of Mesopotamia."

The Syrophoenicians' allegiance with the Roman Empire was economically sound strategy. As the great merchants of the known world, the Syrians/Phoenicians benefitted from the Roman Empire's controversial *Pax Romana*. Pompey's annihilation of sea piracy in the Mediterranean Sea favored the Phoenicians' trade deals (Rawlinson 2005, 540). However, misfortunes also beset the Phoenicians as they did not politically fall in line. In the struggle between Anthony and Octavian (Augustus), the Phoenicians' allegiance to Anthony cost them dearly once Octavian prevailed. According to Dio Cassius, Augustus revoked the privileges the cities of Phoenicia once enjoyed (*Hist. rom.* 48.33–41 [Cary]). Nevertheless, this punishment did not last forever. According to Rawlinson (2005, 542–43), Sidon and Tyre (and Tripolis) eventually rebounded to the status of free cities.

For the zealous liberationists of the Palestinian area, the Judean and Galilean leaders' assimilationist stance with the Syrophoenicians was an abomination. Acts 12:19–20 narrates the collusion of Herod Agrippa I (r. 41–44 CE) with the Tyrians and Sidonians. At first, Agrippa was reluctant to grant the request of the leaders of Tyre and Sidon to support them with food. But after Blastus mediated or lobbied for the Phoenicians, Agrippa agreed to assist. At an appointed time, the Tyrians and Sidonians planned to worship Agrippa for his generosity by saying that Agrippa's voice was that of god and not a human. But an angel of the Lord struck Agrippa down and worms ate him immediately. Acts 12:19–20 seems to be a story of admonition not to collude with the Tyrians and Sidonians, let alone consider oneself a god and not give God what is due. Matthew 11:21–24 further expresses this disdain against Tyre and Sidon by associating them with Sodom. The sour relationship between Syrophoenicians and the Galileans and Judeans worsened as the Syrians apparently did not have any qualms about the Roman plan to use Syria (and Phoenicia) as one of the bulwarks of its empire in the east, especially as a buffer region against the Parthians. The Roman Empire pitted the colonized peoples against one another. In *Against Apion*, Josephus scathingly describes the Tyrians as "notoriously our bitterest enemies" (*C. Ap.* 1.70–71 [Thackeray]). Moreover, the presence of the emperor-appointed Syrian governor and his legion (*Legio Decima Fretensis*) in northern Syria caused even more tensions. One of the controversial enactments that enraged the colonized *ethne* of Judea was the taxation census created by the Syrian governor, Publius Sulpicius Quirinius, in 6 CE (see Luke 2:1–3). Moreover in 66 CE when the Jewish revolt began, the Syrian governor and other client rulers came down to quell the revolt (Josephus, *B.J.* 2.478). By 70–74 CE, the Jewish rebels had lost to the Roman army commanded by Vespasian and then by Titus. As a result of this loss, the *Legio Decima Fretensis* was permanently stationed in Judea. The rebels fought once more against the Roman Empire during the Bar Kokhba revolt (132–136 CE). The failure of this revolt led to the renaming of the entire region as Syria Palestina in 139 CE. This was a response to the need to ultimately destroy any possibility for future revolt and strengthen the presence of the Roman army in the lower regions (Kevin Butcher 2003, 84).

The Animal Mask of the Syrophoenician Woman

The context of a destroyed homeland (even a homeland now experienced only in diaspora) where one's sacred temple, lands, and waters are desecrated must be considered as an influential event that affected the writing of the gospel. In particular, the angst that accompanies trauma as well as political, cultural, and personal insecurity could be inferred in Mark 7:24–30. From the Judean perspective, the Syrophoenicians seemed to be complicit in the demise of Jerusalem. Calling them dogs (κυνάρια) through the mouthpiece that is the Markan Jesus might have been a knee-jerk reaction expected for that time. Jesus's animalizing association of the Syrophoenician woman with a dog is hardly surprising because dogs were powerful symbols in Canaanite religion. Jennifer Koosed (2017, n.p.) argues that "dogs are associated with the goddesses Anat and Astarte and the dog Baal.... [Harkening back to Jezebel, her sudden demise in which] only her palms, feet, and skull remain (2 Kgs 9:35) [alludes to a] Canaanite mythology in which Anat wore a necklace of human skulls and hands." Also, Jezebel, the quintessential "Canaanite" woman, *becomes* canine herself to the extent she is devoured by dogs and incorporated into their flesh. Associating the Syrophoenician woman with Jezebel, the derogatory animalizing comment made by Jesus against the Syrophoenician woman stems from centuries of colonial tensions between the two colonized *ethne*. Jezebel's horrible death is a threat of annihilation to anyone who tries to disrupt the "proper religiosity" of the Israelites (Koosed 2017). Jesus's knee-jerk reaction reflects this colonized mindset in which the other (even if they are fellow colonized *ethne*) has to be eliminated in order to enable one's own survival and prevent imposition of foreign elements on an already fragile state.

Even as a colonized and enslaved *ethnos*, I read the Markan Jesus as a victim of the colonization of the mind. He cannot simply be categorized as a constant victim or labeled as exclusively subjugated. Jesus is both a victim and perpetrator of, using Derrida's neologism, carnophallogocentrism. In unpacking the "scheme of the dominant," Derrida (1995a, 281) explains that the subjectivity of those who view themselves as the dominant or *chef d'Etat* (head of state) operate under carnophallogocentrism. Carnophallogocentrism is a term for a system or machination that considers powerful free adult man to be the ultimate signifier of subjectivity (Derrida 2002, 247). Carnal (carno-) because this system finds power in "carnivorous virility" or the desire to be dominant by being "virile" (contra the "feminine condition"). This virility happens by penetrating others with one's will or so-called rights (phallo-) to impose (Derrida 1995a, 280). This system occurs through carnivorous sacrifice or the sacrifice of others, specifically those who are weaker (women, children, nonhumans, and the rest of those who are viewed inferior) by "eating" or sacrificing them for one's benefit. Carnophallogocentrism's sacrificial machine dictates logocentrically those who are killable or subjected to bare life, and the subjugation of the other becomes the fodder for this carnivorous machinery.

In the Markan episode we have been considering, Jesus mimics the hyper-masculine subjectivity of the free elite male Romans by denigrating the subjectivity of the Syrophoenician woman. Jesus's statement against the Syrophoenician woman in Mark 7:27 reflects his mimicry of the imperial animalization of the other through carnophallogocentrism. A carnophallogocentric reading of the Markan Jesus's utterance in 7:27 resonates with Tat-siong Benny Liew's (1999b, 7–31) cautionary tale of the Markan Jesus's unhindered colonial mimicry in his unquestionable tyranny, his rebuilding of exclusionary boundary formations, and his imitation of "might-is-right" ideology. Moreover, according to Musa Dube (2000, 129), one could also equate the unhindered entry to the Syrophoenician woman's land in 7:24 ("he set out and entered the region of Tyre") with the gendered colonial discourse in which foreign lands are feminized for the purpose of being penetrated by the colonizers.

Nevertheless, the Markan Jesus is not a pure specimen of carnophallogocentric, colonial manhood. His subjectivity is presumed to be impure or flawed by the colonizers. Colonial subjectivity dictates that Jesus's ontology is the negation necessary to the subjectivity of the colonizers, applying Frantz Fanon's (1967, 89–90) definition of colonial neurosis in *Black Skin, White Masks*. The colonizers' gaze "overdetermines" the identity of Jesus from the outside by demanding Jesus to fit into their mold of carnophallogocentrism (95). The colonizers do not simply create a feeling of inferiority; they create a feeling of nonexistence (118). Seeking to break free from this feeling of nonexistence, Fanon expresses the irony of what colonized persons could say: "The colonized ... roar with laughter every time they hear themselves called an animal by the other. For they know they are not animals" (Fanon 1963, 8). But "the colonizer's laughter," as Moore (2017, 82–83) points out, "is even louder when the colonized attempts to turn the animalizing barbs back on him, so confident is he that he is the absolute antithesis of the animal."

The Markan Jesus's denigration of the Syrophoenician woman as a dog, a beast, is a symptom of this overdetermination. He tries to overcome it by unfortunately mimicking the hierarchical binary between himself (as human) versus the Syrophoenician woman (as nonhuman). And yet, the colonizers laugh because this denigration through mimicry unconsciously seeks approval from the colonizers trying to fit into their mold of sacrificial machine that promulgates antithetical relationality with the (animalized) other.

The Markan Jesus's struggle against overdetermination also resonates with Du Bois's (2007, 12) double consciousness, an ambivalence in which it is "at once a deprivation (an inability to see oneself except 'through the eyes of others') and a gift (an endowment of 'second-sight', that seems to allow a deeper or redoubled comprehension of the complexities of 'this American world')."[5] In a similar fashion to Du Bois's double consciousness, the Markan Jesus seems to be in an ambivalent position in which he strives to be true to his colonized identity and people, while at the same time seeks to overcome the imperial carnophallogocentrism by ironically mimicking the colonial image of an overdetermining subject. The Markan Jesus seeks to overcome animalization and garner opportunity to be part of the so-called civilized world. And yet, he seems unable to do so without transgressing against fellow animalized subjects.

---

5. The following sentences expound upon Du Bois's (2007, 34) double consciousness: "After the Egyptian and Indian, the Greek and Roman, the Teuton and Mongolian, the Negro is a sort of seventh son, born with a veil, and gifted with second-sight in this American world—a world which yields him no true self-consciousness, but only lets him see himself through the revelation of the other world. It is a peculiar sensation, this double-consciousness, this sense of always looking at one's self through the eyes of others, of measuring one's soul by the tape of a world that looks on in amused contempt and pity. One ever feels his two-ness—an American, a Negro; two souls, two thoughts, two unreconciled strivings; two warring ideals in one dark body, whose dogged strength alone keeps it from being torn asunder."

The response of the Syrophoenician woman in Mark 7:28b, "Sir, even the dogs under the table eat the children's crumbs," is her refusal to be locked in the "tower of the past," her strategy of "disalienation or her refusal to consider her reality as definitive" (Fanon 1967, 201). Her response is *her* version of double consciousness. As Mitzi J. Smith (2018, 28–45) calls it, her "womanist sass," her "talk back." Her response demonstrates the strength of a double (or even multiple) identity, an identity that manipulates colonial spaces and utterances. Instead of identities warring against each other, they become fluid partners that respond to the needs for various (re/de)territorializations. Her reality is to be continually herded into the fold of those who are animalized and sacrificed to be devoured by carnivorous colonizers. And yet, this reality does not prevent her from finding healing for her daughter even at the expense of being animalized by her fellow colonized *ethne*. In the face of humiliation, the Syrophoenician woman reassembles the carnophallogocentric assemblage that is the Markan Jesus by reconfiguring their encounter as one of Jesus's turning points in the Gospel of Mark. When carnophallogocentrism threatens to divest her of responsivity, making her into τὰ ἄλογα, one of the bestial and "the irrational ones,"[6] she responds in a way that was not expected from those who were deemed lacking in λόγος.

The oppressors, even the Galilean miracle-worker and his entourage, tried to silence her. And yet, the Syrophoenician woman persisted. The Syrophoenician woman's response in Mark 7:28b is her form of an animal mask. According to Ahuja (2009, 558), a performer puts on an animal mask or dons on animal guise in order to unveil "a historical logic of animalization inherent in processes of racial subjection. The performance of the animal mask does not necessarily entail identification with nonhuman species, but it always points to the historical conjunctions of social difference and species discourse. It may also, on occasion, envision alternative multispecies relationships." This ironic performance that provisionally embraces animality "is actually a common strategy for disentangling race and species" (558). The animal mask is Ahuja's response to the clash between racism and speciesism in the struggle to adhere to animality and yet be sensitive to the history of animalization of the minoritized.

---

6. According to Gilhus (2006, 39), the Stoics developed a philosophy on animals as the irrational ones in contrast to humans who are the rational animals: "animals acted according to nature (ἀπό φύσεως) and not according to reason."

Animal mask biblical interpretation is an invitation to question our speciesist take on the Bible. This invitation encourages us to embrace the nonhumans and our own animalization; it calls us not to condone the evils of the bestial logics but to reconfigure our relationality with the nonhumans. This reconfiguration is an invitation to push out the colonial machinations that forced us to hate the nonhumans and the animalized other in order to make ourselves fully human. We are invited to reconfigure and determine our futures, our biblical interpretations, with the nonhumans minus the colonial dictates that have been haunting us.

Instead of running away from Jesus's animalization of her, the Syrophoenician woman provisionally embraces the animal mask, specifically the dog mask. The colonized *ethne* (which includes the Syrophoenician woman) were expected to be "as subservient, obedient, and loyal as a 'devoted dog'" (Kwok 1995, 78). Going against the grain, the Syrophoenician woman performs or wears this mask in order to show Jesus, face to face, the (unintended?) carnophallogocentric violence to which he has subjected her. Her performance is her way of unmasking Jesus's neocolonial tendencies in his mimicry of the colonizers. She reminds Jesus of his mission to reveal the empire of God, and the nature of his messiahship.

More importantly, her response can be read as she reminding Jesus of the animalization of his fellow colonized *ethne*. It is as though she asks, "Have you already forgotten that you and I are both colonized *ethne* who are animalized by the colonizers?" The Syrophoenician woman's animal mask places a mirror in front of Jesus's face in order to remind him that he too is a member of a colonized *ethne* and as such is also animalized. If Hellenism indicated a colonized hybrid identity, we may say that the Syrophoenician woman reminds Jesus that she is also τῷ γένει, one of the (colonized) *ethne* who had to face enforced colonial assimilation to Greco-Roman imperial customs and language. Choi (2015, 85) profoundly argues that the Syrophoenician woman understood or perceived through *phronesis* or embodied wisdom "the brokenness and movement of Jesus' body and utilizes embodied tactics in order to allow her daughter to share his body." Resonating with Choi's interpretation, my reading argues that the Syrophoenician woman performed an affectively embodied assemblage with Jesus (as Choi also argues, this is in contrast to rational knowledge). Her remedy is to remind Jesus of their shared experience of oppression as Syrians and Asiatic Greeks (including Jews), who according to Livy, are considered to be "the most worthless of peoples among mankind and born for slavery" (*Ab urbe cond.* 36.17.5 [Sage]).

The Syrophoenician woman gathered up the messy collective assemblage of enunciation that the Phoenicians and the Galileans/Judeans threw at each other daily. Her short statement subversively reminisced a long history of tension between Jesus's *ethne* and hers. Following Jim Perkinson (1996, 74), the Syrophoenician woman can be said to have reiterated the "discourse of power" thrown at her by Jesus, thereby affectively jolting Jesus with his own statement: "Her word opens a gap in his word: the past catches up to the present. Suddenly there are discontinuous times contentiously present in one discursive space." The Syrophoenician woman did not spare Jesus from his own tainted colonial body and mind. As Perkinson argues, her plea for Jesus to heal her daughter was expressed in both a sly and bold way: "she does (covertly) shame him into honoring her appeal by re-presenting it as the concrete implication of his own reason for refusal" (76). In the end, her plea became the enunciation that healed her own daughter. In Mark 7:29, Jesus did not perform or say anything that would heal her daughter. Instead, Jesus points out that her statement (Διὰ τοῦτον τὸν λόγον, "because of this word/statement"), this bold performance of the animal mask, was the actancy that enabled the healing process. Whereas the Gospel of Matthew's Canaanite woman narrative has Jesus performing in the imperative by healing her daughter through his own words (γενηθήτω σοι ὡς θέλεις, Matt 21:28), Mark does not do this.[7] In Mark her words become the transcorporeal actant that affects not only the colonized mind of the Markan Jesus but also heals the material body of her daughter.

Here, one might wonder if the author of Mark deliberately placed the passage on the Syrophoenician woman right after Jesus's rhetoric on what defiles a person (Mark 7:14–23) and right before the healing of the deaf man (vv. 31–37) in order to highlight the actancy of enunciations. In verse 15, Jesus says: "there is nothing outside of a person that by going in can defile, but the things that come out are what defile." He continues in verses 21–22 by listing the things that are defiling: "adultery, avarice, wickedness, deceit, licentiousness, envy, slander, pride, and folly." This calls us to ask: Did the Markan author place the story of Jesus's encounter with the Syrophoenician woman immediately after the defilement discourse in order to accentuate the transcorporeal capacity of enunciations to affect the other,

---

7. I would like to thank Dr. George Aichele for pointing this crucial difference between Matthew and Mark.

being an actant in itself?[8] Moreover, did the Markan author intentionally redact the healing of the deaf man with speech impediment narrative as the third and last installment that follows the Syrophoenician woman's narrative in order to highlight the astounding healing and transformative actancy of speech and enunciation (and even saliva) upon the colonized and enslaved bodies (vv. 36–37)?

Moreover, the animal mask interpretation moves us away from the patronizing interpretation of τά κυνάρια as endearing "little pet dogs."[9] To interpret the dogs of Mark 7:24–30 as domesticated pets tries to justify Jesus's remarks by claiming that the Syrophoenician woman was not harassed with derogatory words but actually was a recipient of a light banter that used an endearing pet name. Whether it is a wild dog or a cute Schnauzer, animalization cannot be brushed off or explained away just because a lesser form of offensive remark is used.[10] To belittle the issue of animalization in Mark 7:24–30 shows that one has not experienced for oneself the painful reality of animalization. Dismissing or trivializing the historical reality of animalization does not stop the perennial utilization of nonhumans in animalizing the other.

Actancy of the Dogs and Bread Crumbs

So far, I have not yet examined the material bodies of dogs and bread crumbs in 7:24–30. It could be misconstrued that my animal mask interpretation is relegating the nonhumans (again) as flat characters in the clash between two round human characters, Jesus and the Syrophoenician woman. I have not discussed the material bodies of dogs and bread crumbs in this chapter because I presume that they have ontologically transgressed the bodies of Jesus and the Syrophoenician woman (and her daughter as well) through their enunciations. In other words, they have been "eaten" through their heated discussion. I could have resorted to arguing that the dogs and the bread crumbs were "there" in the narrative

---

8. The Gospel of Matthew also has this story preceded by "the things that defile" narrative. See Matt 15:10–28.

9. For the latter, see Donahue and Harrington 2002, 234; 1 Sam 17:43; Isa 56:10–11; 2 Kgs 8:13; Prov 26:11; Matt 7:6; Phil 3:2; 2 Pet 2:22; Rev 22:15.

10. According to David Miller (2008, 487–500), there are passages in the Hebrew Scriptures that portray dogs in positive light: Job 30:1; Tob 6:2; 11:4. For a more ambivalent stance, see Joshua Schwartz (2004, 246–77).

just like the dogs (and serpents) present in the rituals of the Asclepian healing cult, where they were even considered part of the healing process.[11] However, unlike the Asclepian narratives, Mark 7:24–30 does not disclose whether the dogs and bread crumbs were literally present or around them. They were symbolized. I argue that they are ontologically transgressing the narrative, and even unto to us (the audience of Mark), because their symbolic is not confined in the literary. They affectively haunt and penetrate the *ontos* of the other. Dogs and bread crumbs might not be in the text, but they animate us and overflowingly transgress the borders of the text and creep into us. They are not materially present in the text, and yet their animacies are the contentious points of the conversation.

Hence, my question is less of their presence or absence but whether or not we could read Mark 7:24–30 without carnophallogocentrically consuming or eating the nonhumans in order to establish our human arguments. My immediate answer is no. However, in this impasse, Derrida relays a sense of inevitability when it comes to eating nonhumans literally or marginalizing or using nonhumans symbolically for various human purposes. Derrida's (1995a, 282) resolution is *bien manger* or "to eat well." If humans cannot avoid eating the other, then Derrida suggests that we should eat the other in the most respectful way. By eating, Derrida signifies the physical ingestion of the other and metonymically interiorizes the other through symbols, language, and other expressions (282–83). In this eating, "one must begin to identify with the other, who is to be assimilated, interiorized, understood ideally (something one can never do absolutely *without addressing oneself to the other* and without absolutely limiting understanding itself, the identifying appropriation), speak to him or her in words that also pass through the mouth, the ear, the sight, and respect the law that is at once a voice and a court" (283). Moore's 2013 queer temporality and animality reading of the Matthean version (15:21–28) of Mark 7:24–30 invites

---

11. According to Ingvild Sælid Gilhus (2006, 109), "In the temple of Asclepius in Epidaurus, where people came to be healed by the god, serpents and dogs were present and sometimes contributed to effecting a cure…. Not only snakes worked as the god's assistants in Epidaurus; dogs are also mentioned: the blind boy, Lyson of Hermione, had his eyes treated 'by one of the dogs about the sanctuary' [The Epidaurian Miracle Inscriptions A20 (trans. LiDonnici)]). Another boy, from Aigina, was cured of the growth on his neck when 'a dog from the sanctuary took care of him with its tongue while he was awake, and made him well' [The Epidaurian Miracle Inscriptions B6 (trans. LiDonnici)]."

us to identify that the Canaanite woman not only became the proto-disciple but also the portending figure who began the "inhuman" consumption of Jesus. That is, the Canaanite, a member of an ethnic group that should evoke revulsion, became the model of discipleship not just for her care of her daughter but also as the one who first consumed and acknowledged the nourishing grace of the "body" of Jesus.[12] Choi (2015, 106) also invites us to identify the Syrophoenician woman as a member of the ὄχλος (the mass) who "displaced" Jesus's body through her phronetic wisdom, an embodied wisdom that "knows how life is given and nourished against the power of death." Furthermore, Hans Leander identifies the bread crumbs of Mark 7:24–30 with the body of Jesus or the bread of the Eucharist. For Leander (2013, 237), the bread's "predisposition of falling to pieces, its inability to stick together as a unified whole … makes possible the healing of the woman's daughter" (see also Yarbro Collins 2007, 189, 192–93). Following Moore, Choi, and Leander, the actancy of the nonhumans in Mark 7:24–30 is in their capacity to destabilize the subjectivity of Jesus as the Messiah. That is, the nonhumans remind the Markan Jesus that he is also a subject for consumption at the cross. The crumbs that fell on the floor satisfied, but they did not suffice. Much more is needed from the body of Jesus. As a matter of fact, his whole body barely satisfied the hunger of the sacrificial machine of the empire.

Animality, Disability, and The Cross

When I shared an earlier version of the current chapter in a summer institute led by Asian theologians and scholars, Boyung Lee, a leading feminist Korean professor in pastoral theology, reminded me to be vigilant that (gendered) animalization goes both ways.[13] As Heidi J. Nast (2006, 300–327) argues, oppressed communities also use bestial language against their oppressors, Lee admonishes that the oppressed or the minoritized cannot

---

12. Building upon Moore's work, this chapter finds Ahuja's animal mask to be a viable response to an animality reading of Mark 7:24–30 or any other animality interpretations of the Bible. In addition, for readings on the history of relationality between humans and dogs throughout Christianity, Laura Hobgood-Oster's (2008) informative book, *Holy Dogs and Asses*, should be consulted. The chapter on dogs in particular is quite interesting.

13. Boyung Lee is the senior vice president of academic affairs and the dean of the faculty at Iliff School of Theology.

be condoned for using bestial logics no matter their circumstances. The collective assemblage of enunciation that derogatorily identifies the other with nonhuman actants has to be countered not just from one trajectory (oppressor to oppressed) but also vice versa.

Here, I propose another way to eat well in which the assemblage of humans-nonhumans is re-territorialized. This new emerging milieu is to follow Sunaura Taylor's approach in dealing with the intersections of ableism, sexism, racism, and speciesism. Taylor is an artist and a scholar who has arthrogryposis, a medical condition that causes congenital joint contractures in multiple areas of her body. Using her life as a canvas, her paintings and scholarship intersect disability studies and nonhuman issues, focusing on the oppressive systems that animalize, demean, and abuse disabled persons and nonhumans. As a disabled person, to be compared to an animal is downright offensive. And yet, as an animal activist, Taylor has tried to find ways to fight for the disabled while not distancing herself from nonhumans. Her answer is similar to Ahuja's recommendation for an animal mask.

Taylor (2011, 191–92) narrates how during her early childhood she was compared with animals. She writes: "I have been told I walk like a monkey, eat like a dog, have hands like a lobster, and generally resemble a chicken or penguin. ... They meant it to hurt my feelings, which of course it did. However, I wasn't exactly sure why it should hurt my feelings." Taylor is more than aware of animalization or strategies of using animals as tools for denigration. And yet, she seeks to reconfigure this discourse of comparison in a way "that doesn't have to be negative" (192). For her, awareness of oppression is the key to resolving this dilemma: "As a freak, as a patient, I do not deny that I'm like an animal. Instead, I want to be aware of the mistreatment that those labeled 'animal' (human and nonhuman) experience. I am an animal" (194). Echoing Claire Jean Kim's (2017, 52) "ethics of avowal," Taylor further elaborates her assertion for an awareness of oppression by "examin[ing] the system that degrades and devalues both animals and disabled people—systems which are built upon, among, other things, ableist paradigms of language and cognitive capacity."

Taylor's desire for awareness of these issues in the form of art is her way of wearing the animal mask. Her painting, entitled *Animals with Arthrogryposis*, represents Taylor herself nude beside two factory farm pigs and a curly calf. The letters A, B, C, and D are written beside each of them respectively. The image is meant to invoke a medical photo figuring the condition of arthrogryposis.[14] Taylor poses herself in this vulnerable way in order to show how far carnophallogocentrism has infiltrated and denigrated women, the disabled, and nonhumans.

Through her paintings, Taylor is visually force-feeding her audience to "eat well" or be disrupted viscerally by seeing the very animalization of those who are othered. Instead of hiding her disability, Taylor dons the ironic mask of nudity in order to confront ableism, speciesism, sexism, and even racism. The Syrophoenician woman also dons the collective assemblage of animalization enunciated among colonized *ethne*. Instead of running away from Jesus, the Syrophoenician woman shows the negative affect of his colonial utterance. Her self-denuding enunciation disrupts Jesus. Her enunciation perhaps wakes him to the realization that his body-turned-into-meat is also mangled and animalized by the bestial logics of the Roman Empire. He might have covered himself momentarily with robes of carnophallogocentrism, but as Mark's narrative unfolds several chapters later, the Markan Jesus is also laid bare on a wood-framed canvas side by side with two other "rebels" (λῃστάς), one on his right and another on his left (Mark 15:27). And yet, these mutilated carcasses, as Moore (2017a, 59) enunciates, are the "sacred place in which the human encounters the divine in Mark, in which the human shudders before the divine, is affected by the divine." The self-revelation or the unmasking of the Markan Jesus in the assemblage formed at the "cross-torture-victim assemblage" (55), as gruesome as it is, becomes Mark's contact zone for the colonized community. As in Taylor's painting, this visceral encounter disrupts because the sensation of the unwanted, the abhorred crucifixion, is chosen by Mark to be the symbol in which the animalized community is to reassemble. The abject pieces of meat in the eyes of the colonizers have reterritorialized as the rallying cry for the oppressed communities to not be afraid even if the first witnesses were (Mark 16:8). In turn, they are to see their own animalized selves and be emboldened by the butchered bodies because their Messiah and comrades did so first.

---

14. For the image/figure and its descriptions, see Taylor 2011, 204, 218–19.

6
CONCLUSION: (RE)ANIMATING THE BIBLICAL EPISTEMIC GROUND

This book came about as I was somewhat frustrated with the current state of biblical interpretation particularly from the perspective of race and ethnicity. My frustration is that antiracist biblical interpretations disrupt whiteness by inadvertently and ironically centralizing whiteness in their narratives. Others try to decenter whiteness by distancing themselves from "outside interventions" (Asian biblical interpretation should only use Asian stuff). I understand that such distancing is derived from the affirmative need and empowering intention of reference politics in which we are trying to advocate for and support minoritized voices. Nevertheless, antiracist biblical interpretations, even with their liberating and activisms, unfortunately fall for anthropocentric and first-things-first approaches. Of course, I am not arguing that we do not need more race and ethnicity biblical interpretation. I am writing this book after all. And of course, I am not arguing that we do not need to champion the voices of the racially minoritized, as I am advocating for mine.

And yet, my rhizomatic longing to be with the other questions the anthropocentricity of what it means to discuss race and ethnicity especially in biblical interpretation. My epistemic grounds are earth(l)y. My epistemic grounds hope to reanimate my Asian-selves by being grafted in multitudinous ways with other groups (humans and nonhumans) who are interpreting the Bible in liberating and decolonizing ways. Reanimating the epistemic grounds is to admit that hermeneutics that are ethicopolitical, or those that are geared toward uplifting the oppressed and giving voice to those who are suppressed, can still inadvertently conclude with statements that are discriminatory and borderline offensive. Thus it is important to read sensitively through intersectionality. I am not exempt or above this admonition. This is not my unique idea. Rather, communities have already been reimagining a more just world by organizing communities with the nonhumans. Participating in ecojustice-led meetings and activism almost always involves discussing and uplifting the importance of the intersections between humans and nonhumans. For Native Americans and other indigenous groups, this is not even an issue. I find this intersectional endeavor an invitation to reconfigure my Asian race and skin as an assemblage of microbes, water, keratin, dusts, carbon dioxide, nonhuman hair follicles, bread crumbs, and other actants. I want to fully inhabit the flesh because, as Alexander G. Weheliyes (2002, 112) theorizes, "[it] might lead to a different modality of existence." What if this different modality of existence territorializes me into an assemblage with the nonhumans? What then becomes of the Asian in that assemblage?

Can this different modality of existence also happen with(in) biblical studies? Can we reanimate the epistemic grounds of what counts as biblical interpretation? Anna Runesson (2010, 35) in *Exegesis in the Making* unpacks Foucault's (1989, 191) understanding of episteme as "what constitutes the web in which knowledge is possible.... [E]pisteme is composed of the components that determine what knowledge is during a certain historical period." Rupture occurs when those who participate in an episteme do not neatly carry it over to the next period or web of understanding. This failure to transmit meaning is called an epistemic break or rupture. Breaking this episteme is a herculean task in the field of biblical studies. As Moore and Sherwood (2011, 112) rightly point out, such difficulty stems from "fear of breaking with the unwritten regulations that determine our professional style as biblical scholars." Moore and Sherwood locate a colossal epistemic break in the eighteenth-century Enlightenment in which the authority of biblical interpretation shifted from the church (focusing on theological and doctrinal matters) to an emerging culture of critique that analyzed the Bible with a range of scholarly tools (philology, archaeology, history, and so on). The introduction of postmodernism to biblical interpretation in the late twentieth century should have signaled the dawn of a new epistemic break. However, Moore and Sherwood insist, the Enlightenment episteme still has a stranglehold on this supposedly new episteme of biblical interpretation (48).

In all of these, I do see a glimmer of this in-breaking, this rupture here and there, with the rise of activist biblical interpretation or biblical interpretation based on activism. The unhinged atrocities caused by Trump's

6. CONCLUSION: (RE)ANIMATING THE BIBLICAL EPISTEMIC GROUND

presidency created a positive correlation with the rise of activist biblical interpretation or biblical interpretation that are responding to current socioethical and political issues. Although such writings existed before Trump's presidency, many sessions and program units in the Annual Meetings of the Society of Biblical Literature, journal and book publications, and webinars during Trump's presidency saw the remarkable rise of the episteme of interpreting the Bible as expressions of activism. Here, these expressions are not limited to anthropocentric issues. I also have witnessed the rise of biblical interpretations geared toward ecojustice and environmental racism. I see this movement and these expressions as an epistemic break, a reanimation of the epistemic grounds of biblical interpretation. Such a claim does not mean that the field will all of a sudden embrace activist biblical interpretation. I do not expect the Annual Meetings of the Society of Biblical Literature to dramatically shift the call for papers. I also do not have animosity toward historical or textual studies of the Bible. They are needed, in some cases. However, their stranglehold in the field is what needs to be broken or reanimated in order to make way for the animacy of activism and of the nonhumans to inundate the field. Such animacy is my suggestion for, as Moore and Sherwood (2011, 130) advocate, "pick[ing] the locks of the disciplinary mechanism itself and expose its inner operations."

To rephrase the issue with which I am grappling, can we have molecularly 'r'evolutionary[1] interpretations that are rigorous and yet not trapped in the anthropocentrically phallic way of interpreting the Bible? Here, Ivone Gebara's (1999, 25) words come into mind. She asserts that epistemologies are supposed to lead to ethical issues because good scholarship should force us to interrogate the limits and biases of our ways of knowing. In a certain sense, this book is my response to Gebara's mandate by intersecting continental philosophers with the voices of ecojustice scholars and activists. Philosophical, nonhuman-attuned reading of the Gospel of Mark (or the entire Bible) must be responsive to the socioethical demands promulgated by ecojustice scholars and activists. Such responsivity is my contribution to the in-breaking of this new episteme.

---

1. Molecular 'r'evolution is a Guattarian term for decentered, originary, and subversive activities that occur in random moments. The small letter *r* represents Guattari's preference for the molecular or decentered micropolitical nature of social transformations and revolutions against the idea that revolution has to be transcendental or that it requires totalitarian machinations. See Guattari and Rolnik 2007, 261.

To be more specific, I reconfigure the characters in the Markan narrative as actants. This reconfiguration revives the affective interventions of the nonhumans and especially the inanimate entities in a way that does not commodify their presence but actually engages their emergences in assemblages. Moreover, the narratives analyzed in this book are themselves interchangeably called assemblage(s) in order to expose the fragility of any narrative in terms of the presumed centrality of human actants. This fragility also contaminates the efficacy of any criticism, hermeneutics, or theory in providing the ultimate interpretation. The invitation to view any biblical interpretation as always open for further intersectionality due to its unforeseen limitations opens the doors for self-reflexivity in one's interpretations.

This book could be accused of being a heuristic exercise. If heuristic is defined as finding solutions that are not guaranteed optimal or perfect but sufficient for this time, then yes, my reading of the Markan narrative is indeed heuristic. As a matter of fact, this reading is never meant to be optimal or to be *the* interpretation of the text. This reading is heuristic because it relies on dormant possibilities, provisional plausibility, and creative endeavors. Of course, this does not mean that any interpretation of the Bible is acceptable. Instead of arguing that a biblical interpretation is legitimate or acceptable, my reading of the Gospel of Mark expects four stages of reflection. First, this biblical interpretation must acknowledge the agency, context, and ideology of the interpreter(s). Second, it rigorously applies the chosen reading strategies and theoretical practices. Third, it expects critical and ethical checks at various points of interpretations (references, methodologies, interpretative maneuverings, and conclusions). Fourth, it invites communities to engage the interpretation(s). I did not place these four stages of reflection in the introductory chapter of this book because I did not want the readers of this book to be affected by this suggestion. I do not want you, my readers, to be territorialized or molarized by my thoughts; you could be guided by my arguments but the intent is for you to assemble your own line of flight.

When I presented a chapter of this book at a Society of Biblical Literature Annual Meeting, someone from the audience questioned the absurd lowness of my depiction of the Markan Jesus and the Gospel's Christology. That person was worried about how my reading of the Markan Jesus as both bestial and vegetal implied a Christology so low as to border on blasphemy. I empathize with that person's concern, since many Christians feel like they already stand on thin ice when it comes to defending the

6. CONCLUSION: (RE)ANIMATING THE BIBLICAL EPISTEMIC GROUND   129

validity of our faith tradition in the modern world. And yet, one of the reasons why the Christian God tends to recede as a distant unapproachable figure for many is because of a high Christology, an appropriation of Jesus as the Son of God and Son of Man who is detached from the lowliness of humans and especially of nonhumans. In many ways, the suffering messiah of Mark has disappeared in many church pulpits even as the crucifix or the cross continues to reign as a popular fixture behind pulpits. Of course, I am generalizing here; there are many ordained ministers who embody the bestial messiah and participate in the vegetal empire of God. They are the reasons why I still value my own ordination. For the purpose of this book, I mention church life to ground the bestial and vegetal theories of this work.

Could we emphasize then a (Markan) Jesus who is, or a Markan Christology that is, "grounded in the materially embedded sense of responsibility and ethical accountability?" (echoing Braidotti 2006, 137). I offer that this book demonstrates that the author of Mark constructed (even while failing many times) a Jesus who "practice[s] a humble kind of hope, rooted in the ordinary micro-practices of everyday life" (278). Moreover, the empire of Jesus is sustained by the vicissitudes of the bestial, the vegetal, and the inanimate. Moore (2011, 89) has already laid the groundwork for this materially embedded (Markan) Jesus who is ontologically reconfigured in status as the Son of Humanity only through the nonhumans. Turning to Matthew, Moore doubles down his animality reading of the Son of Humanity by closely rereading narratives on the Matthean Jesus's death and its portents. According to Moore (2013, 64), Jesus's humanity is consumed by his (impending) gruesome death through slaughter on the cross. Jesus's dehumanization is also portended by the anthropophagic consumption of his body and blood (Matt 26:26–29) and his animalizing interment: "For just as Jonah was for three days and three nights in the belly of the sea monster, so for three days and three nights the Son of Humanity will be in the heart of the earth" (12:40).

Moore's reflections on the crucifixion, as well as my own earlier chapters, might be further extended. Here, I engage Anne Joh's (2006, xxi) politicized appropriation of the Korean concepts *jeong* and *han*[2] intersected

---

2. Joh here defines *jeong* as "a Korean way of conceiving an often complex constellation of relationality of the self with the other that is deeply associated with compassion, love, vulnerability, and acceptance of heterogeneity as essential to life.... *Jeong* is the power embodied in redemptive relationships." Joh continues: "*han* is a sense of

with Julia Kristeva's (1982, 4) notions of abjection and love in reconceptualizing Christology from the perspective(s) of an Asian American feminist theologian. Joh opens doors for further materially embedding (or embodying) conversations on the cross and Christology. Although Joh (2006, xxii) does not specifically work with nonhumans, her argument that the cross "performs a double gesture as it simultaneously signifies abjection and love, *han* and *jeong*" provides ways to reconfigure animality and the animalization of Jesus on the cross.

For example, I reconfigure a statement from Joh's work with a nonhuman perspective. The parenthetical insertions are the nonhuman additions to Joh's postcolonial Christology: "From a postcolonial perspective of *jeong*, the cross pays homage to the power of horror/abjection(/animalization) while at the same time using mimicry (and/or nonhuman perspectives) to make present the transgressive and transforming power of love (and responsivity toward all actants, both human and nonhuman)" (xxvi). Moreover, Joh's work inspires intersectionalities of *jeong* and *han* with nonhuman biblical interpretations. What does it mean for us humans to have *jeong* and *han* with the nonhumans under the auspices of ecocritical relationality? How do we approach the gruesomeness of the cross and yet still find some form of redemption for those who are animalized, human and nonhuman? If the Markan Jesus is ambivalently striding in the third space of *jeong* and *han*, abjection and love, then how do we translate these concepts to the Markan Jesus's struggle with colonial mentality and mimicry in the form of carnophallogocentrism?

Following Karen Barad's (2016, 178) "ethics of mattering" or responsivity to relationalities of becoming that considers all actants to be part of webs of relations, Barad's concept of sustainability invites us, as biblical interpreters, to break free from technologies that fix our parameters for biblical engagement. This "unfixing" does not seek finality. Like the vegetal, sustainable biblical interpretation grows and dies, blossoms and withers for a negative futurity in which all of our interpretations provide for and respond to our current ethicopolitical issues without being imprisoned in the factory farms of academia. This sustainable biblical interpretation organically encourages "situated knowledge" that participates in dismantling the

---

unresolved resentment against injustices suffered, a sense of helplessness because of the overwhelming odds against one's feeling of total abandonment, a feeling of acute pain and sorrow in one's guts and bowels." See Andrew Sung Park 1993, 120, quoted in Joh 2006, xxi.

6. CONCLUSION: (RE)ANIMATING THE BIBLICAL EPISTEMIC GROUND 131

default (pesticide-ridden) categories of biblical interpretation. By following this recipe, I hope that this book can become a cookbook for organic, free-range, and locally sourced biblical interpretation that provides an alternative to anthropocentrically and carnophallogocentrically modified biblical interpretation.

Other Nonhuman Assemblages in the Gospel of Mark

This is neither the end nor the beginning. The Gospel of Mark creeps, crawls, claws back, and hisses at you and I, demanding to be freed from the territorializations I just made through these chapters. As a matter of fact, the rhizomatic sprawling of these texts has probably burst out of our minds (knowingly and unknowingly) and the texts, forming other territorializations and de-territorializing, affirming while questioning the sanity of this book. This book's epistemic rupture disturbs and haunts. Nevertheless, the rhizomatic hauntings cannot be stopped by anthropocentricism. Whether I intend to do so or not, I have a sense that other Markan passages are rhizomatically forming their assemblages through this book or separately with other assemblages.

I did not turn these narratives below into chapters of this book because I hope that you will form them into your own liberating and decolonizing assemblages. In other words, I offer a nonexhaustive list of possible narratives open for further nonhuman interpretations of Mark.

When it comes to animality, Mark 1:16–20 has Jesus promising his soon-to-be disciples Simon and Andrew that they will become fishers of people (ἁλιεῖς ἀνθρώπων). In Mark 6:34, the crowd (ὄχλος) who seem to be lost are described as sheep (πρόβατα). Both instances describe people in general as nonhumans. Of course, the usual interpretation would argue that these are metaphors. Metaphors are contagious. They transgress into bodies, particularly vulnerable and animalized bodies. Animalization begins, thrives, and even ends with metaphors. To metaphorically call a human actant a monkey brings with it loads of animalizing baggage even if the speaker of such a metaphorical comparison did not intend to do so. With that in mind, further research is needed on the historical baggage and contemporary resonances of fish and sheep. Is calling the colonized *ethne* fish and sheep demeaning, benign, or ambivalently both?

Mark 16:17–18, sidelined by scholars as a secondary addition but devoutly read by countless Christians as scriptural, pictures an apocalyptic expectation in which signs will accompany those who are baptized.

They will cast out demons, speak in new tongues, pick up snakes with their hands, and drink poison but will not die. Here, a nonhuman perspective would question this apocalyptic Eden-like restoration in which predatory animals (here snakes, ὄφεις) are once again defanged. Moreover, the actancy of poison is quite interesting here. The overcoming of the inanimate poison seems to be one of the markers of those who are baptized. The juxtaposition of water and poison, two liquids with supposedly different human purposes (one for sustenance, the other for harm), are now both significations for membership in this baptized community.

From a vegetality perspective, Mark 8:22–25 narrates Jesus's encounter with a blind man in Bethsaida. In the healing process, Jesus puts his saliva on the blind man's eyes. As soon as his saliva was applied, the blind man said: "I can see people, but they look like trees [δένδρα], walking" (8:24). Was the blind man able to see at least partially before? Or was this the first time he was able to see? It seems that the blind man was able to see before since he was able to determine the difference between a tree and a human physique. And yet, why would he describe what he saw as looking like walking trees if humans are supposedly mobile and trees are not? Was the blind man describing liminal entities that blur the ontological and material boundaries between humans and trees?

There are several Markan texts ripe for new materialist and animacies readings. Sandwiched between Jesus's encounter with Jairus, Mark 5:25–34 retells the bravery of a woman who had flow of blood for twelve years. She endured many physicians and spent all she had just to be healed to no avail. Hearing that Jesus was coming to her town, she decides to ask Jesus for help. The large crowd at first prevents her frail body from approaching Jesus. And yet, she persists. Although she was unable to ask Jesus for healing, she believes that she could be healed just by touching his cloak. Here, the issue of the agency of healing becomes an issue. Jesus did not release the healing mechanism because he did not knowingly sanction the healing, but neither did the woman with the flow of blood deploy the healing power through her own agency. The cloak seems to possess the healing power because it encapsulated the actancy to heal for anyone who touched it. The apparent inanimacy of the healing actant in this pericope compels reflection.

Food products in Mark also invite animated readings. First, Jesus cautions his disciples against the yeast of the Pharisees and Herod (Mark 8:14–21). After crossing the Sea of Galilee, the disciples are hungry and have forgotten to bring enough bread. Hearing this, Jesus responds in a way that baffles the disciples: "Watch out—beware of the yeast [ζύμης] of the Pharisees and the yeast of Herod" (8:15). The enigmatic role of yeast, its actancy to puff a small amount of dough into a large fluffy bread, probably is the imagery Jesus uses in describing the puff spewed by the Pharisees and Herod. And yet, for the listeners of Mark, yeast would resonate more with the affect of oral, olfactory, and visual satisfaction through the yeast-puffed bread. The previous actancy, the memory of the whiff and taste of fresh bread, counteracts Jesus's vitriol against the Pharisees and Herod.

Another food product that animates is salt. In Mark 9:49–50, the Markan Jesus presents salt ambivalently in at least three ways (Donahue and Harrington 2002, 288–89). The first way ("everyone will be salted with fire") seems to allude to the testing and purification required before the parousia of Jesus. The second way (on the possibility of salt losing its flavor) shifts the discussion on salt to the importance of faithfulness in discipleship for the followers of Jesus. The third way ("have salt among yourselves, and live in peace with one another") alludes to the use of salt in offerings during sacrifices (see Lev 2:13a) in order to qualify the nature of discipleship. In all three instances, the sayings highlight salt's affective capacity to confer both life and death. What seems inanimate, immobile, and insensate has animated, moved, and sensationalized the nature of discipleship.

Materializing Biblical Interpretation

Adopted in December 2015, the Paris Climate Accord is an agreement among 195 countries with the United Nations Framework Convention on Climate Change (UNFCCC) to curtail polluting mechanisms that contribute to climate change (United Nations 2015). Each country determines its own systems, dates, and goals in mitigating various forms of pollution in their respective countries. On June 1, 2017, former President Trump attempted to justify the United States' historically baffling withdrawal from the accord. He did not resort to scientific or religious arguments. Instead Trump's angle was economic: the United States is paying more than its fair share to the United Nations Green Climate Fund. He wanted to renegotiate so that the United States would have a better deal in this international agreement. The condemnation of this decision, aside from the usual suspects (ecologically-oriented groups), came also from the CEOs of powerful international companies. Goldman Sachs, Disney, Tesla, IBM, and even energy companies such as Shell disapproved of Trump's decision because, among other (environmental) reasons, it was bad for business (David 2017).

Trump's decision and the CEOs' reactions reminded me of Laurel Kearns's (2007, 107) argument that economics and the capitalist market—or what makes economic sense—is the underlying force that manipulates climate change talks and decisions, and not just religion or science. Although we might never fully know the reasons why energy companies condemned Trump's decision, those of us who seek to be protectors of the environment must take heed of Kearns's assertion that "changes must come from deliberately linking a changed worldview with ethical economic practice that challenges the current belief in, and workings of, the market and that promotes a more equitable and just cohabitation of the planet in order to ensure a future for all of creation" (124).

This book focuses on and even reconfigures the parameters of relationality between humans and nonhumans. Not only are the plights of the minoritized and animalized humans highlighted, their ontological relationalities with material nonhumans were central in interpreting various Markan narratives. Beyond such considerations, following Kearns, changes for a more environmentally conscientious biblical interpretation should, among many possibilities, also engage material and economic issues. For those of us who struggle with animalized racism, Kwok Pui-lan (2017, n.p.) invites us to reach out to those who do not see themselves as "minority or animalized" by intersecting our struggle with macrolevel issues: "We have to avoid the tendency of focusing too narrowly on identity issues in the US, without paying attention to larger social, economic, and political forces shaping the world at the macro-level." By being the first to reach out and cross the border, we should strive to tear down the walls of disbelief on climate change and the walls of hatred through animalization of the other. We can do so with unconditional hospitality and socioeconomic coalition and even within biblical interpretation.

WORKS CITED

Ancient Texts

Appian of Alexandria. 1912–1913. *Roman History*. Translated by Horace White. 4 vols. LCL Cambridge: Harvard University Press.

Aristotle. 1933. *Metaphysics, Volume 1: Books 1–9*. Translated by Hugh Tredenick. LCL. Cambridge: Harvard University Press.

———. 1935. *Metaphysics, Volume 2: Books 10–14*. Translated by Hugh Tredenick and G. Cyril Armstrong. LCL. Cambridge: Harvard University Press.

———. 1963. *Minor Works*. Translated by W. S. Hett. LCL. Cambridge: Harvard University Press.

———. 1967. *Politics*. Translated by H. Rackham. LCL. Cambridge: Harvard University Press.

———. 1968. *Nicomachean Ethics*. Translated by H. Rackham. LCL. Cambridge: Harvard University Press.

———. 1975. *On the Soul. Parva Naturalia. On Breath*. Translated by W. S. Hett. Rev. ed. LCL. Cambridge: Harvard University Press.

Cato and Varro. 1934. *On Agriculture*. Translated by W. D. Hooper. LCL. Cambridge: Harvard University Press.

Cicero, Marcus Tullius. 1935. *The Verrine Orations*. Translated by L. H. G. Greenwood. LCL. Cambridge: Harvard University Press.

———. 1963. *Philippics*. Translated by Walter C. A. Ker. LCL. Cambridge: Harvard University Press.

Demosthenes. 1935. *Against Meidias. Androtion. Aristocrates. Timocrates. Aristogeiton*. Translated by J. H. Vince. LCL. Cambridge: Harvard University Press.

———. 1939. *Private Orations L–LIX*. Translated by A. T. Murray. Cambridge: Harvard University Press.

Dio Cassius. 1914–1927. *Roman History*. Translated by Earnest Cary with Herbert Foster. 9 vols. LCL. Cambridge: Harvard University Press.

The Epidaurian Miracle Inscriptions. 1995. Texts, translation, and commentary by L. R. LiDonnici. Atlanta: Scholars Press.

Homer. 1924. *The Iliad, Volume I: Books 1–12*. Translated by A. T. Murray. Revised by William F. Wyatt. LCL. Cambridge: Harvard University Press.

———. 2004. *Odyssey*. Translated by Edward McCrorie. Baltimore: Johns Hopkins University Press.

Josephus, Flavius. 1926. *The Life; Against Apion*. Translated by H. St. J. Thackeray. LCL. Cambridge: Harvard University Press.

———. 1927. *The Jewish War, Volume II: Books 3–4*. Translated by H. St. J. Thackeray. LCL. Cambridge: Harvard University Press.

———. 1943. *Jewish Antiquities, Volume VII: Books 16–17*. Translated by Ralph Marcus. LCL. Cambridge: Harvard University Press.

Justinian. 2011. *The Digest of Justinian, Vol. 1*. Edited by Alan Watson. Philadelphia: University of Philadelphia Press.

Juvenal. 1992. *The Satires*. Translated by Niall Rudd. Oxford: Oxford University Press.

Livy. 1935. *Ab Urbe Condita*. Translated by Evan T. Sage. LCL Cambridge: Harvard University Press.

Manilius. 1977. *Astronomica*. Translated by G. P. Goold. Cambridge: Harvard University Press.

Plato. 1914. *Euthyphro; Apology; Crito; Phaedo; Phaedrus*. Translated by Christopher Emlyn-Jones. LCL. Cambridge: Harvard University Press.

Pliny the Elder. 1938–1962. *Natural History*. Translated by H. Rackham. 10 vols. LCL. Cambridge: Harvard University Press.

Plutarch. 1936. *Moralia, Volume IV*. Translated by Frank Cole Babbitt. LCL. Cambridge: Harvard University Press.

Porphyry. 2000. *On Abstinence from Killing Animals*. Translated by Gillian Clark. Ithaca: Cornell University Press.

Sallustius Crispus, Gaius. 1957. *Catilina; Jugurtha; Fragmenta ampliora*. Edited by Alphons Kurfess. 3rd ed. Leipzig: Teubner.

Strabo. 2014. *The Geography of Strabo: An English Translation, with Introduction and Notes*. Translated by Duane W. Roller. Cambridge: Cambridge University Press.

Suetonius. 2007. *The Twelve Caesars*. Translated by Robert Graves. Rev. ed. New York: Penguin.

Tacitus, Publius Cornelius. 1931. *Histories: Books 4–5; Annals: Books 1–3*. Translated by Clifford H. Moore and John Jackson. LCL. Cambridge: Harvard University Press.

———. 1967. *Agricola; Germany; Dialogue on Orators*. Translation, introduction, and notes by Herbert W. Benario. Indianapolis: Bobbs-Merrill Company.

Theophrastus. 1916. *Enquiry into Plants, Volume II: Books 6–9. On Odours. Weather Signs*. Translated by Arthur Hort. LCL. Cambridge: Harvard University Press.

Modern Sources

Adams, Carol J. 1994. *Neither Man nor Beast: Feminism and the Defense of Animals*. New York: Continuum.

———. 2015. *The Sexual Politics of Meat: A Feminist-Vegetarian Critical Theory*. London: Bloomsbury.

Adams, Carol J., and Josephine Donovan, eds. 1995. *Animals and Women: Feminist Theoretical Explorations*. Durham, NC: Duke University Press.

———. 1996. *Beyond Animal Rights: A Feminist Caring Ethic for the Treatment of Animals*. New York: Continuum.

Adams, Carol J., and Lori Gruen. 2014. *Ecofeminism: Feminist Intersections with Other Animals and the Earth*. New York: Bloomsbury.

Adams, Carol J., and Lisa Kemmerer. 1990. *Sister Species: Women, Animals, and Social Justice*. Champaign, IL: University of Illinois Press.

Adams, James N. 1990. *The Latin Sexual Vocabulary*. Baltimore: Johns Hopkins University Press.

Adamson, Joni. 2001. *American Indian Literature, Environmental Justice, and Ecocriticism: The Middle Place*. Tucson: University of Arizona Press.

Adamson, Joni, Mei Mei Evans, and Rachel Stein, eds. 2002. *The Environmental Justice Reader: Politics, Poetics, and Pedagogy*. Tucson: University of Arizona Press.

Adamson, Joni, and Scott Slovic. 2009. "The Shoulders We Stand On: An Introduction to Ethnicity and Ecocriticism." *MELUS* 34.2:5–24.

Aernie, Jeffrey W. 2014. "Borderless Discipleship: The Syrophoenician Woman as a Christ-Follower in Mark 7:24–30." Pages 191–207 in *Bible, Borders, Belonging(s): Engaging Readings from Oceania*. Edited by Jione Havea, David J. Neville, and Elaine M. Wainwright. SemeiaSt 75. Atlanta: SBL Press.

Agamben, Giorgio. 1998. *Homo Sacer: Sovereign Power and Bare Life.* Translated by Daniel Heller-Roazen. Stanford, CA: Stanford University Press.

Ahmad, Aijaz. 1987. "Jameson's Rhetoric of Otherness and the 'National Allegory.'" *Social Text* 17:3–25.

Ahmed, Sara. 2014. *The Cultural Politics of Emotion.* New York: Routledge.

Ahuja, Neel. 2009. "Postcolonial Critique in a Multispecies World." *PMLA* 124.2:556–63.

Alaimo, Stacy. 2000. *Undomesticated Ground: Recasting Nature as Feminist Space.* Ithaca, NY: Cornell University Press.

———. 2010. *Bodily Natures: Science, Environment, and the Material Self.* Bloomington: Indiana University Press.

———. 2016. *Exposed: Environmental Politics and Pleasures in Posthuman Times.* Minneapolis: University of Minnesota Press.

Alaimo, Stacy, and Susan Hekman, eds. 2008. *Material Feminisms.* Bloomington: Indiana University Press.

Anderson, Hugh. 1976. *The Gospel of Mark.* NCBC 27. Grand Rapids: Eerdmans.

Aquino, Frederick D., and A. Brian McLemore. 1993. "Markan Characterization of Women." Pages 393–424 in *Essays on Women in Earliest Christianity.* Edited by Carroll D. Osburn. Eugene, OR: Wipf & Stock.

Ashkenazi, Eli. 2007. "Seven Sea of Galilee Beaches Closed Due to Pollution, Lifeguard Dearth." *Haaretz.* 27 July. https://tinyurl.com/SBL0700a.

Aus, Roger David. 2003. *My Name Is "Legion": Palestinian Judaic Traditions in Mark 5,1–20 and Other Gospel Texts.* Lanham, MD: University Press of America.

Avotri, Solomon K. 2000. "The Vernacularization of Scripture and African Beliefs: The Story of the Gerasene Demoniac among the Ewe of West Africa." Pages 311–25 in *The Bible in Africa: Transactions, Trajectories and Trends.* Edited by Gerald O. West and Musa W. Dube. Leiden: Brill.

Bae, HyunJu. 2004. "Dancing around Life: An Asian Woman's Perspective." *EcR* 56.4:390–403.

Baird, Mary. 1920. "The Gerasene Demoniac." *ExpTim* 31.4:189.

Baker, Steve. 2001. *Picturing the Beast: Animals, Identity, and Representation.* Champaign: University of Illinois Press.

Balch, David L. 2015. *Contested Ethnicities and Images: Studies in Acts and Art.* WUNT 345. Tübingen: Mohr Siebeck.

Barad, Karen. 2007. *Meeting the Universe Halfway: Quantum Physics and the Entanglement of Matter and Meaning*. Durham, NC: Duke University Press.

Barreto, Eric D. 2010. *Ethnic Negotiations: The Function of Race and Ethnicity in Acts 16*. WUNT 2/294. Tübingen: Mohr Siebeck.

Basofin, Joshua. 2012. "Water Pollution in Israel Threatens People, Animals, Plants." *Green Prophet*. 8 January. https://tinyurl.com/SBL0700b.

Bauckham, Richard. 2011. *Living with Other Creatures: Green Exegesis and Theology*. Waco, TX: Baylor University Press.

Baum, Gregory, and Robert Ellsberg, eds. 1989. *The Logic of Solidarity: Commentaries on Pope John Paul II's Encyclical on Social Concern*. New York: Orbis.

Beavis, Mary Ann. 1988. "Women as Models of Faith in Mark." *BTB* 18:3–9.

Bechtel, Trevor, Matthew Eaton, and Timothy Harvie, eds. 2018. *Encountering Earth: Thinking Theologically with a More-Than-Human World*. Eugene, OR: Wipf & Stock.

Belo, Fernando. 1981. *A Materialist Reading of the Gospel of Mark*. Translated by Matthew J. O'Connell. Maryknoll, NY: Orbis.

Bennett, Jane. 2010. *Vibrant Matter: A Political Ecology of Things*. Durham, NC: Duke University Press.

Benyus, Janine M. 1997. *Biomimicry: Innovation Inspired by Nature*. New York: Morrow.

Best, Ernest. 1983. *Mark: The Gospel of as Story*. Edinburgh: T&T Clark.

Bhattacharya, Sibajiban, ed. 1970. *Jain Philosophy*. Vol. 10 of *The Encyclopedia of Indian Philosophies*. New Delhi: American Institute of Indian Studies.

Birch, Charles. 1990. *On Purpose*. Kensington: University of New South Wales Press.

Birke, Lynda I. A., 1994. *Feminism, Animals and Science: The Naming of the Shrew*. Buckingham: Open University Press.

———. 2002. "Intimate Familiarities? Feminism and Human-Animal Studies." *SocAnim* 10.4:429–36.

Bishop, Eric Francis Fox. 1951. "Jesus and the Lake." *CBQ* 13:398–414.

Blunt, Wilfrid. 2001. *Linnaeus: The Compleat Naturalist*. Introduction by William T. Stearn. Princeton: Princeton University Press.

Bodenheimer, Friedrich Simon. 1935. *Animal Life in Palestine*. Jerusalem: Mayer.

Boer, Roland. 2015. *The Sacred Economy of Ancient Israel*. Louisville: Westminster John Knox.

Boisseron, Bénédicte. 2018. *Afro-Dog: Blackness and the Animal Question*. New York: Columbia University Press.

Bradley, Keith. 2000. "Animalizing the Slave: The Truth of Fiction." *JRS* 90:110–25.

Braidotti, Rosi. 2006. *Transpositions*. Malden, MA: Polity.

———. 2009. "Animals, Anomalies, and Inorganic Others." *PMLA* 124.2:526–32.

Brassier, Ray. 2007. *Nihil Unbound: Enlightenment and Extinction*. New York: Macmillan.

Brenner-Idan, Athalya. 1985. *The Israelite Woman: Social Role and Literary Type in Biblical Narrative*. Sheffield: Sheffield Academic.

Brinkema, Eugenie. 2014. *The Forms of the Affects*. Durham, NC: Duke University Press.

Bryce, Trevor. 2014. *Ancient Syria: A Three Thousand Year History*. Oxford: Oxford University Press.

Buell, Denise K. 2005. *Why This New Race: Ethnic Reasoning in Early Christianity*. New York: Columbia University Press.

Buell, Lawrence. 2005. *The Future of Environmental Criticism: Environmental Crisis and Literary Imagination*. Malden: Blackwell.

Bulosan, Carlos. 1943. *America Is in the Heart*. Seattle: University of Washington Press.

Burdon, Christopher. 2004. "'To the Other Side:' Construction of Evil and Fear of Liberation in Mark 5:1–20." *JSNT* 27.2:149–167.

Butcher, Grace. 1991. *Child, House, World*. Hiram Poetry Review Supplement 12. Hiram, OH: Hiram College Press.

Butcher, Kevin. 2003. *Roman Syria and the Near East*. Los Angeles: J. Paul Getty Museum Publications.

Butler, Judith. 1990. *Gender Trouble: Feminism and the Subversion of Identity*. New York: Routledge.

Calarco, Matthew. 2008. *Zoographies: The Question of the Animal from Heidegger to Derrida*. New York: Columbia University Press.

Callan, Terrance. 2009. "Comparison of Humans to Animals in 2 Peter 2,10b–22." *Bib* 90.1:101–13.

Calpino, Teresa. 2008. "The Gerasene Demoniac (Mark 5:1–20): The Pre-Markan Function of the Pericope." *BR* 53:15–23.

Camery-Hoggatt, Jerry. 1992. *Irony in Mark's Gospel: Text and Subtext*. SNTSMS 72. Cambridge: Cambridge University Press.

Caneday, A. B. 1999. "Mark's Provocative Use of Scripture in Narration: 'He Was with the Wild Animals and Angels Ministered to Him.'" *BBR* 9:19–36.

Cansdale, George. 1970. *Animals of Bible Lands*. Exeter: Paternoster.

Carson, Rachel. 1991. *The Sea around Us*. Introduction by Ann H. Zwinger. Afterword by Jeffrey S. Levinton. Oxford: Oxford University Press.

Carter, Warren. 2014. "Cross-Gendered Romans and Mark's Jesus: Legion Enters the Pigs (Mark 5:1–20)." *JBL* 133:139–55.

Césaire, Aimé. 2001. *Discourse on Colonialism*. Translated by Joan Pinkham. New York: Monthly Review Press.

Chakrabarty, Dipesh. 2012. "Postcolonial Studies and the Challenge of Climate Change." *New Lit. Hist.* 43.1:1–18.

Chamovitz, Daniel. 2013. *What a Plant Knows: A Field Guide to the Senses*. New York: Oneworld.

Chen, Mel Y. 2012. *Animacies: Biopolitics, Racial Mattering, and Queer Affect*. Durham, NC: Duke University Press.

Cho, Grace M. 2008. *Haunting the Korean Diaspora: Shame, Secrecy, and the Forgotten War*. Minneapolis: University of Minneapolis Press.

Choi, Jin Young. 2015. *Postcolonial Discipleship of Embodiment: An Asian and Asian American Feminist Reading of the Gospel of Mark*. New York: Macmillan.

Chow, Rey. 2006. *The Age of the World Target: Self-Referentiality in War, Theory, and Comparative Work*. Durham, NC: Duke University Press.

Cohen, Jeffrey Jerome. 2012. "Introduction: All Things." Pages 1–8 in *Animal, Vegetable, Mineral: Ethics and Objects*. Edited by Jeffrey Jerome Cohen. Washington, DC: Oliphaunt.

Colvin, Jill. 2017. "Trump Pulls US from Global Warming Accord, to Allies' Dismay." Boston.com. 1 June. https://tinyurl.com/SBL0700c.

Connell, Robert W. 1995. *Masculinities*. Berkeley: University of California Press.

Conway, Colleen. 2008. *Behold the Man: Jesus and Greco-Roman Masculinity*. Oxford: Oxford University Press.

Coole, Diana, and Samantha Frost. 2010. "Introducing the New Materialisms." Pages 1–46 in *New Materialisms: Ontology, Agency, and Politics*. Edited by Diana Coole and Samantha Frost. Durham, NC: Duke University Press.

Cotter, Wendy J. 1986. "For It Was Not the Season for Figs." *CBQ* 48:62–66.

———. 1999. *Miracles in Greco-Roman Antiquity: A Sourcebook*. New York: Routledge.

Craghan, John F. 1968. "Gerasene Demoniac." *CBQ* 30:522–36.
Crenshaw, Kimberlé Williams. 1989. "Demarginalizing the Intersection of Race and Sex: A Black Feminist Critique of Antidiscrimination Doctrine, Feminist Theory, and Antiracist Politics." *University of Chicago Legal Forum* 140:139–67.
———. 1991. "Mapping the Margins: Intersectionality, Identity Politics, and Violence against Women of Color." *Stanford Law Review* 43.6:1241–99.
Crossan, John Dominic. 1991. *The Historical Jesus: The Life of a Mediterranean Jewish Peasant.* San Francisco: HarperSanFrancisco.
David, Javier E. 2017. "Big Businesses—Even Energy Companies—Disapprove of Trump's Decision to Walk Away from Climate Deal." CNBC. 1 June. https://tinyurl.com/SBL0700d.
Davidson, Nicola. 2013. "Rivers of Blood: The Dead Pigs Rotting in China's Water Supply." *The Guardian*. 29 March. https://tinyurl.com/SBL0700e.
Deckha, Maneesha. 2012. "Toward A Postcolonial Posthumanist Feminist Theory: Centralizing Race and Culture in Feminist Work on Nonhuman Animals." *Hypatia: Journal of Feminist Philosophy* 27:3:527–45.
DeLanda, Manuel. 2016. *Assemblage Theory.* Edinburgh: Edinburgh University Press.
Deleuze, Gilles, and Claire Parnet. 2002. *Dialogues II.* Oxford: Oxford University Press.
Deleuze, Gilles, and Felix Guattari. 1987. *A Thousand Plateaus: Capitalism and Schizophrenia.* Translated by Brian Massumi. Minneapolis: University of Minnesota Press.
———. 1994. *What Is Philosophy?* New York: Columbia University Press.
DeMello, Margo. 2012. *Animals and Society: An Introduction to Human-Animal Studies.* New York: Columbia University Press.
Derrett, J. Duncan M. 1979. "Contributions to the Study of the Gerasene Demoniac." *JSNT* 2.3:2–17.
Derrida, Jacques. 1988. *Limited, Inc.* Translated by Samuel Weber. Evanston, IL: Northwestern University Press.
———. 1995a. "'Eating Well,' or the Calculation of the Subject." Pages 255–87 in *Points…: Interviews, 1974–1994.* Edited by Elisabeth Weber. Translated by Peggy Kamuf et al. Stanford, CA: Stanford University Press.
———. 1995b. *The Gift of Death.* Translated by David Willis. Chicago: University of Chicago Press.

———. 1999. "L'animal que donc je suis (à suivre)." Pages 251–303 in *L'animal autobiographique*. Edited by Marie-Louise Mallet. Paris: Galilée.

———. 2000. *Of Hospitality: Anne Dufourmantelle Invites Jacques Derrida to Respond*. Translated by Rachel Bowlby. Stanford, CA: Stanford University Press.

———. 2001. "On Forgiveness." Pages 25–60 in *On Cosmopolitanism and Forgiveness*. Translated by Mark Dooley and Michael Hughes. London: Routledge.

———. 2002a. "The Animal That Therefore I Am (More to Follow)." *Crit Inq* 28.2 (2002): 369–418.

———. 2002b. "Force of Law: The 'Mystical Foundation of Authority.'" Pages 228–98 in *Acts of Religion*. Edited and with an Introduction by Gil Anidjar. London: Routledge.

———. 2005a. *Rogues: Two Essays on Reason*. Translated by Pascale-Anne Brault and Michael Naas. Stanford, CA: Stanford University Press.

———. 2005b. *On Touching—Jean-Luc Nancy*. Translated by Christine Irizarry. Stanford, CA: Stanford University Press, 2005.

———. 2008. *The Animal That Therefore I Am*. Edited by Marie-Louise Mallet and David Wills. Perspectives in Continental Philosophy. New York: Fordham University Press.

———. 2009–2011. *The Beast and the Sovereign*. Edited by Michel Lisse et al. Translated by Geoffrey Bennington. 2 vols. Seminars of Jacques Derrida; Chicago: University of Chicago Press.

Dixon, Edward P. 2009. "Descending Spirit and Descending Gods: A 'Greek' Interpretation of the Spirit's 'Descent as a Dove' in Mark 1:10." *JBL* 128:759–80.

Dodd, C. H. 1961. *The Parables of the Kingdom*. Rev. ed. Glasgow: Fontana.

Donahue, John R. and Daniel J. Harrington. 2002. *The Gospel of Mark: A Commentary*. SP 2. Collegeville, MN: Liturgical Press.

Donaldson, Brianne. 2015. *Creaturely Cosmologies: Why Metaphysics Matters for Animal and Planetary Liberation*. Lanham, MD: Lexington.

Donaldson, Laura. 2005. "Gospel Hauntings: The Postcolonial Demons of New Testament Criticism." Pages 97–113 in *Postcolonial Biblical Criticism: Interdisciplinary Intersections*. Edited by Stephen D. Moore and Fernando Segovia. BP 8. London: T&T Clark.

Donner, H. 1982. "The Interdependence of Internal Affairs and Foreign Policy during the Davidic-Solomonic Period." Pages 205–14 in *Studies in the Period of David and Solomon and Other Essays: Papers Read at the International Symposium for Biblical Studies, Tokyo 5–7 December, 1979*. Edited by T. Ishida. Winona Lake, IN: Eisenbrauns.

Dormandy, Richard. 2000. "The Expulsion of Legion: A Political Reading of Mark 5.1–20." *ExpTim* 111:335–37.

Douglas, Mary. 1966. *Purity and Danger: An Analysis of the Concepts of Pollution and Taboo*. New York: Routledge.

Dover, Kenneth James. 1972. *Aristophanic Comedy*. Berkeley: University of California Press.

Doyle, Richard. 2003. *Darwin's Pharmacy: Plants, Sex, and the Noosphere*. Seattle: University of Washington Press.

Dreese, Donelle N. 2002. *Ecocriticism: Creating Self and Place in Environmental and American Indian Literatures*. New York: Lang.

Dube, Musa W. 2000. *Postcolonial Feminist Interpretation of the Bible*. St. Louis: Chalice.

Du Bois, W. E. B. 2007. "The Training of Black Men." Pages 63–76 in *The Souls of Black Folk*. Edited and introduction by Brent Hayes Edwards. Oxford, Oxford University Press.

Dyer, Keith D. 2002. "When Is the End Not the End? The Fate of Earth in Biblical Eschatology (Mark 13)." Pages 44–56 in *The Earth Story in the New Testament*. Edited by Norman C. Habel and Vicky Balabanski. Sheffield: Sheffield Academic.

Earth Bible Team. 2000. "Guiding Ecojustice Principles." Pages 38–53 in *Readings from the Perspective of Earth*. Edited by Norman C. Habel. Sheffield: Sheffield Academic.

———. 2002. "Ecojustice Hermeneutics: Reflections and Challenges." Pages 1–14 in *The Earth Story in the New Testament*. Edited by Norman C. Habel and Vicky Balabanski. Sheffield: Sheffield Academic.

Encyclopedia Britannica. 2017. "Sea of Galilee." *Encyclopedia Britannica*. https://tinyurl.com/SBL0700f.

Egan, Timothy. 2007. "Little Asia on the Hill." *New York Times*. 7 January. http://www.nytimes.com/2007/01/07/education/edlife/07asian.html.

Eisenberg, Ronald L. 2004. "Tu b'Shevat." Pages 252–54 in *JPS Guide to Jewish Traditions*. Philadelphia: The Jewish Publication Society.

Elvey, Anne. 2002. "Storing Up Death, Storing Up Life: An Earth Story in Luke 12:13–34." Pages 95–107 in *The Earth Story in the New Testament*. Edited by Norman C. Habel and Vicky Balabanski. Sheffield: Sheffield Academic.

Esposito, Roberto. 2008. *Bios: Biopolitics and Philosophy.* Translated and introduction by Timothy Campbell. Minneapolis: University of Minneapolis Press.
Ewans, Michael. 2012. *Aristophanes: Archarians, Knights, and Peace.* Norman, OK: University of Oklahoma Press.
Fascher, E. 1965. "Jesus und die Tiere." *TLZ* 90:561–70.
Fanon, Frantz. 1967. *Black Skin, White Masks.* Translated by Charles Larn Markmann. New York: Grove.
———. 2004. *The Wretched of the Earth.* Translated by Richard Philcox. New York: Grove.
Faricy, Robert L. 1982. *Wind and Sea Obey Him: Approaches to a Theology of Nature.* Foreword by Mary Evelyn Jegen. London: SCM.
Flor, Elmer. 2002. "The Cosmic Christ and Ecojustice in the New Cosmos." Pages 137–47 in *The Earth Story in the New Testament.* Edited by Norman C. Habel and Vicky Balabanski. Sheffield: Sheffield Academic.
Focant, Camille. 2004. *L'évangile selon Marc.* Commentaire Biblique Nouveau Testament 2. Paris: Cerf.
Foucault, Michel. 1989. *The Archaeology of Knowledge.* London: Routledge.
Fraiman, Susan. Autumn 2012. "Pussy Panic versus Liking Animals: Tracking Gender in Animal Studies." *Crit Inq* 39:89–115.
Francis, Pope. 2015. *Laudato Sí: On Care for Our Common Home.* Huntington, IN: Our Sunday Visitor.
Freire, Paulo. 1973. *Pedagogy of the Oppressed.* Translated by Myra Bergman Ramos. 9th ed. New York: Seabury.
Funk, Robert W. 1973. "Looking-Glass Tree is for the Birds: Ezekiel 17:22–24; Mark 4:30–32." *Int* 27.1:3–9.
Gaard, Greta. 1993. *Ecofeminism: Living Interconnections with Animals and Nature.* Philadelphia: Temple University Press.
———. 2011. "Ecofeminism Revisited: Rejecting Essentialism and Replacing Species in a Material Feminist Environmentalism." *Fem Form* 23:26–53.
———. 2017. *Critical Ecofeminism.* Lanham, MD: Lexington.
Garnsey, Peter. 1996. *Ideas of Slavery from Aristotle to Augustine.* Cambridge: Cambridge University Press.
Garroway, Joshua. 2009. "The Invasion of a Mustard Seed: A Reading of Mark 5.1–20." *JSNT* 32.1:57–75.
Gebara, Ivone. 1999. *Longing for Running Water: Ecofeminism and Liberation.* Minneapolis: Fortress.
Ghosh, Amitav. 2005. *The Hungry Tide.* Boston: Houghton Mifflin.

Gibson, Jeffrey B. 1995. *The Temptations of Jesus in Early Christianity.* JSNTSup 112. Sheffield: Sheffield Academic.

Gilhus, Ingvild Sælid. 2006. *Animals, Gods and Humans: Changing Attitudes to Animals in Greek, Roman and Early Christian Ideas.* London: Routledge.

Gnanadason, Aruna. 2001. "Jesus and the Asian Woman: A Post-colonial Look at the Syro-Phoenician Woman/Canaanite Woman from an Indian Perspective." *Stud. World Christ.* 7:162–77.

Goethe, Johann Wolfgang. 2009. *Metamorphosis of Plants.* Cambridge: MIT Press.

Goodall, Jane. 1967. *My Friends, the Wild Chimpanzees.* Washington, DC: National Geographic Society.

Gordon, Lewis. 1998. "African-American Philosophy: Theory, Politics, and Pedagogy." *J. Philos. Educ.* 39–46.

Grässer, Erich. 1986. "ΚΑΙ ΗΝ ΜΕΤΑ ΤΩΝ ΘΗΡΙΩΝ (Mk 1,13b): Ansätze einer theologischen Tierschutzethik." Pages 144–57 in *Studien zum Text und zur Ethik des Neuen Testaments: Festschrift zum 80. Geburtstag von Heinrich Greeren.* Edited by Wolfgang Schrage. Berlin: de Gruyter.

Grusin, Richard. 2015. "Introduction." Pages vii–xxix in *The Nonhuman Turn.* Edited by Richard Grusin. Minneapolis: University of Minneapolis Press.

Guardiola-Säenz, Leticia. 1997. "Borderless Women and Borderless Texts: A Cultural Reading of Matthew 15:21–28." *Semeia* 78:69–81.

Guattari, Félix. 1995. *Chaomosis: An Ethico-aesthetic Paradigm.* Bloomington: Indiana University Press.

———. 1996. *The Guattari Reader.* Edited by Gary Genosko. Oxford: Blackwell.

———. 2011. *The Machinic Unconscious: Essays in Schizoanalysis.* Translated by Taylor Adkins. Los Angeles: Semiotext(e).

Guattari, Félix, and Suely Rolnik. 2007. *Molecular Revolution in Brazil.* Translated by Karel Clapshow and Brian Holmes. Los Angeles: Semiotext(e).

Guelich, Robert A. 1989. *Mark 1–8:26.* WBC 34A. Edited by David A. Hubbard and Glenn W. Baker. Waco, TX: Word.

Gundry, Robert H. 1993. *Mark: A Commentary on His Apology for the Cross.* Grand Rapids: Eerdmans.

Habel, Norman C. 2000a. *The Earth Story in Psalms and Prophets.* Sheffield: Sheffield Academic.

———. 2000b. "Introducing the Earth Bible." Pages 25–37 in *Readings from the Perspective of Earth*. Edited by Norman C. Habel. Sheffield: Sheffield Academic.

———. 2008. "Introducing Ecological Hermeneutics." Pages 1–8 in *Exploring Ecological Hermeneutics*. Edited by Norman C. Habel and Peter Trudinger. SymS 46. Atlanta: Society of Biblical Literature.

Habel, Norman C., and S. Wurst, eds. 2000. *The Earth Story in Genesis*. Sheffield: Sheffield Academic.

———, eds. 2001. *The Earth Story in Wisdom Traditions*. Sheffield: Sheffield Academic.

Haenchen, E. 1968. *Der Weg Jesu*. Berlin: de Gruyter.

Hagedorn, Jessica. 1990. *Dogeaters*. New York: Penguin.

Hall, Matthew. 2010. *Plants as Persons*. Albany, NY: SUNY Press.

Halle, Francis. 2002. *In Praise of Plants*. Translated by David Lee. Portland: Timber.

Hamel, Gildas. 1990. *Poverty and Charity in Roman Palestine, First Three Centuries CE*. Berkeley: University of California Press.

Haraway, Donna. 1990. *Primate Visions: Gender, Race, and Nature in the World of Modern Science*. New York: Routledge.

———. 1991. *Simians, Cyborgs, and Women: The Reinvention of Nature*. New York: Routledge.

———. 2003. *The Companion Species Manifesto: Dogs, People, and Significant Otherness*. Chicago: Prickly Paradigm Press.

———. 2007. *When Species Meet*. Minneapolis: University of Minnesota Press.

Harman, Graham. 2011. *The Quadruple Object*. Hants: Zero.

Harris, Marvin. 1974. "Pig Lovers and Pig Haters." Pages 35–57 in *Cows, Pigs, Wars, and Witches: The Riddles of Culture*. New York: Vintage.

Harris, Melanie L. 2011. *Gifts of Virtue, Alice Walker, and Womanist Ethics*. New York: Macmillan.

———. 2016. "Ecowomanism: An Introduction." *Worldviews* 20:1–3.

———. 2017. *Ecowomanism: African American Women and Earth-Honoring Faiths* Maryknoll, NY: Orbis.

Harrod, Howard L. 2000. *The Animals Came Dancing: Native American Sacred Ecology, and Animal Kinship*. Tuscon: University of Arizona Press.

Hearne, Vicki. 1986. *Adam's Task: Calling Animals by Name*. New York: Skyhorse.

Hedrick, Charles W. 1994. *Parables as Poetic Fictions: The Creative Voice of Jesus.* Peabody, MA: Hendrickson.

Heil, John Paul. 2006. "Jesus with the Wild Animals in Mark 1:13." *CBQ* 68:63–78.

Henderson, Jeffrey. 1975. *The Maculate Muse: Obscene Language in Attic Comedy.* New Haven: Yale University Press.

———. 1998. *Aristophanes: Acharnians. Knights.* LCL. Cambridge: Harvard University Press.

Herm, Gerhard. 1975. *The Phoenicians: The Purple Empire of the Ancient World.* New York: Morrow.

Herzog, William R., II. 1994. *Parables as Subversive Speech: Jesus as Pedagogue of the Oppressed.* Louisville: Westminster John Knox.

———. 2012. "Sowing Discord: The Parable of the Sower (Mark 4:1–9)." *RevExp* 109:187–98.

Hird, Myra J., and Celia Roberts. 2011. "Feminism Theorizes the Nonhuman." *Fem. Theory* 12.2:109–17.

Hobgood-Oster, Laura. 2008. *Holy Dogs and Asses: Animals in the Christian Tradition.* Urbana: University of Illinois Press.

Holland, Eugene W. 2013. *Deleuze and Guattari's A Thousand Plateaus.* London: Bloomsbury.

Holland, Sharon Patricia. 2012. *The Erotic Life of Racism.* Durham, NC: Duke University Press.

Hollenbach, Paul W. 1981. "Jesus, Demoniacs, and Public Authorities: A Socio-historical Study." *JAAR* 49.4:567–88.

Horsley, Richard A. 1998. "Submerged Biblical Histories and Imperial Biblical Studies." Pages 152–73 in *The Postcolonial Bible.* Edited by R. S. Sugirtharajah; Sheffield: Sheffield Academic.

———. 2001. *Hearing the Whole Story: The Politics of Plot in Mark's Gospel.* Louisville: Westminster John Knox.

———. 2003. *Jesus and Empire: The Kingdom of God and the New World Disorder.* Minneapolis: Fortress.

Howard-Brook, Wes, and Anthony Gwyther. 1999. *Unveiling Empire: Reading Revelation Then and Now.* Maryknoll, NY: Orbis.

Huggan, Graham, and Helen Tiffin. 2010. *Postcolonial Ecocriticism: Literature, Animals, Environment.* London: Routledge.

Hunzinger, Claus-Hunno. 1971. "συκῆ κτλ." *TDNT* 7:751–59.

Hurtado, Larry W. 1983. *Mark.* NIBCNT 2. Peabody, MA: Hendrickson.

Iersel, Bas M. F. van. 1998. *Mark: A Reader-Response Commentary*. Translated by W. H. Bisscheroux. JSNTSup 164. Sheffield: Sheffield Academic.

Infante, Manuela. 2010. "Estado Vegetal." Southern Exposure Arts. Chile: Mid Atlantic Arts Foundation.

Irigaray, Luce and Michael Marder. 2016. *Through Vegetal Being: Two Philosophical Perspectives*. New York: Columbia University Press.

Isaac, Benjamin. 2004. *The Invention of Racism in Classical Antiquity*. Princeton: Princeton University Press.

Iverson, Kelly. 2007. *Gentiles in the Gospel of Mark: "Even the Dogs under the Table Eat the Children's Crumbs."* LNTS 339. London: T&T Clark.

Jackson, Zakiyyah Iman. 2013. "Animal: New Directions in the Theorization of Race and Posthumanism." *Feminist Studies* 39: 669–85.

———. 2020. *Becoming Human: Matter and Meaning in an Antiblack World*. New York: New York University Press.

Jameson, Frederic. 1986. "Third World Literature in the Era of Multinational Capitalism." *Social Text* 15:65–88.

Jeremias, Joachim. 1972. *The Parables of Jesus*. Translated by H. S. Hooke. 2nd ed. New York: Scribner's Sons.

Joh, Wonhee Anne. 2006. *Heart of the Cross: A Postcolonial Christology*. Louisville: Westminster John Knox.

Jones, A. H. M. 1971. *The Cities of the Eastern Roman Provinces*. 2nd ed. Oxford: Clarendon Press.

Joy, David. 2008. *Mark and Its Subalterns: A Hermeneutical Paradigm for a Postcolonial Context*. Oakville, CT: Equinox.

Juel, Donald. 1994. *A Master of Surprise: Mark Reinterpreted*. Minneapolis: Fortress.

Kamuf, Peggy. 2005. *Book of Addresses*. Stanford, CA: Stanford University Press.

Kearns, Laurel. 2007. "Cooking the Truth: Faith, Science, the Market, and Global Warming." Pages 97–124 in *Ecospirit: Religions and Philosophies for the Earth*. Edited by Laurel Kearns and Catherine Keller. TTC. New York: Fordham University Press.

Keegan, Terence J. 1994. "The Parable of the Sower and Mark's Jewish Leaders." *CBQ* 56:501–18.

Keller, Catherine. 2003. *The Face of the Deep: A Theology of Becoming*. London: Routledge.

———. 2000. "No More Sea: The Lost Chaos of the Eschaton." Pages 183–98 in *Christianity and Ecology*. Edited by Dieter T. Hessel and Rosemary Radford Ruether. Cambridge: Harvard University Press.

Keller, Catherine, and Mary-Jane Rubenstein. 2017. *Religion, Science, and New Materialisms* TTC. New York: Fordham University Press.

Kernaghan, Ronald J. 2007. *Mark*. Downers Grove: InterVarsity.

Kim, Claire Jean. 2015. *Dangerous Crossings: Race, Species, and Nature in a Multicultural Age*. Cambridge: Cambridge University Press.

Kimmerer, Robin Wall. 2013. *Braiding Sweetgrass: Indigenous Wisdom, Scientific Knowledge, and the Teachings of Plants*. Minneapolis: Milkweed.

Kingston, Maxine Hong. 1976. *The Woman Warrior: Memoirs of a Girlhood among Ghosts*. New York: Random.

Kinukawa, Hisako. 1994. *Women and Jesus in Mark: A Japanese Feminist Perspective*. Maryknoll, NY: Orbis.

———. 2004. "De-colonizing Ourselves as Readers: The Story of the Syro-Phoenician Woman as a Text." Pages 131–44 in *Distant Voices Drawing Near: Essays in Honor of Antoinette Clark Wire*. Edited by Holly E. Hearon. Collegeville, MN: Liturgical Press.

Kloppenborg, John. 1987. *The Formation of Q: Trajectories in Ancient Wisdom Collections*. Philadelphia: Fortress.

Knauf, Ernst Axel. 1991. "King Solomon's Copper Supply." Pages 167–86 in *Phoenicia and the Bible: Proceedings of the Conference held at the University of Leuven on the 15th and 16th of March 1990*. Edited by Edward Lipinski. Leuven: Peeters.

Kohn, Eduardo. 2013. *How Forests Think: Toward an Anthropology Beyond the Human*. Berkeley: University of California Press.

Koosed, Jennifer L. ed. 2013. *The Bible and Posthumanism*. SemeiaSt 74. Atlanta: Society of Biblical Literature.

———. 2017. "Death of Jezebel." Bible Odyssey. https://tinyurl.com/SBL0700g.

Kraeling, Carl H., ed. 1938. "The History of Gerasa." Pages 27–69 in *Gerasa: City of the Decapolis*. Edited by Carl H. Kraeling. New Haven: American Schools of Oriental Research.

Kristeva, Julia. 1982. *Powers of Horror: An Essay on Abjection*. New York: Columbia University Press.

Kwok, Pui-lan. 1995. *Discovering the Bible in the Non-biblical World*. BL. Maryknoll, NY: Orbis.

———. 2005. *Postcolonial Imagination and Feminist Theology*. Louisville: Westminster John Knox.

———. 2017. "Trump, Democracy, and Empire." Wabash Center. 11 May. https://tinyurl.com/SBL0700h.
Laist, Randy. ed. 2013. *Plants and Literature: Essays in Critical Plant Studies*. New York: Rodopi.
Latour, Bruno. 1993. *We Have Never Been Modern*. Translated by Catherine Porter. Cambridge: Harvard University Press.
———. 1996. "On Actor-Network Theory: A Few Clarifications." *Soziale Welt* 47.4:369–81.
———. 2004. *Politics of Nature: How to Bring the Sciences into Democracy*. Translated by Catherine Porter. Cambridge: Harvard University Press.
———. 2005. *Reassembling the Social: An Introduction to Actor-Network-Theory*. Oxford: Oxford University Press.
Leander, Hans. 2013. *Discourses of Empire: The Gospel of Mark from a Postcolonial Perspective*. Atlanta: Society of Biblical Literature.
Lee, Rachel C. 2014. *The Exquisite Corpse of Asian America: Biopolitics, Biosociality, and Posthuman Ecologies*. New York: New York University Press.
Leopold, Aldo. 1950. *A Sand County Almanac and Sketches Here and There*. Illustration by Charles W. Schwartz. Oxford: Oxford University Press.
Levine, Amy-Jill. 2004. "The Disease of Postcolonial New Testament Studies and the Hermeneutics of Healing." *JFSR* 20.1:91–99.
Liew, Tat-siong Benny. 1999a. *Politics of Parousia: Reading Mark Inter(Con)Textually*. Leiden: Brill.
———.1999b. "Tyranny, Boundary, and Might: Colonial Mimicry in Mark's Gospel." *JSNT* 73:7–31.
———. 2008a. "Postcolonial Criticism." Pages 211–31 in *Mark and Method: New Approaches in Biblical Studies*. Edited by Janice Capel Anderson and Stephen D. Moore. 2nd ed. Minneapolis: Fortress.
———. 2008b. *What Is Asian American Biblical Hermeneutics? Reading the New Testament*. Honolulu: University of Hawai'i Press.
Liew, Tat-siong Benny, and Fernando Segovia, eds. 2022. *Reading Biblical Texts Together: Pursuing Minoritized Biblical Criticism*. SemeiaSt 98. Atlanta: SBL Press.
Lin, Yii-Jan. 2016. *The Erotic Life of Manuscripts: New Testament Textual Criticism and the Biological Sciences*. Oxford: Oxford University Press.
Linmark, R. Zamora. 2006. *Rolling the R's*. New York: Kaya.
Linzey, Andrew. 2000. *Animal Gospel*. Louisville: Westminster John Knox.
Lloyd-Jones, Hugh. 1975. *Females of the Species: Semonides on Women*. Park Ridge, NJ: Noyes.

Lloyd-Paige, Michelle R. 2010. "Thinking and Eating at the Same Time: Reflections of a Sistah Vegan." Pages 1–7 in *Sistah Vegan: Black Female Vegans Speak on Food, Identity, Health, and Society*. Edited by A. Breeze Harper. Brooklyn: Lantern.

Loader, William. 2002. "Good News—For the Earth? Reflections on Mark 1.1–15." Pages 8–43 in *The Earth Story in the New Testament*. Edited by Norman C. Habel and Vicky Balabanski. Sheffield: Sheffield Academic.

Locy, William A. 1925. *The Growth of Biology: Zoology from Aristotle to Cuvier, Botany from Theophrastus to Hofmeister, Physiology from Harvey to Claude Bernard*. New York: Holt.

Lopez, Davina C. 2010. *Apostle to the Conquered: Reimagining Paul's Mission*. Minneapolis: Fortress.

Lorde, Audre. 1984. "The Master's Tools Will Never Dismantle the Master's House." Pages 110–13 in *Sister Outsider: Essays and Speeches*. Trumansburg, NY: The Crossing.

Luz, Ulrich. 2001. *Matthew 8–20: A Commentary*. Hermeneia. Minneapolis: Fortress.

Malbon, Elizabeth Struthers. 1984."The Jesus of Mark and the Sea of Galilee." *JBL* 103:363–77.

———. 1986. *Narrative Space and Mythic Meaning in Mark*. San Francisco: Harper & Row.

Malina, Bruce J., and J. H. Neyrey. 1996. *Portraits of Paul: An Archaeology of Ancient Personality*. Louisville: Westminster John Knox.

Manes, Christopher. 1997. *Other Creations: Rediscovering the Spirituality of Animals*. New York: Doubleday.

Marcus, Joel. 1985. *The Mystery of the Kingdom of God*. Atlanta: Scholars Press.

———. 1997. "Blanks and Gaps in the Markan Parable of the Sower." *Biblical Interpretation* 5.3:247–62.

———. 2000. *Mark 1–8: A New Translation with Introduction and Commentary*. AB 27. New York: Doubleday.

Marder, Michael. 2013. *Plant-Thinking: A Philosophy of Vegetal Life*. New York: Columbia University Press.

———. 2014. *The Philosopher's Plant: An Intellectual Herbarium*. New York: Columbia University Press.

McClintock, Anne. 1995. *Imperial Leather: Race, Gender and Sexuality in the Colonial Contest*. London: Routledge.

McGann, Diarmuid. 1985. *The Journeying Self: The Gospel of Mark through A Jungian Perspective*. New York: Paulist.

McNicol, Allan J. 1984. "The Lesson of the Fig Tree in Mark 13:28–32: A Comparison Between Two Exegetical Methodologies." *ResQ* 27.4:193–207.

Meillassoux, Quentin. 2008. *After Finitude: An Essay on the Necessity of Contingency*. Translated by Ray Brassier. London: Continuum.

Mell, Ulrich. 1996. "Jesu Taufe durch Johannes (Markus 1,9–15) zur Narrative Christologie vom Neuen Adam." *BZ* 40:161–78.

Miller, David. 2008. "Attitudes Toward Dogs in Ancient Israel: A Reassessment." *JSOT* 32.4:487–500.

Miller, Elaine. 2002. *Vegetative Soul: From Philosophy of Nature to Subjectivity in the Feminine*. Albany, NY: SUNY Press.

Miller, Susan. 2008. "The Descent of Darkness over the Land: Listening to the Voice of Earth in Mark 15:33." Pages 123–30 in *Exploring Ecological Hermeneutics*. Edited by Norman C. Habel and Peter Trudinger. SymS 46. Atlanta: Society of Biblical Literature.

Miller, William Ian. 1997. *The Anatomy of Disgust*. Cambridge: Harvard University Press.

Moloney, Francis J. 2002. *The Gospel of Mark: A Commentary*. Peabody, MA: Hendrickson.

Moore, Stephen D. 2006. *Empire and Apocalypse: Postcolonialism and the New Testament*. BMW 12. Sheffield: Sheffield Press.

———. 2011. "Why There Are No Humans or Animals in the Gospel of Mark." Pages 71–93 in *Mark as Story: Retrospect and Prospect*. Edited by Kelly R. Iverson and Christopher W. Skinner. RBS 65. Atlanta: Society of Biblical Literature.

———. 2013. "The Dog-Woman of Canaan, and Other Animal Tales in the Gospel of Matthew." Pages 57–71 in *Soundings in Cultural Criticism: Perspectives and Methods in Culture, Power, and Identity in New Testament Interpretation*. Edited by Francisco Lozada Jr. and Greg Carey. Minneapolis: Fortress.

———, ed. 2014. *Divinanimality: Animal Theory, Creaturely Theology*. TTC. New York: Fordham University Press.

———. 2017a. *Gospel Jesuses and Other Nonhumans: Biblical Criticism Postpoststructuralism*. SemeiaSt 89. Atlanta: SBL Press.

———. 2017b. "Why the Johannine Jesus Weeps at the Tomb of Lazarus." Pages 287–310 in *Mixed Feelings and Vexed Passions: Exploring Emotions in Biblical Literature*. Edited by F. Scott Spencer. Atlanta: SBL Press.

Moore, Stephen D., and Yvonne Sherwood. 2011. *The Invention of the Biblical Scholar: A Critical Manifesto*. Minneapolis: Fortress.

Morton, Timothy. 2009. *Ecology without Nature: Rethinking Environmental Aesthetics*. Cambridge: Harvard University Press.

———. 2012. *Hyperobjects: Philosophy and Ecology after the End of the World*. Surrey: Ashgate.

Moscati, Sabatino. 1968. *The World of the Phoenicians*. New York: Praeger.

———. 1989. *The Phoenicians*. New York: Abbeville.

Murray, Robert. 1992. *The Cosmic Covenant*. HeyM 7. London: Sheed & Ward.

Myers, Ched. 1988. *Binding the Strong Man: A Political Reading of Mark's Story of Jesus*. Maryknoll, NY: Orbis.

Myers, Jeffrey. 2005. *Converging Stories: Race, Ecology, and Environmental Justice in American Literature*. Athens: University of Georgia.

Nandy, Ashis. 1983. *The Intimate Enemy: Loss and Recovery of Self under Colonialism*. Oxford: Oxford University Press.

Nast, Heidi J. 2006. "Loving … Whatever: Alienation, Neoliberalism and Pet-Love in the Twenty-First Century." *ACME* 5.2:300–327.

Nealon, Jeffrey T. 1998. *Alterity Politics: Ethics and Performative Subjectivity*. Durham, NC: Duke University Press.

———. 2016. *Plant Theory: Biopower and Vegetable Life*. Stanford, CA: Stanford University Press.

Nelavala, Surekha. 2009. *Liberation beyond Borders: Dalit Hermeneutics and Four Gospel Women*. Saarbrücken: Lambert Academic.

Newheart, Michael Willett. 2004. *My Name Is Legion: The Story and Soul of the Gerasene Demoniac*. Collegeville, MN: Liturgical Press.

Nineham, Dennis. 1963. *St. Mark*. Pelican 2. New York: Penguin.

Northcott, Michael S. 1996. *The Environment and Christian Ethics*. Cambridge: Cambridge University Press.

Notley, R. Steven. 2009. "The Sea of Galilee: Development of an Early Christian Toponym." *JBL* 128:183–88.

Oakman, Douglas E. 1993. "Cursing Fig Trees and Robbers' Dens: Pronouncement Stories Within Social-Systemic Perspective: Mark 11:12–25 and Parallels." *Semeia* 64:253–72.

O'Brien, Susie. 2002. "The Garden and the World: Jamaic Kinkaid and the Cultural Borders of Ecocriticism." *Mosaic* 35.2:167–84.

Oh, Jea Sophia. 2011. *A Postcolonial Theology of Life: Planetarity East and West*. Upland, CA: Sopher.

Olajubu, Oyeronke. 2002. "Reconnecting with the Waters: John 9:1–11." Pages 108–21 in *The Earth Story in the New Testament*. Edited by Norman C. Habel and Vicky Balabanski. Sheffield: Sheffield Academic.

Oliver, Kelly. 2009. *Animal Lessons: How They Teach Us to Be Human*. New York: Columbia University Press.

Olley, John. 2001. "Animals in Heaven and Earth: Attitudes in Ezekiel." *Colloq* 33:47–57.

Oranekwu, George Nnaemeka. 2006. *"... Indeed, He Would Never Speak to Them Except in Parables" (Mark 4:34): A Hermeneutical Correlation of Parables in Mark 4 to the Traditional Igbo Culture*. Frankfurt: IKO.

Palmer, G. D. 2016. "When Does a Fig Tree Bear Fruit?" SFGATE. 5 September. http://homeguides.sfgate.com/fig-tree-bear-fruit-49324.html.

Park, Andrew Sung. 1993. *The Wounded Heart of God: The Asian Concept of Han and the Christian Doctrine of Sin*. Nashville: Abingdon.

Park, Madison, and Dayu Zhang. 2013. "Chinese Farm Says It Dumped Dead Pigs in River." CNN. 14 March. https://tinyurl.com/SBL0700i.

Park, Wongi. 2021. "Multiracial Biblical Studies." *JBL* 140:435–59.

Parsons, John J. 2016. "Tu B'Shevat—Rosh Hashanah for Trees." Hebrew4Christians. 17 September. https://tinyurl.com/SBL0700j.

Parsons, Mikeal C. 2011. *Body and Character in Luke and Acts: The Subversion of Physiognomy in Early Christianity*. Waco, TX: Baylor University Press.

Peckham, Brian. 1992. "Phoenicia, History of." *ABD* 5:349–63.

Perkins, Pheme. 1994–2004. "Gospel of Mark." *NIB* 8:507–734.

Perkinson, Jim. 1996. "A Canaanitic Word in the Logos of Christ; or the Difference the Syrophoenician Woman Makes to Jesus." *Semeia* 75:61–85.

Peterson, Christopher. 2012. *Bestial Traces: Race, Sexuality, Animality*. New York: Fordham University Press.

Plumwood, Val. 1993. *Feminism and the Mastery of Nature*. Feminism for Today. London: Routledge.

———. 2002. *Environmental Culture: The Ecological Crisis in Reason*. New York: Routledge.

Pollan, Michael. 2002. *The Botany of Desire: A Plant's-Eye View of the World*. New York: Random.

Pratt, Mary Louis. 1992. *Imperial Eyes: Travel Writing and Transculturation*. London: Routledge.

Puar, Jasbir. 2007. *Terrorist Assemblages: Homonationalism in Queer Times*. Durham, NC: Duke University Press.

———. 2012. "'I Would Rather be a Cyborg Than a Goddess': Becoming-Intersectional in Assemblage Theory." *PhiloSOPHIA* 2.1:49–66.

Radl, Walter. 1991. "μετα." *EDNT* 2:413–14.

Ravitz, Jessica. 2016. "The Sacred Land at the Center of the Dakota Pipeline Dispute." CNN. 1 November. https://tinyurl.com/SBL0700k.

Rawlinson, George. 2005. *Phoenicia: History of Civilization*. London: Tauris.

Razack, Sherene. 1998. *Looking White People in the Eye: Gender, Race, and Culture in Courtrooms and Classrooms*. Toronto: University of Toronto Press.

Reid, Barbara E. 1999. *Parables for Preachers: The Gospel of Mark Year B*. Collegeville, MN: Liturgical Press.

Rhoads, David M. 1994. "Jesus and the Syrophoenician Woman in Mark: A Narrative-Critical Study." *JAAR* 62:343–75.

———. 2004. "Who Will Speak for the Sparrow? Eco-Justice Criticism of the New Testament." Pages 64–86 in *Literary Encounters with the Reign of God*. Edited by Sharon H. Ringe and H. C. Paul Kim. London: T&T Clark.

Rhoads, David M., Joanna Dewey, and Donald Michie. 2012. *Mark as Story: An Introduction to the Narrative of a Gospel*. Minneapolis: Fortress.

Riddehough, G. B. 1959. "Man-into-Beast Changes in Ovid." *Phoenix* 13.4:201–9.

Ringe, Sharon H. 1985. "A Gentile Woman's Story." Pages 65–72 in *Feminist Interpretation of the Bible*. Edited by Letty M. Russell. Philadelphia: Westminster.

———. 2001. "A Gentile Woman's Story Revisited: Re-reading Mark 7:23–31." Pages 79–100 in *A Feminist Companion to Mark*. Edited by Amy-Jill Levine with Marianne Blickenstaff. Sheffield: Sheffield Academic.

Ritvo, Harriet. 1989. *The Animal Estate: The English and Other Creatures in the Victorian Age*. Cambridge: Harvard University Press.

———. 1997. *The Platypus and the Mermaid and Other Figments of the Classifying Imagination*. Cambridge: Harvard University Press.

Robbins, Wayne G. 1999. *Soul and Psyche: The Bible in Psychological Perspective*. Minneapolis: Fortress.

Roffe, Jon, and Hannah Stark. 2015a. "Deleuze and the Nonhuman Turn: An Interview with Elizabeth Grosz." Pages 17–24 in *Deleuze and the Non/Human*. Edited by Jon Roffe and Hannah Stark. New York: Macmillan.

———. 2015b. "Introduction: Deleuze and the Nonhuman Turn." Pages 1–16 in *Deleuze and the Non/Human*. Edited by Jon Roffe and Hannah Stark. New York: Macmillan.
Rohman, Carrie. 2009. *Stalking the Subject: Modernism and the Animal*. New York: Columbia University Press.
Roth, Philip. 2001. *The Human Stain*. New York: Vintage International.
Roy, Siddharta. 2016. "Legionnaire's Disease Possibly Associated with Flint River Water Supply." Flint Water Study Updates. January 15, 2016. http://flintwaterstudy.org/?s=legionnaire.
Ruether, Rosemary Radford, ed. 1996. *Women Healing Earth: Third World Women on Ecology, Feminism, and Religion*. Maryknoll, NY: Orbis.
Runesson, Anna. 2010. *Exegesis in the Making: Postcolonialism and New Testament Studies*. Leiden: Brill.
Samuel, Simon. 2007. *A Postcolonial Reading of Mark's Story of Jesus*. London: T&T Clark.
Savoy, Lauret E. 2015. *Trace: Memory, History, Race, and the American Landscape*. Berkeley: Counterpoint.
Schiller, Friedrich. 2004. *On the Aesthetic Education of Man*. Translated by Reginald Snell. New York: Dover.
Scott, James C. 1990. *Domination and the Arts of Resistance: Hidden Transcripts*. New Haven: Yale University Press.
Schüssler Fiorenza, Elisabeth. 1992. *But She Said: Feminist Practices of Biblical Interpretation*. Boston: Beacon.
Schwartz, Joshua. 2004. "Dogs in Jewish Society in the Second Temple Period and in the Time of the Mishnah and Talmud." *JJS* 55.2:246–77.
Schwartz, Seth. 2001. *Imperialism and Jewish Society: 200 BCE to 640 CE*. Princeton: Princeton University Press.
Sherwood, Yvonne. 2014. "Cutting up Life: Sacrifice as a Device for Clarifying—and Tormenting—Fundamental Distinctions between Human, Animal, and Divine." Pages 247–300 in *The Bible and Posthumanism*. Edited by Jennifer L. Koosed. SemeiaSt 74. Atlanta: SBL Press.
Simon, Stephen. 1987. "Monuments of Empire: Allegory/Counter-Discourse/Post-Colonial Writing." *Kunapipi* 9:1–16.
Smith, C. W. 1960. "No Time for Figs." *JBL* 79:315–27.
Smith, Mitzi J. 2018. *Womanist Sass and Talk Back: Social (In)Justice, Intersectionality, and Biblical Interpretation*. Eugene, OR: Wipf & Stock.
Sommerstein, Alan H. 1980. *Acharnians*. Warminster: Aris & Phillips.
Spalde Annika, and Pelle Strindlund. 2012. "Doesn't Jesus Treat Animals as Property?" Pages 101–13 in *A Faith Embracing All Creatures: Address-*

ing Commonly Asked Questions about Christian Care for Animals. Edited by Tripp York and Andy Alexis-Baker. Eugene, OR: Cascade.

Speiser, E. A. 1936. "The Name Phoinikes." *Language* 12:121–26.

Spiegel, Marjorie. 1996. *The Dreaded Comparison: Human and Animal Slavery*. Stanford, CA: Stanford University Press.

Spillers, Hortense J. 1987. "Mama's Baby, Papa's Maybe: An American Grammar Book." *Diacritics* 17:64–81.

———. 2003. *Black, White, and in Color: Essays on American Literature and Culture*. Chicago: University of Chicago Press.

Spivak, Gayatri Chakravorty. 1988. "Can the Subaltern Speak?" Pages 271–316 in *Marxism and the Interpretation of Culture*. Edited by Cary Nelson and Lawrence Grossberg. Urbana: University of Illinois Press.

Staley, Jeffrey L. 2006. "'Clothed and in Her Right Mind:' Mark 5:1–20 and Postcolonial Discourse." Pages 319–27 in *Voices from the Margin: Interpreting the Bible in the Third World*. Edited by R. S. Sugirtharajah. Maryknoll, NY: Orbis.

Stark, Hannah. 2015. "Deleuze and Critical Plant Studies." Pages 180–96 in *Deleuze and the Non/Human*. Edited by Jon Roffe and Hannah Stark. New York: Macmillan.

Steinberg, Paul. 2007. *Celebrating the Jewish Year. The Winter Holidays: Hanukkah, Tu b'Shevat, Purim*. Edited by Janet Greenstein Potter. Philadelphia: The Jewish Publication Society.

Stone, Ken. 2017. *Reading the Hebrew Bible with Animal Studies*. Stanford, CA: Stanford University Press.

Story, J. Lyle. 2011. "The Parable of the Budding Fig Tree (Mark 13:28-31)." *ATI (Online)* 4.1:85–94.

Strømmen, Hannah M. 2018. *Biblical Animality after Jacques Derrida*. SemeiaSt 91. Atlanta: SBL Press.

Sudworth, John. 2013. "China Pulls Nearly 6,000 Dead Pigs from Shanghai River." BBC. March 13, 2013. https://tinyurl.com/SBL0700m.

Sugirtharajah, R. S. 1986. "The Syrophoenician Woman." *ExpTim* 98:13–15.

———. 2002. *Postcolonial Criticism and Biblical Interpretation*. Oxford: Oxford University Press.

Sun, Poling. 2010. "Naming the Dog: Another Asian Reading of Mark 7:24–30." *RevExp* 107:381–94.

Taylor, Sunaura. 2011. "Beasts of Burden: Disability Studies and Animal Rights." *Qui Parle* 19.2:191–222.

———. 2017. *Beasts of Burden: Animal and Disability Liberation*. New York: The New Press.

Telford, William R. 1980. *The Barren Temple and the Withered Tree: A Redaction-Critical Analysis of the Cursing of the Fig-Tree Pericope in Mark's Gospel and Its Relation to the Cleansing of the Temple Tradition*. JSNTSup 1. Sheffield: Sheffield Academic.

———. 1991. "More Fruit from the Withered Tree: Temple and Fig-Tree in Mark from Greco-Roman Perspective." Pages 264–304 in *Templum Amicitiae: Essays on the Second Temple Presented to Ernst Bammel*. Edited by William Horbury. JSNTSup 48. Sheffield: JSOT Press.

Theissen, Gerd. 1991. *The Gospels in Context: Social and Political History in the Synoptic Tradition*. Translated by L. M. Maloney. Minneapolis: Fortress.

Thiongo, Ngũgĩ wa. 1994. "The Language of African Literature." Pages 435–55 in *Colonial Discourse and Post-colonial Theory: A Reader*. Edited by Patrick Williams and Laura Chrisman. New York: Columbia University Press.

Tolbert, Mary Ann. 1989. *Sowing the Gospel: Mark's Literary-Historical Perspective*. Minneapolis: Fortress.

———. 1992. "Mark." Pages 263–74 in *Women's Bible Commentary*. Edited by Carol A. Newsom and Sharon H. Ringe. Exp. ed. London: SPCK.

Tristram, Henry Baker. 1911. *The Natural History of the Bible*. London: SPCK.

Tsing, Anna. 2004. *Friction: An Ethnography of Global Connection*. Durham, NC: Duke University Press.

Tucker, Gene M. 2000. "The Peaceable Kingdom and a Covenant with the Wild Animals." Pages 215–25 in *God Who Creates: Essays in Honor of W. Sibley Towner*. Edited by William P. Brown and S. Dean McBride. Grand Rapids: Eerdmans.

United Nations. 2015. "Chapter XXVII: Environment." *United Nations Treaty Collection*. 12 December. https://tinyurl.com/SBL0700n.

Valentine, Kendra Haloviak. 2017. "Liberating Legion: An Ecocritical, Postcolonial Reading of Mark 5:1–20." Pages 199–216 in *Ecotheology and Nonhuman Ethics in Society: A Community of Compassion*. Edited by Melissa J. Brotton. Lanham, MD: Lexington.

Victor, Royce M. 2010. *Colonial Education and Class Formation in Early Judaism: A Postcolonial Reading*. London: Bloomsbury.

Vieira, Patricia, Monica Gagliano, and John Ryan, eds. 2016. *The Green Thread: Dialogues with the Vegetal World*. Lanham, MD: Lexington.

Wachsmann, Shelley. 1995. *The Sea of Galilee Boat: An Extraordinary 2000 Year Old Discovery.* New York: Plenum.

Waetjen, Herman C. 1989. *A Reordering of Power: A Socio-political Reading of Mark's Gospel.* Minneapolis: Fortress.

Wainwright, Elaine. 2001. "Not Without My Daughter: Gender and Demon Possession in Matthew 15:21–28." Pages 126–37 in *A Feminist Companion to Matthew.* Edited by Amy-Jill Levine and Marianne Blickenstaff. Sheffield: Sheffield Academic.

———. 2008. "Healing Ointment/Healing Bodies: Gift and Identification in an Ecofeminist Reading of Mark 14:3–9." Pages 131–40 in *Exploring Ecological Hermeneutics.* Edited by Norman C. Habel and Peter Trudinger. SymS 46. Atlanta: Society of Biblical Literature.

Waldau, Paul, and Kimberley Patton. 2009. "Introduction." Pages 11–23 in *A Communion of Subjects: Animals in Religion, Science, and Ethics.* Edited by Paul Waldau and Kimberley Patton. New York: Columbia University Press.

Warren, Karen. 2000. *Ecofeminist Philosophy: A Western Perspective on What It Is and Why It Matters.* Lanham, MD: Rowman & Littlefield.

Weheliye, Alexander G. 2014. *Habeas Viscus: Racializing Assemblages, Biopolitics, and Black Feminist Theories of the Human.* Durham, NC: Duke University Press Books.

Weil, Kari. 2012. *Thinking Animals: Why Animal Studies Now?* New York: Columbia University Press.

Weissenrieder, Annette. 2010. "The Didactics of Image: The Fig Tree in Mark 11:12–14 and 20–21." Pages 260–82 in *The Interface of Orality and Writing: Speaking, Seeing, Writing in the Shaping of New Genres.* Edited by A. Weissenrieder and R. Coote. Tübingen: Mohr Siebeck.

———. 2013. "Cultural Translation: The Fig Tree and Politics of Representation under Nero in Rome (Mark 11:13–15, 19–20; Matthew 21:18–19; Luke 13:1–19)." Pages 201–30 in *Miracles Revisited: New Testament Miracle Stories and their Concepts of Reality.* Edited by Stefan Alkier and Annette Weissenrieder. Berlin: de Gruyter.

William, Watty W. 1982. "Jesus and the Temple: Cleansing or Cursing?" *ExpTim* 93.8:235–39.

Wimbush, Vincent L., and Tat-siong Benny Liew. 2002. "Contact Zones and Zoning Contexts: From the Los Angeles 'Riot' to a New York Symposium." *USQR* 56.1–2:21–40.

Winter, Paul. 1974. *On the Trial of Jesus.* Studia Judaica: Forschungen zur Wissenschaft des Judentums. 2nd ed. Berlin: de Gruyter.

Witherington, Ben, III. 1984. *Women in the Ministry of Jesus: A Study of Jesus' Attitudes to Women and Their Roles as Reflected in His Early Life.* SNTSMS 51. Cambridge: Cambridge University Press.
Wolfe, Cary. 2003a. *Animal Rites: American Culture, The Discourse of Species, and Posthumanist Theory.* Chicago: University of Chicago Press.
———. 2003b. "Introduction." Pages xi–xxiii in *Zoontologies: The Question of the Animal.* Edited by Cary Wolfe. Minneapolis: University of Minnesota Press.
———. 2009. "Human, All Too Human: 'Animal Studies' and the Humanities." *PMLA* 124.2:564–75.
———. 2010. *What Is Posthumanism?* Minnesota: University of Minnesota Press.
———. 2012. *Before the Law: Humans and Other Animals in a Biopolitical Frame.* Chicago: University of Chicago Press.
Wu, Ellen D. 2014. *The Color of Success: Asian Americans and the Origins of the Model Minority.* Princeton: Princeton University Press.
Wynter, Sylvia. 2003. "Unsettling the Coloniality of Being/Power/Truth/Freedom: Toward the Human, After Man, Its Overrepresentation—An Argument." *CR* 3:257–337.
Yarbro Collins, Adela. 2007. *Mark: A Commentary.* Hermeneia. Minneapolis: Fortress.
Young, Eugene B., Gary Genosko, and Janell Watson. 2013. *The Deleuze and Guattari Dictionary.* London: Bloomsbury.

ANCIENT SOURCES INDEX

Hebrew Bible/Old Testament

Genesis
- 1:11–12 — 63
- 1:26–28 — 93
- 3:2 (LXX) — 37
- 6:20 — 37
- 7:20 — 37
- 10:15 — 107
- 10:19a — 108
- 37:20 — 37

Exodus
- 6:15 — 107
- 16:35 — 107
- 23:31 — 93

Leviticus
- 2:13a — 133
- 19:23–25 — 65
- 25:5 (LXX) — 66
- 25:6–7 — 67
- 25:11 (LXX) — 66
- 26:3–4 — 65
- 26:22 — 37

Numbers
- 34:6–7 — 93
- 34:11 — 90

Deuteronomy
- 7:22 — 36
- 8:15 — 36
- 14:28 — 65
- 22:22–27 — 65

Joshua
- 1:4 — 93
- 5:1 — 107
- 5:12 — 107
- 9:1 — 93
- 12:3 — 90
- 13:27 — 90
- 15:47 — 93

1 Samuel
- 17:43 — 119

1 Kings
- 5 — 108
- 5:8 — 108
- 5:11–12 — 108
- 7:13–14 — 108
- 9 — 108
- 9:10–14 — 108
- 9:11 — 108
- 9:14 — 108
- 11:5 — 109
- 11:33 — 109
- 14:22–23 — 109
- 15:3 — 109
- 15:12–14 — 110
- 16:32–33 — 109
- 18:12 — 45
- 21:1–17 — 109
- 21:23 — 109
- 21:25–26 — 109

2 Kings
- 2:16 — 45
- 8:13 — 119

2 Kings (cont.)
9:22	109
9:32–37	109
9:35	113
10:1–27	110
10:18–31	109
10:28	110
10:30	110
23:13	109

Ezra
3:7	110
9–10	110

Nehemiah
13:16	110
13:17–18	110
13:23–27	110

Job
5:22–3	37
30:1	119
38:8–11	91–92

Psalms
10:9	37
17:12	37
22:12–13	37
22:16	37
22:21	37
58:4–6	37
91:11–13	36
91:13	37
104:7	91
107:23–29	92
118:12	37
140:3	37
148:7	91
148:10	37

Proverbs
26:11	119

Ecclesiastes
1:9	2

Isaiah
9:1	90
11:1–9	35
13:10	79
28:24–6	60
34:4	79
56:10–11	119

Jeremiah
3:13	76
4:3	60
8:13	68
27:1–7	110
27:3	110
27:22	110

Ezekiel
8:3	45
17:22–23	73
26	109
27	109
27:17	109
31:1–9	73
32:7–8	79
34:5	36
36:9	60
47:10	93
47:15	93
47:20	93

Daniel
4:20–22	73

Hosea
2:12	76
2:18	37
4:13 (LXX)	37
9:10	68
13:8 (LXX)	37

Joel
1:7	76
1:12	76
2:10–11	79
2:22	77

2:31	79	Testament of Naphtali	
3:4	79	8.4	36
3:15	79		

Ancient Jewish Writers

Amos
8:9	79	1 Enoch	
		7.5	37

Micah
4:4	68	Apocalypse of Moses	
7:1	68	29.13	37

Nahum
1:4	91	Joseph and Aseneth	
		12.9–10	37

Haggai
		Josephus, *Antiquitates judaicae*	
2:6	79	2.35	37
2:19	76	14.74–76	98
2:21	79	17.117	37
		17.120	37

Zechariah
3:10	68, 77	Josephus, *Bellum judaicum*	
9:3	109	2.258–64	38
		2.478	113

Deuterocanonical Books

		Josephus, *Contra Apionem*	
1 Maccabees		1.70–71	112
14:12	68		

New Testament

Tobit
6:2	119	Matthew	
11:4	119	1:1–17	44
		4:1	45

Pseudepigrapha

		4:12b–16	90
		7:6	119
Gospel of Thomas		11:21–24	112
20	60	12:40	129
		13:31–32	73
		15:10–28	119
Jubilees		15:21–28	120
11.11	60	26:26–29	129

Testament of Benjamin
5.2	36	Mark	
		1:1	89
Testament of Issachar		1:1–8	44
7.7	36	1:8	45

Mark (cont.)

1:9	89
1:10	45
1:11	89
1:12	44, 45
1:13b	15, 33–35, 38, 43, 48
1:16	89
1:16–20	131
1:19	89
1:20	89
1:23	45
1:23–28	44
1:26	45
1:27	45
1:32–34	44
1:34	45
1:39	44–45
2:8	45
2:13	89
3:7	89
3:11	44–45, 89
3:15	44–45
3:22	45
3:23	45
3:29	45
3:30	45
4:1	89
4:1–11	34
4:1–20	15, 54, 59–62
4:4	62
4:13	63
4:15	44, 62
4:26–29	15, 54, 62–66, 70–71, 74
4:28a	66
4:30–32	15, 54, 62, 72–74
4:32	74
4:35	89
4:35–41	63, 91–93, 96
4:39	96
4:40b	96
4:41	96
5:1	89
5:1–20	16, 44, 50, 82–90, 92–96, 99, 101
5:2	45
5:8	45
5:9	97
5:13	45
5:16–17	82
5:17	99
5:21	89
5:25–34	60, 132
5:40	45
6:7	44–45
6:13	45
6:34	131
6:45	89
6:45–52	63
6:45–56	89
6:53	89
7:14–23	118
7:15	118
7:21–22	118
7:24	114
7:24–30	16, 44, 50, 103–6, 111, 113, 119–21
7:25	45
7:26	45
7:27	103, 105–6, 114
7:28b	116
7:29	118
7:31–33	118
7:36–37	119
8:10	89
8:12	45
8:13	89
8:13–21	89
8:14–21	132
8:15	133
8:17–21	63
8:22–25	132
8:34–35	65
9:7	89
9:14–29	44
9:17	45
9:18	45
9:20	45
9:25	45
9:28	45
9:35–37	72

9:38	45	Luke	
9:38–41	44	1:5–25	44
9:42	92	2:1–3	112
9:47	45	4:1	45
9:49–50	133	4:1–13	34
10:13–16	72	5:1	90
10:17–22	60	5:2	90
10:35–41	63	8:22	90
10:42–45	64, 72	8:23	90
10:45	75	8:33	90
11:12–14	15, 50, 54, 68–70	10:19	37
11:13d	69	13:6–9	68
11:15	45	13:10–17	40
11:20–21	15, 50, 54, 68–70	13:18–19	73
11:23	92		
12:8	45	John	
12:36	45	1:1–18	44
13	75–77	6:1	90
13:7	76	21:1	90
13:11	45		
13:21–22	75	Acts	
13:24	79	11:6	37
13:24–25	79	12:19–20	112
13:25	79	28:4–5	37
13:27	78		
13:28	75–77	Galatians	
13:28–31	15, 54	4:3	79
13:30	76		
13:32–37	75	Philippians	
13:34	72	3:2	119
13:37	80		
14:3–9	11, 63	Colossians	
14:9	63	2:8	79
14:22–25	67	2:20	79
14:38	45		
15:21–37	44	Titus	
15:24	87	1:12	37
15:27	123		
15:34	33, 46	James	
15:39	89	3:7	37
16:8	123		
16:9	45	1 Peter	
16:17	45	5:8	37
16:17–18	131		

2 Peter
    2:22   119
    3:10   79
    3:12   79

Revelation
    5:5   36
    8:8–11   91
    13   93
    16:3–4   91
    16:12   91
    21:1   92
    22:15   119

Rabbinic Works

b. Shabbat
    73a–b   60

m. Ketubbot
    5:8   68

m. Shabbat
    7:2   60

Early Christian Writings

Epistle of Barnabas
    6.8   37

Ignatius, *To the Ephesians*
    7.1   37

Ignatius, *To the Romans*
    4.1–2   37
    5.2   37

Ignatius, *To the Smyrnaeans*
    4.2   37

Shepherd of Hermas, *Similitudes*
    9.26.1   37
    9.26.7   37

Greco–Roman Literature

Appian of Alexandria, *Historia romana*
    11.50   111

Aristotle, *De anima*
    410b   55

(Pseudo-)Aristotle, *De plantis*
    816a35–40   55
    816b5–10   55

Aristotle, *Ethica Nicomachea*
    1149a4–7   42

Aristotle, *Metaphysica*
    1022b24   55

Aristotle, *Politica*
    1253a   42
    1254b   42

Cato, *De agricultura*
    2.7   42

Cicero, *In Verrem*
    2.5.109   41

Cicero, *Orationes philippicae*
    4.5.12   41

Demosthenes, *Contra Timotheum*
    24.143   40

Demosthenes, *De Chersoneso*
    5.8   40

Demosthenes, *In Theocrinem*
    49.8   40

Dio Cassius, *Historia romana*
    48.33–41   112

ANCIENT SOURCES INDEX

Homer, *Ilias*
   2.87   3
   2.459   3
   2.469   3
   23.743   108

Homer, *Odyssea*
   14.287–91   108

Justinian, *Digesta seu Pandectae*
   9.2.2   43

Juvenal, *Satirae*
   3.62–63   111

Livy, *Ab urbe condita*
   36.17.5   117

Manilius, *Astronomica*
   4.794   41

Philostratus, *Vita Apollonii*
   4.38   37

Plato, *Phaedrus*
   230d   55

Pliny the Elder, *Naturalis historia*
   5.17–19   111
   16.49   69
   18.176   60

Plutarch, *De Alexandri magni fortuna aut virtute*
   6 [329b]   24

Porphyry, *De Abstinentia*
   3.17.1   43

Sallust, *Bellum jugurthinum*
   18.1   41

Strabo, *Geographica*
   5.2.7   41

Suetonius, *Gaius Caligula*
   27   24–5

Tacitus, *Agricola*
   46.4   41

Theophrastus, *Historia plantarum*
   1.3–4   56

Varro, *De re rustica*
   1.17.1   42

MODERN AUTHORS INDEX

Adams, Carol J. 12, 15, 20–21, 29, 34, 46–47
Adams, James N. 86
Adamson, Joni 13, 101
Aernie, Jeffrey W. 106
Agamben, Giorgio 7, 38
Ahmad, Aijaz 87
Ahmed, Sara 16, 97, 100
Ahuja, Neel 3, 16, 116, 121–22
Aichele, George 118
Alaimo, Stacy 12, 20, 95
Anderson, Hugh 98
Aquino, Frederick D. 103
Ashkenazi, Eli 100
Aus, Roger David 84
Avotri, Solomon K. 85
Bae, HyunJu 104
Baird, Mary 85
Balabanski, Vicky 11
Balch, David L. 24
Barad, Karen 12, 130
Basofin, Joshua 100
Bauckham, Richard 34–35, 37–38, 72, 88
Beavis, Mary Ann 104
Bechtel, Trevor 15
Belo, Fernando 70
Bennett, Jane 4, 17–20, 32
Benyus, Janine 57–58
Berry, Thomas 20
Best, Ernest 36
Bishop, Eric Francis Fox 90
Blunt, Wilfrid 58
Boer, Roland 88
Boisseron, Bénédicte 8
Bradley, Keith 42
Braidotti, Rosi 129
Brassier, Ray 32
Brenner-Idan, Athalya 109
Brinkema, Eugenie 82, 99
Bryce, Trevor 107, 111
Bulosan, Carlos 7
Burdon, Christopher 97
Butcher, Kevin 111
Butler, Judith 8
Calarco, Matthew 28
Callan, Terrence 43
Calpino, Teresa 85
Camery-Hoggatt Jerry 103
Caneday, A. B. 36
Carson, Rachel 99
Carter, Warren 86–87
Césaire, Aimé 7
Chadwick, George Alexander 86
Chakrabarty, Dipesh 13
Chamovitz, Daniel 57
Chen, Mel Y. 16, 32, 49, 83, 93–94, 96
Cho, Grace M. 44
Choi, Jin Young 4, 104, 117, 121
Chow, Rey 22
Cohen, Jeffrey Jerome 28
Conway, Colleen 86
Cotter, Wendy 69, 90
Craghan, John F. 84
Crenshaw, Kimberlé Williams 20–22
Crossan, John Dominic 97
David, Javier E. 134
Davidson, Nicola 81
Deckha, Maneesha 12
DeLanda, Manuel 18–20, 105

MODERN AUTHORS INDEX

Deleuze, Gilles 14–15, 18–20, 22, 29, 30–31, 58, 71, 105–6
Derrett, Duncan J. 84
Derrida, Jacques 4, 7, 11, 15, 26, 28–29, 34, 46, 49–50, 53–54, 59, 67, 78, 83–84, 98, 114, 120
Dewey, Joanna 90
Dixon, Edward P. 44
Donahue, John R. 35, 45, 67, 72, 76, 79, 119, 133
Donaldson, Laura 104
Donner, H. 108
Donovan, Josephine 12
Dormandy, Richard 85
Douglas, Mary 88
Dover, Kenneth James 86
Doyle, Richard 31
Dreese, Donelle 13
Du Bois, W.E.B. 8, 115
Dube, Musa 104, 114
Dyer, Keith D. 76, 79–80
Earth Bible Team 11, 20
Eaton, Matthew 15
Egan, Timothy 6
Eisenberg, Ronald L. 65
Elvey, Anne 11
Esposito, Roberto 71
Evans, Mei Mei 13
Ewans, Michael 86
Fanon, Frantz 6–8, 114–16
Faricy, Robert L. 92
Flor, Elmer 11
Focant, Camille 35
Foucault, Michel 7, 126
Fraiman, Susan 11–12
Francis, Pope 10
Freire, Paulo 54
Funk, Robert W. 72–73
Gaard, Greta 12, 27, 100
Garnsey, Peter 42
Garroway, Joshua 85
Gebara, Ivone 127
Genosko, Gary 106
Ghosh, Amitav 94
Gibson, Jeffrey B. 35
Gilhus, Ingvild Saelid 38, 42–43, 49, 116, 120
Goethe, Johann Wolfgang 79
Goodall, Jane 12, 29
Gordon, Lewis 7
Grässer, Erich 36
Gruen, Lori 12
Grusin, Richard 26–27
Guardiola-Sáenz, Leticia 104
Guattari, Félix 14–15, 18–20, 22, 29–31, 56, 58, 71, 105–6, 127
Guelich, Robert A. 103
Gundry, Robert H. 45, 84
Gwyther, Anthony 4
Habel, Norman C. 11, 93
Haenchen, E. 85
Hagedorn, Jessica 7
Hall, Matthew 31
Halle, Francis 57
Hamel, Gildas 69
Haraway, Donna 12, 29–30
Harman, Graham 32
Harrington, Daniel J. 35, 45, 67, 72, 76, 79, 119, 133
Harris, Marvin 88
Harris, Melanie 12
Harrod, Howard 101
Harvie, Timothy 15
Hearne, Vicki 12
Heil, John Paul 36
Hekman, Susan 12
Henderson, Jeffrey 86
Herm, Gerhard 107–8
Herzog, William R. 54–55, 61
Hobgood-Oster, Laura 43
Holland, Eugene 105
Holland, Sharon Patricia 7
Hollenbach, Paul W. 85
Horsley, Richard A. 64, 97
Howard-Brook, Wes 4
Huggan, Graham 12–13, 94
Hunzinger, Claus-Hunno 68
Hurtado, Larry W. 104
Iersel, Bas M. F. van 45
Infante, Manuela 78

Irigaray, Luce	31, 57–58	Marder, Michael	15, 30, 31, 55, 57–59, 63–64, 66, 67, 71–72, 74–75, 77–80
Isaac, Benjamin	39–42		
Iverson, Kelly	103	McGann, Diarmuid	85
Jackson, Zakiyyah Iman	7–8	McLemore, Brian	103
Jameson, Frederic	87	McNicol, Allan J.	76
Jeremias, Joachim	60	Meillassoux, Quentin	32
Joh, Anne Wonhee	129	Mell, Ulrich	35
John Paul II, Pope	10	Michie, Donald	90
Juel, Donald	97	Miller, David	119
Kamuf, Peggy	49	Miller, William Ian	98
Kearns, Laurel	134	Moloney, Francis J.	45
Keegan, Terence J.	62	Moore, Stephen D.	4, 10, 25, 29, 44, 49, 53, 72, 82–83, 85, 87, 96, 98, 103, 107, 115, 121, 123, 126–27, 129
Keller, Catherine	92–93		
Kernaghan, Ronald J.	45		
Kim, Claire Jean	21, 25, 122	Morton, Timothy	31–32
Kimmerer, Lisa	12, 101	Moscati, Sabatino	107
Kingston, Maxine Hong	7	Myers, Ched	70, 85
Kinukawa, Hisako	104	Myers, Jeffrey	13
Kloppenborg, John	36	Nast, Heidi J.	121
Knauf, Ernst Axel	108	Nealon, Jeffrey T.	31, 58, 66, 70–71
Kohn, Eduardo	31	Nelavala, Surekha	104
Koosed, Jennifer	113	Newheart, Michael Willett	85
Kraeling, Carl H.	98	Nineham, Dennis	69
Kristeva, Julia	130	Northcott, Michael	88
Kwok, Pui-lan	12, 104, 117, 134	Notley, R. Steven	90
Lacan, Jacques	83, 84	Oakman, Douglas E.	68–69
Laist, Randy	57	Oh, Jea Sophia	12
Latour, Bruno	17	Olajubu, Oyeronke	11
Leander, Hans	86, 104, 121	Oliver, Kelly	53–54
Lee, Boyung	121	Oranekwu, George Nnaemeka	61
Lee, Rachel C.	7	Palmer, G. D.	68
Leopold, Aldo	15, 34, 46–48	Park, Madison	81–82
Levine, Amy-Jill	104	Park, Andrew Sung	130
Liew, Tat-siong Benny	4, 25, 28, 114	Park, Wongi	4
Lin, Yii-Jan	58	Parnet, Claire	18, 105
Linmark, R. Zamora	7	Parsons, John J.	65
Linzey, Andrew	84	Parsons, Mikeal C.	40
Lloyd-Jones, Hugh	39	Patton, Kimberley	20
Lloyd-Paige, Michelle	12	Peckham, Brian	108
Loader, William	35, 38, 45, 88	Perkins, Pheme	66, 73
Locy, William A.	56	Perkinson, Jim	118
Lopez, Davina	23	Peterson, Christopher	40, 49–50
Luz, Ulrich	107	Plumwood, Val	27
Malbon, Elizabeth Struthers	89, 92	Pollan, Michael	57
Marcus, Joel	35, 60, 97, 103	Pratt, Mary Louis	3

Puar, Jasbir	22–23	Trudinger, Peter L.	11
Ravitz, Jessica	101	Tsing, Anna	56
Rawlinson, George	112	Valentine, Kendra Haloviak	88–89
Reid, Barbara	60–61	Victor, Royce M.	24
Rhoads, David M.	88, 90, 104	Vieira, Patricia	57
Riddehough, G. B.	39	Waetjen, Herman	97
Ringe, Sharon H.	104	Wainwright, Elaine	11, 104
Ritvo, Harriet	3, 12	Waldau, Karen	20
Roffe, Jon	19	Watson, Janell	106
Rolnik, Suely	127	Weheliye, Alexander G.	7, 126
Robbins, Wayne G.	85	Weissenrieder, Anette	70
Roy, Siddharta	100	William, Watty	70
Ruether, Rosemary Radford	11	Wimbush, Vincent	28
Runesson, Anna	126	Winter, Paul	97
Samuel, Simon	87, 98, 106–7	Wynter, Sylvia	7
Savoy, Lauret, E.	101	Wolfe, Cary	7, 13, 29
Schüssler-Fiorenza, Elisabeth	104	Wu, Ellen D.	6
Schwartz, Joshua	119	Wurst, Shirley	11
Schwartz, Seth	25	Yarbro Collins, Adela	121
Scott, James C.	61	Young, Eugene B.	106
Segovia, Fernando	4	Zhang, Dayu	81–82
Sherwood, Yvonne	25, 98, 126–27		
Smith, Mitzi J.	4, 116		
Sommerstein, Alan H.	86		
Spalde, Annika	84		
Speiser, E. A.	107		
Spiegel, Marjorie	8		
Spillers, Hortense J.	7		
Spivak, Gayatri	13		
Staley, Jeffrey L.	85		
Stark, Hannah	19		
Stein, Rachel	13		
Steinberg, Paul	65		
Stone, Ken	36		
Story, J. Lyle	77		
Strindlund, Pelle	84		
Sudworth, John	81		
Sugirtharajah, R. S.	84–85, 104		
Sun, Poling	104		
Taylor, Sunaura	122–123		
Telford, William R.	70		
Theissen, Gerd	104		
Thiongo, Ngũgĩ wa	5		
Tiffin, Helen	12–13, 94		
Tolbert, Mary Ann	60, 62, 104		

SUBJECT INDEX

AAPI, 1–3
   anti-AAPI hatred, 1
   Asian, 4–7, 9, 12, 25–26, 48, 85–86, 104, 121, 125–26
   Asian American(s), 6–7, 25, 130
   Asian American feminist theology/ian, 130
ableism, 8, 122–23
actant/cy, 7, 15–20, 23, 29, 31–32, 44, 49, 55–65, 67, 69–71, 75, 78, 83–84, 88–90, 93–95, 101, 105–6, 118–19, 121–22, 126, 128, 130–33
   Necro-, 87, 95
affect(ive), 1–3, 11–12, 15–17, 20, 22, 29–32, 34, 40, 56, 65–67, 71–72, 82–84, 87–90, 94–96, 99–101, 106, 108, 113, 117–18, 123, 128, 133
   actant/cy, 89, 93–94
   animacy, 87
   assemblage, 95, 101, 117
   capacities, 30, 34, 133
   (close) reading, 82–83, 95
   of disgust, 16, 82–83, 96, 100–101
   emergence, 71
   encounter, 9, 83
   haunt, 120
   interventions, 128
   ontologically, 49
   potentialities, 16, 83, 89
   relationality, 4
   responsivity, 83
agencement, 18
agent/cy, 11, 44–45, 91, 94–95, 105, 128, 132

alterity, 15, 57, 66–69, 78, 91
ambivalent/ce, 49–51, 85–87, 97–98, 104, 107, 115, 119
animacy/ies, 7, 10, 16, 20, 26, 28, 32, 45, 83, 87, 93–97, 100, 127, 132
   of toxicity, 96–97
animal mask, 16, 103–4, 107, 113, 116–19, 121–22
animality, 7–8, 10, 15–16, 20, 28–29, 31, 34, 46, 116, 120–21, 129–31
animalizing/ed/ation, 1–8, 16, 23–25, 33–34, 37–43, 47–48, 51, 103–4, 106, 114–17, 119, 121–23, 129–31, 134
animalséance, 46
anthropocentric/ism, 3, 5, 8–9, 11–13, 15, 17, 19, 26, 29, 30, 33–34, 36–37, 46, 48–51, 53–54, 57–63, 66–68, 71, 74–75, 79, 84, 90, 92, 94–95, 125, 127, 131
anthropomorphic/ized, 24, 91
assemblage(s), 4, 14, 16–20, 22–24, 26, 28, 31, 34, 37–38, 44, 48, 56, 58, 63–64, 67–68, 75, 78, 93, 95, 99, 101, 103, 105–6, 108, 116–18, 122–23, 126, 128, 131
   colonized, 4
   definition, 4, 17–19
atelic (collective being), 15, 57, 60, 64, 67, 75
auto-immunitary (logic), 26, 50
   of democracy, 50
bestial logics, 7, 15–16, 25, 39–40, 48, 50, 56, 87, 104–5, 117, 122–23
bestial messiah, 4, 15, 33, 44, 98, 129
bestialization, 39, 41, 100
beastly sovereignty, 50

biomimicry, 57–58
biopolitics, 31, 39, 48, 54, 70
　vegetal, 70–71
biopower, 38, 71
carnivorous virility, 98–99, 114
carnophallogocentrism, 16, 66, 95, 107, 114–17, 120, 123, 130–31
Cartesian logic, 5, 13, 29, 83
　hierarchy, 27–28, 49
climate change, 5, 89, 133–34
collective assemblage of enunciation, 16, 105–8, 118, 122–23
colonial mentality, 6, 130
colonial neurosis, 6, 114
colonization, 3–4, 8, 25, 38, 57, 85, 101, 113
communion of subjects, 20
COVID-19 pandemic, 1–2, 5
crab mentality, 2
critical plant studies, 30–31, 57
cross-racial, 4
decolonize/ing, 9, 28, 47, 66, 95, 125, 131
disabled, 3, 122–23
disavowal of disavowal, 49
divinanimal/ity, 29, 49
Earth Bible principles, 76, 93
earthother, 27
earth pedagogy, 53
ecocritical/ism, 13–14, 88–89, 130
　postcolonial, 12, 94
ecofeminist/ism, 11–12, 20, 27–28, 95
ecojustice, 2, 5, 10–12, 15, 17, 20, 31–32, 57, 83–84, 87, 126–27
ecowomanist/ism, 11–12, 28, 95
Eden, 35, 132
embarrassed *et cetera*, 8–9
embrace/ing, 3–5, 9, 11, 32, 48–50, 56, 104, 116–17, 127
empire of God, 4, 15, 32, 46, 51, 54–55, 57, 59–60, 62–66, 70–75, 77–79, 87, 90, 117, 129
enslaved, 3, 24–25, 41, 75, 99, 113, 119
episteme/ic, 28, 56, 125–27, 131
eschatology/ical, 34–35, 76
ethics of avowal, 122

ethics of mattering, 130
ethne (colonized), 3–7, 14–17, 23–25, 32, 34, 38, 40–42, 48–50, 57, 64, 66, 68–69, 72–80, 87, 90, 98–99, 103, 105, 107, 112–13, 116–18, 123, 131
ethnic(ity), 6–8, 15, 23–24, 101, 111, 121, 125
ex-scription, 80
feminist/m, 11, 47, 104, 121, 130
Filipinx/Philippines, 5–6, 9, 12, 48
first-things-first approach, 2, 12–13, 88, 125
fluidity, 7–9, 23, 25, 28, 54, 63
gaps, 14, 56, 57, 83
geophysical force, 13
Gerasa/enes, 16, 50, 82, 84, 85–88, 90, 94–99, 101
han, 129, 130
heteronomy, 64
hidden transcript, 61–62
hoarding, 69
hospitality, 53–54
　unconditional, 49, 54, 67, 134
hyperbolic ethics, 53–54
identity politics, 23
imperial cult, 111
inanimate (entities), 2–3, 10, 15–17, 26–27, 32, 83, 92, 94–95, 97, 101, 128–29, 132–33
incorporeal transformation, 106
indigenous, 101, 126
interconnected(ness), 20–21, 76
intersectional(ity), 4, 8–9, 11–12, 14, 17, 20–23, 26, 28, 101, 126, 128, 130, 134
iterability, 67, 78
jeong, 129–130
kinship, 53–54
(South) Korea(n), 5–6, 9, 44, 121, 130
land acknowledgment, 9
legion, 41, 82, 84–88, 98, 101–102
　tenth Roman, 85–86, 88, 97–98, 112–13
liberation to come, 50
Linnaean taxonomy, 58, 70
logocentrism, 46, 95, 114

masculinity, 86
  hyper-/toxic, 87, 107
misogyny, 12, 30
mimeticism, 50
(colonial) mimic(ry), 4, 6, 15–16, 25, 34, 50, 57–58, 67, 69, 85–86, 98, 106–7, 114–15, 117, 130
model minority myth, 1
molarize/ation, 62, 128
molecular ('r'evolution), 31, 127
more-than-human, 14, 20, 27
multioptic approach, 12, 21, 25
Native American(s), 13, 100–101, 126
negative futurity, 77, 130
new materialist/m, 7–8, 12, 28, 32, 132
NoDAPL, 100–101
nonhumans, 2–5, 7–15, 17–30, 32–36, 38, 43–50, 53, 56–58, 60–68, 70, 72, 74–75, 77–79, 83–84, 87, 90, 93–96, 98–101, 114–17, 119–23, 125–32, 134
orientalism, 6
ontology/ies/ical, 5, 8, 13, 19, 23, 29, 31, 59, 65, 75, 99, 114
  boundaries, 10, 32, 132
  essentialism/uniqueness, 7, 34
  exhaustion, 67
  fluid(ity), 7, 9, 28
  irreducibility, 22
  reconfigure, 129
  relational(ities), 99, 134
  threat/s, 49
  transgress, 119–20
ontophytology, 31, 75, 77. *See also* vegetal: ontology
panentheism, 65
patriarchy/al, 59, 104
phallogocentricism, 12, 58, 59
phronesis, 117
physiognomy/ics, 39–40
phytophallogocentrism, 59
postcolonial(ism), 24, 26, 85–89, 98, 104, 130
  ecocriticism, 12, 14, 94
posthumanist/ism, 8, 10–11, 20, 27, 53
postmodern(ism), 126

postposthumanism, 10, 20
poststructuralist/m, 22, 58
quasi-causal operator, 17
queer, 5, 22, 96
  temporality, 120
race, 7, 15, 21–22, 32, 71, 86, 101, 116, 125–26
racism, 1–3, 6, 8, 12, 21, 86, 116, 122–23, 134. *See also* white supremacy
  antiracism, 4, 13, 125
  environmental, 12–13, 127
  transcorporeality, 1
reconfigure/ation, 8, 15, 17, 20, 23, 31, 34–35, 46, 48–49, 54, 83, 93–94, 117, 122, 126, 128, 130
relationality, 3–5, 12, 15, 19–20, 24–26, 30, 34, 37, 43, 46, 48, 50, 56, 59, 61, 74, 79, 94, 115, 117, 121, 129, 130, 134
responsivity, 3–4, 15, 34, 46, 83, 116, 127, 130
rhizome(s)/atic, 31, 58, 67, 70, 75, 125, 131
Roman Catholic Church, 10, 20
Sea of Galilee, 16, 18, 24, 81–85, 87–100, 132
sexism, 8, 21, 122–23
Son of Humanity, 49, 75, 129
speciesist/m, 1, 8, 21, 116–17, 122–23
  antispecieist/m, 4, 13
stain, 50
subjectivity, 11, 13, 17, 20, 22–23, 26, 54, 114, 121
Syrophoenician (woman), 16, 18, 50, 103–5, 107, 113–19, 121, 123
tehomicide, 90, 93
tehomophilia, 92
tehomophobia/c, 92–93
(re/de-) territorialize, 15–16, 18–19, 62, 71, 75, 105, 116, 122–23, 126, 128, 131
transcorporeal(ity), 1, 20, 99–100, 118
trauma(tized), 1–3, 25, 41, 47, 82, 105, 113
Tu B'Shevat, 65
vegetal
  assemblage(s), 75

vegetal (cont.)
    empire (of God), 4, 61–64, 71–72, 74–75, 79
    fidelity, 64
    generosity, 72, 74
    lesson(s), 15, 54, 57, 62–63, 66, 72, 75
    messiah, 98
    ontology, 31, 75
    play, 71
    potentialities, 77
    temporality, 15, 57, 71, 75–77, 79
vegetal(ity), 7–8, 10, 15, 20, 28, 30–31, 53, 55–68, 70–72, 74, 77–80, 128–30, 132. *See also* critical plant studies
    Marderian, 57, 63
vegetarian, 47
vibrant matter, 4, 19, 32
white supremacist/y, 1–3
whiteness, 6, 10, 125
(wild) beasts, 15, 29, 33–41, 43–44, 46, 48–51
wilderness, 33–34, 36, 38, 44–45, 48
xenophobia/c, 1

www.ingramcontent.com/pod-product-compliance
Lightning Source LLC
Chambersburg PA
CBHW030818090425
24824CB00002B/321